# FOUNDATIONS AND FRONTIERS
# OF DELIBERATIVE GOVERNANCE

# Foundations and Frontiers of Deliberative Governance

JOHN S. DRYZEK

with Simon Niemeyer

OXFORD
UNIVERSITY PRESS

# OXFORD
UNIVERSITY PRESS

Great Clarendon Street, Oxford OX2 6DP
United Kingdom

Oxford University Press is a department of the University of Oxford.
It furthers the University's objective of excellence in research, scholarship,
and education by publishing worldwide. Oxford is a registered trade mark of
Oxford University Press in the UK and in certain other countries

© John Dryzek 2010, except chapters 3 and 5, both: © John Dryzek and Simon Niemeyer

The moral rights of the author have been asserted

First published 2010
First published in paperback 2012
Reprinted 2013

British Library Cataloguing in Publication Data
Data available

Library of Congress Cataloging in Publication Data
Data available

ISBN 978-0-19-964485-8

# Preface

Deliberative democracy has been ascendant in the theory and practice of democracy for some time. A president of the United States has declared his belief in deliberative democracy (in Barack Obama's book *The Audacity of Hope*), and the hierarchy of the Chinese Communist Party appears open to deliberative experimentation. These two extremes illustrate the variety of meanings that can be ascribed to deliberative democracy, and the variety of practices it can inspire (just like democracy itself).

This book is designed as a statement about deliberative democracy in theory and practice, reaching from its conceptual underpinnings to the key challenges faced in its applications to an ever-increasing range of problems and issues. Its intended location is at the several cutting edges of deliberative democracy and deliberative governance. Part I, which consists of an introductory chapter, surveys the life and times of deliberative democracy, the turns it has taken, and contemplates the basic logic of deliberative systems. Part II is about the foundations of the theory. These cannot be taken for granted and simply built upon. As befits a live field, contentious issues require attention. Part II therefore attends to how deliberative legitimacy can be achieved in large-scale societies where face-to-face deliberation is implausible, to what representation can and should mean in such systems, to the kinds of communication that ought to be valued (rhetoric in particular), and to the competing appeals of pluralism and consensus. Some new concepts are developed along the way: discursive legitimacy, discursive representation, systemic tests for rhetoric, and several forms of meta-consensus. Part III builds upon these foundations (and on more established concepts) and shows how deliberative democracy can be applied fruitfully and effectively to areas where democratic theory is not normally taken. These areas are networked governance, the democratization of authoritarian states, and global politics. The role of designed mini-publics in these larger processes receives a chapter of its own. Part IV integrates the discussions of foundations and frontiers.

A lot happened in the first decade of deliberative democracy, between two earlier books: *Discursive Democracy* (Cambridge University Press, 1990), and *Deliberative Democracy and Beyond* (Oxford University Press, 2000). A lot more has happened in the second decade of the deliberative era since 2000; so much that it is hard to keep track of all the developments in the ever-expanding areas of political theory, social science, and political practice into which deliberative democracy is taken. It gets ever harder to write a comprehensive statement that would address the major outstanding questions in the field. This book tries to do so, but doubtless there are astute readers who will say "but what about . . . ?" And obviously, it is selective in the questions and areas that it picked, though selection was most certainly not on the basis of ease of treatment.

The Australian National University somehow manages to be a great research university despite some of its administrative follies (in which respect it is probably far from unique). This book owes much to all those once part of the Social and Political Theory Program in the Research School of Social Sciences, to all those subsequently gathered around what eventually became the Centre for Deliberative Democracy and Global Governance, and to the many scholars who have visited us over the years. Deliberative democracy never appeared in any strategic plan, but we still managed to amass the world's largest (and arguably strongest) concentration of deliberative democracy scholars. It has been a pleasure working among them.

A large part of the reason for this success comes from the generosity of the Australian Research Council in financing various projects. Much of the research reported in these chapters was supported by ARC Discovery Grants DP0342795 (to John Dryzek and Robert Goodin), DP0558573 (to John Dryzek and Simon Niemeyer), and DP0773626 (to John Dryzek and Bora Kanra); Linkage Grant LP0882714 (to John Dryzek, Simon Niemeyer, Lyn Carson, Janette Hartz-Karp, Luca Belgiorno-Nettis, and Ian Marsh) and Federation Fellowship FF0883522 (to John Dryzek). The New Democracy Foundation was a funding partner on the Linkage Grant.

Arguments from these chapters were presented to the Political Theory Seminar at the London School of Economics, the Conference on Rethinking Democratic Representation, University of British Columbia, 2006; the PATH Conference on Participatory Approaches in Science and Technology, Edinburgh, 2006; the THEMES Workshop on Complexity and Sustainable Development, Autonomous University of Barcelona, 2006; the Into the Void Workshop, Commonwealth Scientific and Industrial Research Organization, Canberra, 2006; the Department of Political Science, University of Stockholm; the Centre for Democratic Network Governance, Roskilde University; the Symposium on Representation and Democracy, University of Birmingham, 2007; the 2003, 2007, and 2008 Conferences of the American Political Science Association; the Nagoya University Conference on Constructivist Political Theory, 2008; the Conference on Unity and Diversity in Deliberative Democracy, University of Bern, 2008; the Conference on Rhetorical Citizenship and Public Deliberation at the University of Copenhagen, 2008; the Colloquium on the Media and Deliberative Democracy, Federal University of Minas Gerais (Brazil), 2009; the Bellagio Conference on Rethinking Representation: A

North–South Dialogue, 2008; the Interpretive Policy Analysis Conference, Kassel, 2009; and the Department of Political Science, Leiden University. For comments, suggestions, and criticism, thanks to Selen Ayirtman, André Bächtiger, Peter Balint, Henrik Bang, James Bohman, Simone Chambers, Louise Clery, Molly Cochran, Katherine Curchin, Mary Dietz, Robyn Eckersley, Lindy Edwards, Archon Fung, Robert Goodin, Carol Gould, Kasper Moller Hansen, Baogang He, Carolyn Hendriks, Christian Hunold, Alnoor Ibrahim, Kerstin Jacobsson, Bora Kanra, John Keane, Andrew Knops, Christian Kock, Christian List, Carolyn Lukensmeyer, Gerry Mackie, Eric MacGilvray, Rousiley Maia, Jane Mansbridge, Ricardo Fabrino Mendonça, Karolina Milewicz, Laura Montanero, Richard Mulgan, Michael Neblo, John Parkinson, Anne Phillips, Bernard Reber, Shawn Rosenberg, Jensen Sass, Michael Saward, Vivien Schmidt, Philippe Schmitter, Graham Smith, Eva Sørensen, Hayley Stevenson, Lawrence Susskind, Paul 't Hart, Dennis Thompson, Jacob Torfing, Douglas Torgerson, Aviezer Tucker, John Uhr, Shikegi Uno, Mark Warren, and Laura Zurita. Dominic Byatt was, as always, a terrific editor to work with at Oxford University Press. Thanks also to Rose Dryzek for finding an image for the cover, and to Alessandra Pecci for preparing the index.

Several of the chapters draw upon previously published articles, though they have been heavily revised for this book. Thanks to the publishers for permission to use them, as follows:

Chapter 2: John S. Dryzek, "Legitimacy and Economy in Deliberative Democracy," *Political Theory* 29 (2001): 651–69, by permission of Sage Publishers.

Chapter 3: John S. Dryzek and Simon Niemeyer, "Discursive Representation," *American Political Science Review* 102 (2008): 481–93, by permission of Cambridge University Press.

Chapter 4: John S. Dryzek, "Rhetoric in Democracy: A Systemic Appreciation," *Political Theory* 38 (2010): 319–39, by permission of Sage Publishers.

Chapter 5: John S. Dryzek and Simon Niemeyer, "Reconciling Pluralism and Consensus as Political Ideals," *American Journal of Political Science* 50 (2006): 634–49, by permission of Blackwell Publishers, © 2006 Midwest Political Science Association.

Chapter 7: John S. Dryzek, "Democratization as Deliberative Capacity Building," *Comparative Political Studies* 42 (2009): 1379–402, by permission of Sage Publishers.

J.S.D.
*Aranda, Australian Capital Territory*
*February 2010*

# Contents

# List of Tables and Figures

# List of Abbreviations

| | |
|---|---|
| ANC | African National Congress |
| CFCs | Chlorofluorocarbons |
| DGCA | Deliberative Global Citizens' Assembly |
| EU | European Union |
| GM | Genetically modified |
| IMF | International Monetary Fund |
| NGOs | Nongovernmental Organizations |
| OPECST | *Office Parlementaire d'Evaluation des Choix Scientifiques et Technologiques* |
| STS | Science and technology studies |
| STV | Single transferable vote |
| UN | United Nations |
| UNFCCC | United Nations Framework Convention on Climate Change |
| UNPA | United Nations Parliamentary Assembly |
| WTO | World Trade Organization |

# Part I

# Introduction

# 1

## Deliberative Turns

Since the deliberative turn taken by democratic theory around 1990, deliberative democracy has gone from strength to strength. This turn put communication and reflection at the center of democracy. Democracy, in other words, is not just about the making of decisions through the aggregation of preferences. Instead, it is also about processes of judgment and preference formation and transformation within informed, respectful, and competent dialogue. Democratic legitimacy is sought in the participation in consequential deliberation of those subject to a decision (or their representatives). No longer confined to an ever-expanding body of political theory, deliberative democracy now also describes:

- A central topic for inquiry in fields as varied as communications (Gastil 2008; Kock 2007), planning (Forester 1999b), ecological economics (Norgaard 2007), science and technology studies (STS) (Reber 2007), philosophy (Estlund 2007), policy analysis (Hajer and Wagenaar 2003), game theory (Landa and Meirowitz 2006), constitutional law (Sunstein 1993), criminal justice (De Grieff 2002; Parkinson and Roche 2004), conflict resolution (Susskind 2006), journalism (Dzur 2002), international relations (Smith and Brassett 2008), development studies (Crocker 2008; Morrison and Singer 2007), and social psychology (Eggins et al. 2007).
- A program of empirical research in a variety of these disciplines and interdisciplinary areas, designed either to test claims about the possibility and efficacy of deliberation (Mutz 2006, 2008; Ryfe 2005) or to inform the normative project of deliberative democracy (Rosenberg 2007; Steiner et al. 2004).
- An international movement for political reform. This reform can involve improvements to the practice of existing institutions, such as legislatures (Bessette 1994; Uhr 1998); the introduction of new institutions, involving, for example, systematic procedures for facilitating the input into policy making of deliberative citizen forums (Fung 2003; Gastil and Levine 2005); and the reworking of political systems in their entirety to facilitate

deliberative exchanges (Eriksen and Fossum 2007). An emerging profession of forum design and facilitation both takes advantage of, and contributes to, the reform movement – though not without some hazards attending this commercialization (Hendriks and Carson 2008).

- A way to interpret the point of whole political systems. As President Barack Obama (2006: 92) put it in his book *The Audacity of Hope*:

What the framework of our constitution can do is organize the way in which we argue about our future. All of its elaborate machinery – its separation of powers and checks and balances and federalist principles and Bill of Rights – are designed to force us into a conversation, a "deliberative democracy" in which all citizens are required to engage in a process of testing their ideas against an external reality, persuading others of their point of view, and building shifting alliances of consent.

The expanding reach of deliberative democracy is reflected in an ever-growing number of books, articles, conferences, courses, experiments, speeches, and institutional innovations. Those of us who have been working in this field for a long time are generally gratified and sometimes astonished at the ever-expanding range and ever-increasing depth of deliberative analysis, invocation, and innovation, whatever reservations we may have about some specific applications.

With the expansion of the field comes diversification in both theory and practice. The time for truly comprehensive integrated statements of the essence of deliberative democracy (of the sort offered by, among others, Cohen 1989; Dryzek 1990, 2000; Benhabib 1996; Gutmann and Thompson 1996; Habermas 1996; Bohman 1996; Niño 1996; Young 2000) may soon be past, if it has not gone already (though see Talisse 2005; Rostbøll 2008). But there is still plenty of work to be done on the foundations of the theory – and this is what Part II of this book is about. The chapters in Part II develop positions on some central questions of deliberative theory. That theory needs to be rendered applicable to contexts not easily reached by formulations of deliberative democracy tied to the constitutional structure and politics of the liberal democratic state. A decade ago, the pervasiveness of such formulations was blunting the critical edge of deliberative democracy (Dryzek 2000), though that danger has now receded. Part III of this book will take a look at some of the frontier areas into which deliberative democracy can now be taken. The particular areas emphasized in Part III are networked governance that may have only a tenuous connection to the formal authority of any sovereign state, the democratization of authoritarian regimes, the use of designed citizen forums in different sorts of states, and global governance. All of these applications drive home the need to make deliberative democracy applicable beyond the constitutionally constrained politics of developed liberal democracies. Part III is not supposed to be an exhaustive survey of the long frontier, though it is a set of areas of particular importance and growing interest. Another application of crucial importance is to deeply divided societies and deep disputes in the international system – but the contribution of deliberative democracy to resolving deep differences is the topic of a separate book (Dryzek 2006).

A particularly telling indicator of the importance of deliberative democracy is the degree to which some social scientists have tried to claim that what they are studying fits under the heading of "deliberation." Often, the object of the claim bears little relation to anything a deliberative democrat would recognize as belonging under that heading (Steiner 2008). Even articles in the political science discipline's top journal, the *American Political Science Review*, are not immune from this kind of dubious claim (Austen-Smith and Feddersen 2006).

With the expansion of the field also comes criticism. But that is itself a cause for celebration rather than concern. Some of the critics are theorists and philosophers (e.g., Van Mill 1996; Mouffe 1999; Shapiro 1999; Saward 2000; Norval 2007). Political theorists and political philosophers make their living largely by criticism of other theories and other philosophies. So the most important political theories are those that receive the largest volume of criticism, and by that yardstick alone deliberative democracy is among the most important contemporary political theories. In political science for its part, there is a long and dismal history of scholars trying to demonstrate that anything more than a minimal liberal democracy demands too much of the time, energy, and competence of ordinary citizens, as well as being subject to all kinds of paradoxes and pathologies (see Mackie 2003: 2–3). The fact that political scientists in the empirical tradition (e.g., Mutz 2006; Hibbing and Theiss-Morse 2002) have now turned their attention to trying to debunk the claims that *deliberative* democracy makes about the potential of citizen deliberation is again cause for celebration. This attention is one more indicator of the fact that deliberative democracy merits serious consideration.

The arguments of philosophical critics and the results of empirical political science should not be rejected out of hand. Most of the philosophical arguments are at least interesting, and some have led to important reformulations in how deliberative democracy is stated. Indeed, a substantial part of the material in Part II of this book is inspired by these critics. It takes on critics who, for example, charge deliberative democracy with an inability to deliver on its central claim to provide an account of how legitimacy is achieved in contemporary political systems, with neglect of the fact that contemporary democracies are mostly *representative* democracies, with an approach to political communication that rules out the essential rhetorical vitality of democratic communication, and with an unrealistic stress on the pursuit of consensus in political life. Some of the critical empirical research misses the point by oversimplifying or distorting what its authors take to be the claims made by deliberative theory, and some is, unfortunately, badly constructed and badly executed social science. However, some of this research poses some interesting challenges. A different strand in empirical research contributes quite directly to the project of deliberative democracy – indeed, some of it is designed to do so, including some of the work at the core of later chapters of this book.

## TURN, TURN, TURN, TURN

As noted at the outset, deliberative democracy can be said to have taken identifiable shape with the deliberate turn in democratic theory that occurred around 1990.[1] After 2000, further turns come thick and fast.

- An *institutional turn* in deliberative democracy is identified by Chambers (2003): one in which deliberative democrats increasingly focus on the shape taken by particular forums, while (she claims) losing sight of the larger ambitions of deliberative democracy to provide an account of democratic politics in its entirety. Of particular interest here is the focus on "mini-publics" composed of small numbers of citizens, who may be self-selected, or randomly selected from the larger population (Fung 2003). Some treatments do sometimes proceed as though deliberative democracy is something that can be sought and assessed in a single forum, such as a deliberative poll (Fishkin 2009), citizens' assembly (Warren and Pearse 2008), citizens' jury (Smith and Wales 2000), legislature (Bessette 1994), or Supreme Court (Rawls 1993: 231). Chambers tries to find support for the idea that adherents of this turn are (in her eyes, mistakenly) pinning their hopes for effective deliberation exclusively on mini-publics and other designed forums (see also Chambers 2009). However, a large part of the motivation for this emphasis may be simply that deliberation in such small-scale forums is much easier to study than in large-scale political

---

[1] The antecedents do, however, go back around 2,500 years to Aristotle's conception of life in the *polis*. Over 200 years ago, the great conservative politician and philosopher Edmund Burke spoke of parliament as a "deliberative assembly." The term "deliberative democracy" can be credited to Bessette (1980), for whom it was a particular interpretation of the politics intended by the Constitution of the United States. Goodin (2008: 2, fn 2) erroneously credits "deliberative turn" to Bohman (1998), but the earliest use of the expression may be Dryzek (2000: 1).

systems with many interacting elements (see discussion of the empirical turn below). Thus, people who work on single forums do not have to be committed to the idea that it is only in such forums that genuine deliberation can be sought.

- A *systemic turn* is the antidote to the institutional turn alleged by Chambers. The focus here is firmly on whole systems, of which any single deliberative forum is just a part. Contemporary political systems do of course feature multiple interacting parts. Interactions are necessary for the sake of constitutional checks and balances, coordination across the layers of multilevel governance, the variable capacity of different kinds of actors to participate in different venues, and coordination of policies across multiple jurisdictions. This systemic aspect has actually been there all along, particularly in the work of those such as Benhabib (1996), Dryzek (2000), and Habermas (1996) who emphasize the importance of the broader public sphere in constituting any deliberative democracy along with more formally constructed political authority structures. Kanra (2007) speaks of "binary deliberation" with separate "social-learning" and "decision-making" phases. But the systemic aspect is sharpened in the introduction by Mansbridge (1999*a*) of the idea of a "deliberative system" reaching from everyday talk among friends and associates to formal debate in the legislature. The aspects of a deliberative system are elaborated by Parkinson (2006*a*: 166–73). For Parkinson, social movement activism, expert testimony, bureaucracy and administrative consultation, public hearings, designed forums, media, legislature, and referenda or petitions can each contribute in their own particular and different ways to the achievement of deliberatively legitimate public policy. Different kinds of communication might be appropriate in different places: Parkinson (2006a: 172) thinks that rhetoric has a place in agenda setting by activists, but not elsewhere (chapter 4 will argue that rhetoric merits broader application). Constitutional courts (easily added to Parkinson's scheme) may feature skillful application of argument in public interest terms to legal and policy issues – but rarely do justices (at least on the U.S. Supreme Court) actually talk to each other, still less subject themselves to public accountability. Thus, constitutional courts can only contribute one particular piece to the deliberative democracy puzzle. Hendriks (2006) speaks of an "integrated deliberative system" linking microscale citizen forums (ideally incorporating partisans as well as ordinary citizens) with the macroscale political system. The public sphere in such a system could feature informal networks, enclaves of like-minded individuals, social movements, media, and Internet activity. Goodin (2005, 2008: 186–203) speaks of a representative democracy "sequencing deliberative moments" that can be found in a party caucus, parliamentary debate, election campaigns, and postelection bargaining. For Goodin, different deliberative virtues should be sought in each of these locations. The existing treatments of Mansbridge, Parkinson, Hendriks, and Goodin are all tied to the institutional specifics of developed liberal democratic states, but the basic notion of a deliberative system can actually be generalized to any kind of political setting – including ones where legislatures and even states are completely absent (see the following section for more detail).

- A *practical turn*, where the emphasis is on the strengthening or introduction of deliberative democracy in the real world of politics. This might involve efforts to make parliaments more deliberative (Uhr 1998), or the introduction of designed mini-publics such as citizens' juries, deliberative polls, consensus conferences, and citizens' assemblies. Some of these innovations, such as citizens' juries and consensus conferences, actually predate the idea of deliberative democracy in political theory. Others (such as deliberative polls) are very much the invention of deliberative democrats (see Fishkin 1991 for the deliberative poll). But with time, deliberative democrats have become interested in both the analysis and design of such forums, and in some cases have played substantial roles in making such forums happen (including the Australian National University Deliberative Democracy group's role in the creation of the world's first Citizens' Parliament, in Australia in 2009; see Dryzek et al. 2009*b*). Chambers (2003, 2009) might interpret such developments as further proof of the degree to which deliberative democracy has turned its back on the larger political system, but there is absolutely no reason why this has to be the case. Some practical deliberative democrats (e.g., Fishkin) might advocate one particular model as the embodiment of deliberative democratic ideals. But practitioners of the practical turn might just as easily devote themselves to the harder task of thinking through the shape of whole systems. Any such ambition would, however, bring into sharp focus the question of whether or not deliberative democrats should, if they are true to their own ideals, actually be designers – as opposed to participants in a democratic process of design that would itself involve broad deliberative participation.

- An *empirical turn* in which deliberative democratic theory starts to inspire systematic empirical work to test or refine its claims (for summary treatments, see Bächtiger, Steenbergen, and Niemeyer 2007; Dryzek 2007*b*; Rosenberg 2007; Sunstein 2007; Thompson 2008; Bächtiger et al. 2010). Some of those doing the work are social scientists who feel that deliberative democracy merits their attention simply because of the claims now made for it by theorists and advocates (e.g., Hibbing and Theiss-Morse 2002; Conover, Searing, and Crewe 2002). Such social scientists can even treat deliberative democracy in its entirety as a hypothesis that can be corroborated or refuted by empirical work (Mutz 2008) – though most deliberative democrats would insist that, as a normative project, deliberative democracy should not be treated in those terms. Other empirical analysts are true to the notion that deliberative democracy is indeed a project, but one that cannot ignore what we know about the way the political world actually works (Neblo 2005: 173). They engage in empirical work in order to refine claims about what deliberative democracy can and cannot do, and how its better practice might be informed by understandings of what is and is not possible and likely under particular conditions (e.g., McLean et al. 2000; Niemeyer 2004; Steiner et al. 2004). As suggested earlier, part of the reason for the institutional turn alleged by Chambers is that isolated deliberative forums are much easier to study empirically than are large-scale deliberative systems. Those involved in the design and analysis of such forums are therefore often motivated by reasons of tractability in empirical inquiry. It is possible, for example, to study how, why, and to what effect preferences, judgments, and values get transformed in deliberation. Concepts developed and refined in the study of small-scale forums (e.g., the meta-consensus concept addressed at length in chapter 5) can then be applied to large-scale systems. And we can ask how any positive effects we observe in small forums (e.g., greater consistency between underlying worldviews and expressed preferences) can be achieved in these larger systems. Correspondingly, we can also ask how any observed negative effects (e.g., the group polarization observed by Sunstein 2002) can be avoided in the larger system. Such studies will be addressed at greater length in chapter 8. Studying larger real-world deliberative systems poses greater challenges – but such studies are beginning to appear (and some will be reported in subsequent chapters).

In light of all this empirical work, it is hard to see how Habermas (2006*b*: 411) can maintain that "the deliberative model of democracy . . . appears to exemplify the widening gap between normative and empirical approaches toward politics" (though in fairness to Habermas, the real empirical explosion was only beginning in 2006 when he wrote these words). With a bit of simplification, the history might actually be something like the following. In the 1950s, there was an area of social science styling itself "empirical democratic theory" that used survey research findings about mass political incompetence to develop a "realistic" model of minimal democracy that demanded very little of ordinary citizens. Political theorists disgusted with this work recoiled from empirical inquiry altogether, confirming what Gunnell (1986) calls "the alienation of political theory." Influential theories such as that of Rawls (1971) made use of no facts at all, just assumptions. Eventually stylized facts are allowed, such as "the fact of reasonable pluralism" at the core of Rawls's restatement of his theory of justice (1993). The popularity of deliberative democracy later led some social scientists who are methodologically sophisticated but theoretically challenged to stumble into the field with studies that often miss the point. Eventually, there is real productive cooperation between political theory and social science, to the point that in some cases it is hard to tell whether a particular author is a political theorist, an empirical social scientist, or both. This book will endeavor to make use of this last category of studies, and many are cited in the chapters that follow.

This proliferation of turns is further proof, if any were needed, of the growth, vitality, and diversity of the deliberative democracy field.

## THE CAPACITY OF DELIBERATIVE SYSTEMS

The chapters that follow can be situated in the wake of the systemic, practical, and empirical turns in deliberative democracy. As such, we need to think at the outset about how to assess the completeness and effectiveness of actual and potential deliberative systems.

A system can be said to possess deliberative capacity to the degree it has structures to accommodate deliberation that is *authentic, inclusive,* and *consequential.* To be authentic, deliberation ought to be able to induce reflection upon preferences in noncoercive fashion (Dryzek 2000: 68), and involve communicating in terms that those who do not share one's point of view can find meaningful and accept (this is what Gutmann and Thompson (1996) call "reciprocity," though they are concerned with argument in particular, rather than communication in general). To be inclusive, deliberation requires the opportunity and ability of all affected actors (or their representatives) to participate. To be consequential, deliberation must somehow make a difference when it comes to determining or influencing collective outcomes. Such outcomes might include laws and other explicit and codified public policy decisions, international treaties, the more informal outcomes reached by governance networks, or even cultural change (e.g., if groups in a divided society learn through deliberation how to live together).

The specific deliberative systems sketched by Mansbridge (1999a), Hendriks (2006), Parkinson (2006a), and Goodin (2008) are, as already noted, tied to the institutional details of developed liberal democracies. However, the basic idea of a deliberative system can be generalized to make it applicable to a wide variety of settings, including those that do not contain legislatures, political parties, citizen forums, or elections. One such setting is the international system, but informal governance networks at many levels (from the local to the global) can also produce outcomes without any of the standard liberal democratic accoutrements just mentioned. A more generally applicable scheme for the analysis of deliberative systems is made up of the following items:

1. *Public space*, ideally hosting free-ranging and wide-ranging communication, with no barriers limiting who can communicate, and few legal restrictions on what they can say. Contributions to such spaces can come from political advocates and activists, media commentators, social movements, and ordinary citizens, as well as politicians. The locations might involve Internet forums, the physical places where people gather and talk (e.g., cafés, classrooms, bars, and public squares), public hearings, and designed citizen forums of various sorts (which limit participation on the basis of numbers, but do not restrict the kinds of persons who can deliberate).

2. *Empowered space*, home to deliberation among actors in institutions clearly producing collective decisions. The institution in question might be a legislature, a policy-making council in a corporatist state with representatives from government, business, and labor union federations, a cabinet, a constitutional court, an empowered stakeholder dialogue, an international organization, or a set of international negotiations. Institutions here need not be *formally* constituted and empowered. Thus, informal networks producing collective outcomes could also constitute empowered (and potentially deliberative) space.

3. *Transmission*, some means through which deliberation in public space can influence that in empowered space. Relevant mechanisms could include activist campaigns, the use of rhetoric and other performances designed to attract publicity for a cause, the making of arguments, new ideas and associated cultural change of the kind often sought by social movements that eventually can be accepted by formally empowered actors, and personal links between actors in public space and empowered space. Transmission might be in the form of advocacy, or criticism, or questioning, or support, or some combination of all four.

4. *Accountability*, whereby empowered space answers to public space. Accountability is necessary when it comes to securing deliberative legitimacy for collective outcomes. In liberal democratic states, election campaigns are an important accountability mechanism, as the actions of empowered politicians are judged by the voting public. But accountability can also

mean simply being required to give an account justifying decisions and actions, and that can happen without any necessary reference to election campaigns. Accountability and transmission may sometimes be combined in what Neblo (2005: 178) calls "symmetric inter-public deliberation" where representations from empowered space and public space deliberate together (his example is the New England town meeting). The idea of public consultation, however poor and asymmetric its general practice in deliberative terms, should in principle provide opportunities for this kind of exchange.

5. *Meta-deliberation*, or deliberation, about how the deliberative system itself should be organized. As Thompson (2008: 15) puts it, deliberative democrats should "not insist that every practice in deliberative democracy be deliberative but rather that every practice should at some point in time be deliberatively justified." A healthy deliberative system therefore needs a capacity for self-examination and self-transformation if need be. Examples are provided in Ackerman's account (1991) of three key moments in U.S. constitutional history: the constitutional founding, the Civil War amendments to the constitution, and the New Deal in the 1930s. These three crises involved broad deliberation, spanning all the institutions in the polity about what the polity itself should subsequently look like.

6. *Decisiveness*, the degree to which these five elements together determine the content of collective decisions. Conceivably, a parliament could be a flourishing deliberative chamber under item (2) listed above – but have little impact on the decisions of a president who rules by decree. Or the government of a state in its entirety might seem quite deliberative, but produce major policy decisions on the instructions of the international financial institutions to which it is indebted.

On the face of it, the deliberative system is diminished by any non-deliberative substitute for any of the first five elements. For example, transmission might happen due to those in empowered space fearing the political instability that those in public space might unleash if they are ignored. This kind of mechanism might, for example, be the only one available for local deliberations to have much of an effect on (mostly non-deliberative) empowered space in influencing economic development in China (He and Warren 2008). This is also how some social movements have secured influence in Western liberal democracies: by those in government fearing the disruption the movement might otherwise cause (Piven and Cloward 1971). However, the idea of meta-deliberation allows that the system as a whole might determine that some non-deliberative mechanism (such as opinion polling as a transmission mechanism) is allowable. Meta-deliberation might also recognize that effective deliberation sometimes benefits from moments of secrecy, allowing representatives to try to understand each other without immediately being pulled back by skeptical constituents (Chambers 2004). The deliberative virtue of publicity can then enter later, or elsewhere in the deliberative system.

While some examples have been given, a deliberative system and its component elements do not require any specific institutions, be they competitive elections or a constitutional separation of powers. Many different sorts of deliberative system are possible, with many different kinds of components. So the sorts found, for example, in a transnational network will be different from those that might exist in the European Union (EU), which in turn will differ from those available in an adversarial Anglo-American liberal democracy, which will not resemble those feasible in a consensual Confucian state. The same set of formal institutions may at different times coexist with very different deliberative systems – if (for example) informal channels and high degrees of publicity are sometimes activated by a social movement, while at other times there is little movement activity. In transnational regulatory networks, empowered space may sometimes be coterminous with public space, as the content of (say) forest certification regulation is negotiated in dialogue encompassing nongovernmental organizations (NGOs), timber corporations, certifiers, government officials, and consumer representatives. For the EU, the open method of coordination linking the European Commission and the policy decisions of member states is a unique kind of potentially deliberative form in empowered space that is decisive in producing collective outcomes (Eriksen, Joerges, and Neyer 2004). In most EU institutions, the practice is also that state representatives should argue in terms of shared legal principles and/or common interest justifications, and this norm contributes to the deliberative character of empowered space. However, the EU falls short on public space, given the lack of a European public sphere, with NGOs, parties, and the media all organized only on a national basis. European elections are fought by national parties on national issues, and no accountability mechanism effectively substitutes for this accountability deficit in elections.

Particular institutions can, then, constitute and interact within a deliberative system in complex and variable ways. Apparently poor deliberative quality in one place (say, the legislature) may be compensated by, or even inspire, higher deliberative quality in another location (say, a flourishing informal public sphere). On the other hand, high deliberative quality in one location might diminish deliberative quality in another location. For example, if legislators know that their more dubious collective decisions will be overruled by a constitutional court, they are free to engage in irresponsible rhetoric. For these kinds of reasons, it is important to look at the deliberative system in its entirety, rather than assess component parts in isolation.

A well-functioning deliberative system will feature authentic deliberation in elements 1–5, will be inclusive in elements 1, 2, and 5, and will also be decisive when it comes to collective outcomes. Real-world cases will always come up short to some degree, and may conceivably be missing one or more elements entirely. These ideas will inform several of the chapters that follow.

## PREVIEW

The reexamination of the foundations of deliberative democracy of Part II begins in chapter 2 with a look at key idea of legitimacy. In the classic works of Manin (1987) and Cohen (1989), the theory of deliberative democracy actually arrived as an account of legitimacy: collective outcomes are legitimate to the extent that all those subject to them have the right, capacity, and opportunity to participate in consequential deliberation about their content. But immediately, a scale problem arises when it comes to political systems of any size: face-to-face deliberation can only ever be for a few people. Several solutions to the scale problem are canvassed. The problem can be solved most effectively by conceptualizing discursive legitimacy as existing to the extent of the resonance of collective decisions with the outcome of the engagement of discourses in the public sphere, to the extent this engagement is itself practiced by a broad variety of competent actors.

If the engagement of discourses in the public sphere is central to democracy, what are the implications for the idea of representation, which is also widely seen as central to contemporary notions of democracy? It is possible to think of the representation of discourses as well as persons. In chapter 3, the idea of discursive representation is developed and explored, quite literally in terms of the constitution of a formal Chamber of Discourses, more informally in a way that sees this "Chamber" as existing within the broader public sphere. Discursive representation turns out to be applicable in many contexts where electoral notions of representation are problematic – such as the international system.

Treating deliberation in systemic terms and representation in discursive terms illuminates the kinds of communication that can be sought (and the kinds condemned) in a deliberative democracy. Deliberation is unquestionably a particular kind of communication; but how exactly do we distinguish between deliberative and non-deliberative form and content? Particularly, when it comes to large-scale processes in the broader public sphere, many deliberative democrats now recognize that rhetoric has an important place. This is especially true when it comes to communication linking the components of a deliberative system. Yet, rhetoric also has its well-known hazards, especially in the hands of demagogues and deceivers. Chapter 4 takes a look at the place of rhetoric in deliberative systems, and points to the need for systemic as well as categorical tests for the sort of rhetoric that is defensible and desirable. Categorical tests focus on the content of the rhetoric itself. Systemic tests look too at the degree to which the rhetoric in question contributes to the construction of an effective deliberative system – or undermines any such system.

Consensus was once thought of as the gold standard of political legitimacy in deliberative democracy, especially by Habermas (1996) and thinkers influenced by him. The idea of consensus has also been a soft target for critics of deliberative democracy in a plural society, because it seems so unrealistic when faced with political conflicts of any depth. Chapter 5 argues that apparently competing ideals of consensus and pluralism can be reconciled by the idea that the purpose of deliberation is *not* to secure consensus. Instead, the key goal of deliberation is to produce meta-consensus that structures continued dispute. Meta-consensus can refer to agreement on the legitimacy of contested values, on the validity of disputed judgments, on the acceptability and structure of competing preferences, and on the applicability of contested discourses. It can be applied as a standard for the evaluation of deliberative systems, as well as to particular forums. But it should not be sought and celebrated uncritically. Instead, we need to pay careful attention to the deliberative qualities of the processes that produce it.

The first frontier of deliberative democracy addressed in Part III is networked governance. Traditionally, democratic theorists have located democracy in the accountable institutions of the sovereign state. The rise of networked governance undercuts notions of sovereignty and accountability, for networks often do not correspond to traditional political units. They are informal, sometimes transnational, and engaged by public and private actors from many different locations. Traditional aggregative and electoral ideas about democracy are helpless in the face of these developments. Chapter 6 shows how governance networks can be interpreted as deliberative systems, and how democratic standards can therefore be applied in the evaluation of such governance.

Deliberation is now ubiquitous in the theory and practice of democracy – except when it comes to comparative studies of the democratization of states emerging from authoritarianism. This absence is remedied in chapter 7, which shows that democratization itself can be conceptualized in terms of the building of deliberative capacity in a political system. This capacity can be distributed in variable ways in the deliberative systems of states. Deliberative capacity proves to be an important determinant of democratic transition and consolidation, such that the concept has substantial analytical and evaluative purchase. The ambit claim is that all democratization studies need to be recalled and reframed in a deliberative light, but even if this claim is resisted by traditional democratization scholars, the deliberative aspect merits attention. Countries such as China that resist democracy conceptualized in terms of competitive elections, constitutions, and human rights recognized by the state might nonetheless prove susceptible to a deliberative path of democratization.

Designed citizen forums are increasingly seen as important elements of any agenda for deliberative democratization. Mini-publics are at the same time potential components of deliberative governance, and sources of lessons about what deliberation ought to both seek and avoid, and the challenges it faces, in those larger systems. Chapter 8 explores the many roles that mini-publics can play, and the different sorts of impacts they can have. The global movement to institutionalize lay citizen deliberation has, however, generally ignored variability in the characteristics of the different kinds of political systems in which these forums are implemented. Using comparative studies of citizen forums, chapter 8 shows that the democratic potential of such "mini-publics" is actually quite different in different sorts of political systems. For example, in actively inclusive Denmark, mini-publics are deployed in integrative fashion; in exclusive France, in managerial fashion; in the passively inclusive United States, in advocacy fashion. If mini-publics are to contribute to deliberative democratization, they need supportive structures and processes in government and the broader public sphere. The kinds of structures and processes required will again vary by political system type.

In today's world, political authority increasingly eludes sovereign states to be located instead in transnational and sometimes global political and economic processes. If legitimate authority is to be democratic, then this requirement applies no less to legitimate international authority. Chapter 9 looks at global governance in deliberative democratic light, emphasizing in the first instance the construction of transnational publics and the engagement of discourses in transnational public spheres. As hegemony yields to contestation in global politics, the prospects for such engagement improve. All the ideas about legitimacy, representation, rhetoric, and meta-consensus developed in Part II prove applicable to global deliberative systems. There may even be a place for mini-publics at the global level.

The long frontier of deliberative governance does, then, extend from mini-publics to the global system. With this examination of points on the long frontier complete, the concluding chapter returns to the more foundational concepts set out in Part II. Chapter 10 synthesizes the discussion of foundations and frontiers to demonstrate how they can be joined in a coherent systemic view of deliberative democracy and its many applications. There may be limits to the deliberative democratization of politics, but they have not yet been reached.

# Part II

# Foundations

# 2

## Legitimacy

Deliberative democracy began as a theory of democratic legitimacy, and remains so to a considerable degree. Legitimacy is one of those perennial issues in thinking about democracy that never quite receives a treatment that would satisfy those who worry about it. That in itself is not a problem. Democracy is, after all, the best example of what Gallie (1956) calls an "essentially contested concept," requiring that continued dispute over the key components of what democracy means is actually integral to the very idea of democracy itself. Legitimacy is one of these key components. But the specifically *deliberative* account of legitimacy actually faces some potentially devastating challenges that are invited by the way this account is normally stated. This chapter attempts to provide an answer to these challenges.

If something (be it an institution, a value, a policy, a decision, or a practice) is legitimate, that means it is accepted as proper by those to whom it is supposed to apply. Acceptance so defined could of course be secured by coercion, or in ignorance of what the people in question are actually being asked to accept. So we need to add a moral dimension: those granting legitimacy must do so because they believe it is morally right to do so. We also need to add a freedom dimension: those granting legitimacy must do so freely. We then need to add a competence dimension: those granting legitimacy must do so in full awareness of what they are being asked to accept. So legitimacy does not just mean acceptance, it also refers to moral rightness, as well as freedom, transparency, and competence in the process of acceptance. When it comes to political structures and public policies in particular, it is also common to add a requirement of legality: to be legitimate, a decision must be legal or constitutional. In addition, legitimacy in a democracy seems to require some notion of public authorization of decision makers actually to make decisions, and accountability of decision makers to the public (for further discussions of legitimacy in political philosophy, see among others Beetham 1991; Simmons 2001; Føllesdal 2006; Peter 2007).

Deliberative democrats generally believe that legitimacy is achieved by deliberative participation on the part of those subject to a collective decision. Moreover, this participation should have substantial influence on the content of the decision. But then the problem becomes one of somehow involving large numbers of people in deliberation, given that deliberation at its most straightforward cannot easily involve at the very most more than about twenty or so individuals reasoning together. This is the *scale* problem. The problem has been recognized and treated at length by Parkinson (2006*a*). Parkinson's solution appeals to the idea of a deliberative system, of the kind examined in chapter 1. For Parkinson, different deliberative sites can all make their contributions to the legitimacy of the system as a whole. In the specific case of health policy making in the United Kingdom, which he considers at length, the relevant sites include parliament, social movement activist networks, petitions, elections, citizen forums, public hearings, the media, and bureaucracy. So roles are played at different places and times by activists, experts, bureaucrats, local and national politicians, journalists, and ordinary citizens. Parkinson himself recognizes that he has not fully solved the scale problem, because it is still the case that the consequential deliberation of anything like *all* subject to a decision has not been achieved. Yet if he has not solved the problem, he has at least shown how it can be ameliorated, and that deliberative legitimacy can be promoted, if never fully achieved in any ideal sense. His treatment of legitimacy stands as the most thoughtful and comprehensive within the deliberative democracy literature.

This chapter does not dispute Parkinson's basic argument for the importance of multiple interactions in a deliberative system in producing legitimacy. All it seeks to do is highlight a particular angle on how deliberative legitimacy can be sought in large-scale political systems. This angle stresses the engagement and contestation of discourses in the public sphere, yielding public opinion characterized as the provisional outcome of this engagement as transmitted to some kind of public authority (most often, a government). Legitimacy is then achieved to the degree collective outcomes respond to the balance of discourses in the polity, to the extent this balance is itself subject to dispersed and competent political control. This idea is consistent with the general notion of a deliberative system sketched in chapter 1, which emphasizes the interaction between the public space and the empowered space where decisions are produced. (Parkinson's deliberative system is tied to the more specific case of a reasonably well-functioning liberal democracy.)

## LEGITIMACY AND LARGE SCALE

Deliberative democracy arrived as a theory of legitimacy in Joshua Cohen's classic formulation (1989) (see also Manin 1987), and this is still the claim at the theory's core: that outcomes are legitimate to the extent they receive reflective assent through participation in authentic deliberation by all those subject to the decision in question. This deliberation should in turn be consequential when it comes to affecting the content of collective decisions. As Benhabib (1996: 68) puts it, "legitimacy in complex democratic societies must be thought to result from the free and unconstrained deliberation *of all* about matters of common concern" [emphasis added]. The essence of deliberation is generally taken to be that claims for or against collective decisions need to be justified to those subject to these decisions in terms that, given the chance to reflect, these individuals can accept. But in real-world deliberations all or even very many of those affected cannot easily participate, thus rendering deliberative democracy vulnerable to demolition of its legitimacy claims. In the context of the supposedly exemplary case of health-care rationing in Oregon (see, for example, Gutmann and Thompson 1996: 144), Shapiro (1999: 33) asks "why should we attach legitimacy at all to a deliberative process that involved very few of those whose health care priorities were actually being discussed?"

There are ways to fudge the issue. For example, Cohen (1989: 22) specifies only that "outcomes are democratically legitimate if and only if they could be the object of a free and reasoned agreement among equals" – *could* be, rather than actually being. Casting matters in terms of the universal right, capacity, or opportunity to deliberate, rather than actual exercise of that right, capacity, or opportunity, makes deliberative democracy more plausible. So for Manin (1987: 352), "As political decisions are characteristically imposed on *all*, it seems reasonable to seek, as an essential condition for legitimacy, the deliberation of *all* or, more precisely, the right of all to participate in deliberation" [emphasis in original]. However, this sort of qualification places a major question mark next to legitimacy. For surely, the theory hangs by a slender thread if its viability depends crucially on the vast majority always choosing not to exercise the rights and capacities that are so fundamental to the theory – and whose exercise is taken by most proponents of deliberative democracy to be what makes for good citizens to begin with. Relying on mass apathy to make the theory work would return us to the dark days of the elitist models of democracy that deliberative democrats are otherwise so keen to reject. Foremost among these elitist models is the kind of theory advanced by Schumpeter (1942) and his many successors, in which democracy is seen as a competition among elites, with ordinary people having a say only at election times, and then only to confer the right to rule. Given Schumpeter thought citizens "infantile" when it came to politics, their more general apathy was actually thought by him and his successors to be good for the stability of democratic systems.

The scale constraint that deliberative democracy seems to have trouble respecting can be restated as a matter of economy: deliberative democracy seems to demand way too much of the time and energy of citizens. Dahl (1970) and many others have pointed out that meaningful participation in collective decision making by anything more than a tiny minority is inconceivable in contemporary nation-states (and, indeed, in most of their component units). The time demands on participants are simply impossible in anything beyond a very small-scale political unit. As Walzer (1999: 68) puts it, "deliberation is not an activity for the demos ... 100 million of them, or even 1 million or 100,000, can't plausibly 'reason together'."

Jacobs, Cook, and Delli Carpini (2009) have demonstrated that around two-thirds of the U.S. citizenry do reason with others by participating in public discussions about political issues, so in one sense Walzer is wrong. Deliberation really is an activity for the entire demos. However, all this public discussion is not necessarily connected into a common conversation, or integrated into collective decision making (and it is not necessarily especially deliberative). So Walzer is right in the sense that all the people do not reason together in consequential fashion.

This chapter will now briefly survey and criticize some of the more obvious solutions to this problem, and then propose a way to think about securing legitimacy while respecting the basic constraint of deliberative economy.[1] This proposed interpretation highlights deliberation in the broad public sphere – the "public space" of the deliberative system. Deliberation in public space can be conceptualized as a multifaceted interchange or contestation across discourses. Discursive legitimacy is then secured to the degree that collective outcomes are responsive to the balance of competing discourses in the public sphere, to the extent that this balance is itself subject to dispersed and competent control. Much less is said here about how deliberation within the institutions of empowered space can contribute to the generation of legitimacy; for that, the reader is again referred to Parkinson (2006a).

## PARTIAL SOLUTIONS TO THE SCALE PROBLEM

Three current solutions to the problem of achieving deliberative legitimacy under conditions of large scale are laid out in this section. They involve,

[1] Not to be confused with Gutmann and Thompson's proposed "economy of moral disagreement" (1996), which refers to the idea that deliberators who disagree on fundamental matters should nevertheless seek to identify points where they can agree.

respectively, limiting the occasions when deliberation is needed, limiting deliberation itself to representatives of the relevant people, and limiting deliberation to those best able to discern the interests and needs of others. These solutions are not mutually exclusive, and can indeed be combined.

## Limiting the times when deliberation is needed

To begin, deliberative democracy can be restricted to a small number of occasions when popular deliberation is required. Rawls (1993) believes that extended deliberation is appropriate only to matters concerning the constitution, and legislation inasmuch as "basic justice" (equality of opportunity and material distribution) is at issue. Yet the problem of scale remains even on such special occasions. Take, for example, a 1999 referendum in Australia on whether or not to ditch the British monarch in favor of a proposed republic. The failure of the republican proposal in the referendum compared to the overwhelming success of the model in a setting provided by a deliberative opinion poll (of which more shortly) suggests that this occasion, at least, was a deliberative failure at the national level – even in a population of (only) 19 million. The sheer impossibility of involving more than a handful of members of the population in deliberation remains overwhelming. However, as we shall see shortly, Rawls himself in the end sees no problem in restricting deliberation to a well-qualified handful.

The number of occasions for society-wide deliberation is restricted still further by Ackerman (1991), who argues that the political history of the United States has, rightly, seen just three such occasions: the constitutional founding, the Civil War amendments to the constitution, and the New Deal. But even on these rare great crises of the state, it certainly was not a matter of *all* the people deliberating, however much deliberative circles may have been widened. And even if these three occasions were the only three rightful candidates, it would seem odd to rest an account of democratic legitimacy on events that most citizens may well go through their lives without ever seeing.

## Limiting deliberation to a small number of representatives

The second solution, perhaps more straightforward than the first, is somehow to restrict the number of people involved in deliberation, making sure that the individuals who do participate be in some way representative of those who do not. Currently, there are two main available ways of securing representativeness: by popular election and by random selection. Popular elections are, of course, central to representative democracy, and so should be attractive to those who see deliberation as an aspect of, rather than substitute for, conventional sorts of representative democracy (e.g., Bessette 1994; Sunstein 1997: 94). But such an easy assimilation to representative democracy cannot straightforwardly deliver on the legitimacy requirements of deliberative democrats such as Cohen, Benhabib, and Manin. For to do so, election campaigns themselves would have potentially to involve the deliberation *of all*. So the problem of scale reappears, only this time in a slightly different electoral location, and a legitimacy claim cannot be established at one remove simply by appeal to the electoral process.

Deliberative democracy's legitimation problems are compounded here to the degree elections themselves are not exactly deliberative affairs even for those who do participate in them – deliberation often has to be subordinated to strategy in the interests of winning. Gastil (2008: 87–96) catalogs the deliberative failures of existing electoral politics. The failures include safe incumbents with no viable opposition candidates; negative advertising; manipulative and misleading rhetoric; media coverage that presents elections as reassuring rituals, or as horse races in that all that matters is the competitive spectacle rather than any issues; sensationalism and the pursuit of scandal in media reporting – and complete lack of media coverage if there is no horse race, scandal, or sensation to be had.

As antidotes to these problems, Gastil (2000: 104–9) proposes a number of reforms. These would include changes to the voting system away from simple plurality rule (as used in the United States) to induce voters to consider more than two options; campaign finance reform to reduce the role of money in elections; the preelection "Deliberation Day" national holiday proposed by Ackerman and Fishkin (2004) on which citizens would gather locally and be connected electronically to a national discussion; and the use of citizens' panels to deliberate over what should go into voters' pamphlets distributed in connection with referenda on specific issues, in the hope that voters will be influenced by "the deliberative judgement of their peers"(Gastil 2000: 109). Any such reforms might indeed make election campaigns more deliberative. But would they make these campaigns deliberative enough? Only the Deliberation Day proposal would involve anything like the deliberation of all citizens in the election campaign. And with personal experience of organizing a national Australian Citizens' Parliament in 2009 in mind, it is doubtful that a day is long enough for citizens to get to the point of even beginning to deliberate complex issues.

An alternative way to organize representation is to select deliberators by lot rather than election. This mechanism is actually much older than popular elections, dating back to ancient Greece. A host of contemporary examples of "mini-publics" now includes citizens' juries (Smith and Wales 2000), Danish-style consensus conferences (see chapter 8), planning cells (Hendriks 2005), deliberative polls (Fishkin 1991, 1995), citizens' assemblies (Warren and Pearse 2008), and the Australian Citizens' Parliament (Dryzek et al. 2009*b*). Leib (2004) suggests these mini-publics could constitute a fourth branch of government, both generating proposals and scrutinizing proposals made in executive, legislative, and judicial branches. In the context of reform of the House of Lords in the United Kingdom in the late 1990s, the Demos think tank proposed an upper chamber of citizens selected at random. While such forums are usually issue specific and advisory, the Leib proposal shows how they could be incorporated more formally into the institutions of government. The British Columbia Citizens' Assembly of 2004 was constituted to formulate a proposal that was put to a binding referendum, suggesting one possible means of formal incorporation. The Demos proposal points to a possible role for a citizens' forum as a general-purpose legislature.

Random sampling of the relevant population followed by deliberation in a mini-public gives a simulation of what the population as a whole would decide if everyone were allowed to deliberate. This simulation may not hold if the deliberation so organized fails to capture the differentiated character of political interchange, that is, the fact that in reality people encounter each other largely within or across groups, as opposed to an undifferentiated forum. (Sanders (1999: 12) suggests that this means deliberative polls misrepresent group processes.) However, even if we grant the simulation claim, it does not solve the scale problem, because decisions still have to be justified to those who did not participate. Moreover, nonparticipants would need to understand the logic of random sampling, and the idea that everyone has an equal chance of being chosen. Getting acceptance of both the existence of the mini-public and the logic of its selection through deliberative means is a real challenge here. Simply televising and publicizing the poll is insufficient – as perhaps the Australian deliberative poll on monarchy versus republic mentioned earlier indicates, where the majority of those voting in the referendum chose the opposite of the deliberators' recommendation. In a larger environment of partisan conflict, those not satisfied with the recommendation that a forum reaches can try to undermine its legitimacy. Reacting to the results of the Australian deliberative poll, one of the leaders of the "real republic" faction urging a "no" vote to the model of the republic on offer dismissed the deliberative poll as an exercise in "push-polling" (Phil Cleary, quoted in *The Age*, Melbourne, October 25, 1999: 1).[2]

Another problem that may arise is that mini-publics normally require that well-defined boundaries can be drawn around issues. Sometimes they can (e.g., when it comes to a constitutional question such as the Australian transition from monarchy to republic), but for some issues there will be a variety of important interactions across issues (e.g., concerning issues of free trade and capital mobility, which have major ramifications for environmental affairs and social justice).

## Limiting deliberation to those best able to discern the public's interest

Representation is not the only way to limit the number of deliberators to a manageable set. It is also possible to select on how well individuals can discern what is in the interests of the public as a whole. Consider in this light how Rawls (1993, 1997) specifies deliberative practice in terms of the exercise of public reason. Public reason is a standard for the substantive content of arguments, which have to be framed in terms that can be accepted by *all*, thus excluding self-interest and partial perspectives. Public reason for Rawls is singular and universal: its terms are identical for all, and all individuals who exercise it properly will reach the same conclusions. It is defined by a body of principles that people must accept before they enter a political setting, not what they will be prompted to discover after they have entered the public arena (see Benhabib 1996: 75). There is no notion that individuals might actually learn something from their encounters with others (Rostbøll 2008: 109–32). Thus, any reflective individual can reach the correct conclusions, and so all that is really needed is one individual to deliberate about the content of a decision – an obvious solution to the problem presented by large scale. If some people are better able to reflect than others, perhaps political philosophers and legal theorists, then they should be the ones to whom society entrusts public reason. This perhaps helps to explain Rawls's own enthusiasm (1993: 231) for the U.S. Supreme Court as an exemplary deliberative institution.

Restriction of numbers of deliberators along Rawlsian lines means that public reason does not *have* to be tested in political interaction, and there is in

---

[2] Push-polling is a marketing tactic where interviewees are asked leading questions and given biased information in order to induce them to buy a product – or support a position or candidate.

fact no reason why it *should* be so tested in interaction. Political venues for deliberation, be they courts or legislatures (Rawls's favorite places), function so as to provide opportunity for expression; in this light, there is nothing interactive about them that induces proper public reason. Rawls (1997: 771–2) is a deliberative theorist, but not a deliberative democrat, his own self-description notwithstanding. The Supreme Court is a deliberative institution, but not really an interactive one, because justices do not actually make arguments to each other when they are considering the merits of cases. The Supreme Court is most certainly not a democratic institution. The problem of legitimation arises still more acutely for such nondemocratic deliberation than for deliberation on the part of representatives. Institutions such as the Supreme Court can only contribute to legitimacy to the extent that the public accepts that public reason is indeed singular, and that professional experts in the exercise of public reason do indeed know best.

Like Rawls, Goodin (2000, 2003) believes that deliberation can occur quite effectively within the mind of a single individual. Goodin wants those who do participate in deliberative proceedings to call to mind the interests of those who do not participate. Thus, those who cannot or choose not to participate still have their interests entered into the collective deliberation of a decision-making body – but it is via "internal-individual" deliberation as cogitation, which takes place within the minds of those who do participate. This sort of deliberation resembles Rawlsian public reason, at least inasmuch as deliberation is seen mainly as a matter of personal cogitation in light of public concerns, not as a social or interactive process. Goodin recognizes these social processes taking place among political elites – but it is the "internal-individual" deliberation of members of the elite that solves the scale problem.

This kind of partial substitution of internal-individual deliberation for real interaction is advocated in a somewhat different context by Eckersley (2000), whose concern is with extending deliberation to a "community of the affected" that encompasses future generations and the nonhuman world. Given that there is no conceivable way that future persons or nonhumans can give literal voice to their concerns, they can only be made virtually present in deliberations.[3] One could also imagine this sort of presence being used in connection with the extension of deliberative democracy across national boundaries as proposed by Thompson (1999), who wants participants in decision making in state structures to be induced to internalize the interests of those residing in other states. Thompson himself does not advocate internal-individual deliberation, but he does stress the role of a particular

---

[3] For an argument that communications from nonhuman entities can be received by deliberators, see Dryzek (1995).

kind of expert in discerning the interests of others in the form of a "tribune for noncitizens" (1999: 122).

Goodin's solution presupposes that we have already restricted the number of deliberators. Given the criticisms he levels at selection by lot, in contrast with the free passage he grants more conventional representation, he appears to have the latter in mind. But in specifying a key role for "deliberation within," Goodin intensifies the legitimation problem for elected representatives. For he is asking members of the broader public to take it on trust that the deliberators really are calling to mind and internalizing broader sets of interests. At least in the case of the Supreme Court a public record (or at least rationalization) of internal-individual deliberation is supplied, against which members of the public could, if so inclined, check the justices' version of public reason against their own. Goodin hints at no such check.

While none of the three categories of "limiting" solutions that have been canvassed provides an adequate and compelling solution to the problem of scale that confronts deliberative approaches to legitimation, the second is on the right track in seeing representation as a key ingredient. But those advocating representation are burdened by ideas about representation inherited from long traditions of non-deliberative approaches to democracy. Required here is some more expansive thinking about what gets represented, and how.

## LEGITIMACY IN THE ENGAGEMENT OF DISCOURSES

This expansive thinking requires to begin letting go of the idea that legitimacy must be based on a head count of (real or imaginary) reflectively consenting citizens. Such a move might on the face of it seem to invite rejection of both the very idea of legitimation and of deliberative democracy itself. But on closer inspection, all it will prove to require is thinking in a slightly different direction about the entities that populate the political world – not all of which need to be reduced to individuals. This approach builds on a conception of discursive democracy that emphasizes the contestation of discourses in the public sphere (Dryzek 2000).[4]

---

[4] It remains useful to retain the idea of discursive democracy as a critical subcategory of deliberative democracy. Fraser (1992) too speaks of contestation in the public sphere, though engaged by publics rather than discourses. Specifically, contestation for Fraser characterizes the orientation of "subaltern counterpublics" to dominant power structures. She treats contestation as an alternative to deliberation, rather than a category of deliberation.

Deliberative democrats influenced by Habermas (e.g., Benhabib 1996; Bohman 1996; Dryzek 1990, 2000) have emphasized the public sphere as a key site of deliberative politics. Habermas (1996) himself has tried to work out what this might mean in contemporary complex and plural societies, as opposed to the far smaller scale and personal context of his earlier exemplar, the early bourgeois public sphere (Habermas 1989). He speaks of dispersed "subjectless communication" that generates public opinion, whose influence can in turn be converted into communicative power via elections, and then into administrative power via law making. Similarly, Benhabib (1996: 74) speaks of an "anonymous public conversation" in "interlocking and overlapping networks and associations of deliberation, contestation, and argumentation."

In order to give more substance to the idea of diffuse deliberation in the public sphere than the sometimes rather imprecise formulations of Habermas and Benhabib, we can recognize that the public sphere is at any time home to constellations of discourses. A discourse may be defined in somewhat un-Habermasian terms as a shared way of comprehending the world embedded in language. In this sense, a discourse is a set of concepts, categories, and ideas that will always feature particular assumptions, judgments, contentions, dispositions, intentions, and capabilities. These common terms mean that adherents who subscribe in whole or in part to a given discourse will be able to recognize and process sensory inputs into coherent stories or accounts, which in turn can be shared in intersubjectively meaningful fashion. Accordingly, any discourse will have at its center a story line, which may involve opinions about both facts and values. Discourses involve practices, not just words, as social actions are generally accompanied by words that indicate the meaning of action.

Consider, for example, the area of criminal justice, which is currently home to at least four competing discourses. One treats crime as a matter of rational calculation on the part of potential lawbreakers; the story line is one of fully competent individuals weighing in their minds the expected subjective benefit of the crime against the probability of being caught and the severity of the punishment. A second emphasizes instead the circumstances of poverty and deprivation that cause individuals in desperation to commit criminal acts. A third emphasizes the psychopathology of criminals. A fourth emphasizes the social dislocation of the criminal, and the consequent need to reintegrate that individual into the community. Each discourse has at its heart a different model of the (criminal) human being, his or her capacity for autonomous agency, and likely motivations, as well as a model of the society surrounding the criminal. Each is also entwined with values about what constitutes normal, criminal, and deviant behavior; and about what kind of punishment or treatment is desirable. Each can be both backed and undermined by empirical studies that are unlikely immediately to convince adherents of different discourses. Each is entwined with ideological positions taken by politicians. The content of public policy at any time and place depends crucially on the relative weight of these discourses.

Other contemporary examples of particularly powerful discourses would include market liberalism – arguably the dominant policy discourse of our time, at least until the financial crash of 2008 and subsequent reassertion of state economic management; sustainable development, which since the mid-1980s has dominated global environmental affairs; and various feminisms.

Any discourse embodies some conception of common sense and acceptable knowledge; it may embody power by recognizing some interests as valid, while repressing others. However, discourses are not just a surface manifestation of interests, because discourses help constitute identities and their associated interests. The relevant array of discourses depends upon the issue at hand (though some discourses can apply to a range of different issues), and can evolve with time. For example, when it comes to economic issues, relevant discourses might include market liberalism, antiglobalization, social democracy, and sustainable development. When it comes to international security, pervasive discourses might include realism, counterterrorism, Islamic radicalism, and neoconservatism.

Followers of Michel Foucault often treat discourses as power/knowledge formations that condition – to the extent of imprisoning – human subjects. If so, it is hard to be a Foucauldian *and* a deliberative democrat, because deliberation across discourses would be hard to imagine. However, discursive democrats can quite straightforwardly reject this sort of position, and point out that reflective choice across discourses is indeed possible, though not easy. (If it were easy, discourses would lack any organizing force.) A more subtle Foucauldian position toward deliberation is articulated by Walter (2008), who points out that expert discourses such as economics are very hard to escape; it is very hard to talk about the subject matter of economics, which is pervasive, without also implicitly accepting the terms of economic discourse.

Yet discourses enable as well as constrain communication,[5] and deliberation can enter when discourses intersect. Though most actions, practices, and uses of language reinforce the prevailing constellation of discourses, more reflective interventions can sometimes challenge that configuration. While they do not use the "discourse" terminology, the notion of a reflexive modernity as advanced by Ulrich Beck and Anthony Giddens suggests that such choices across discourses become increasingly possible and likely with the "de-traditionalization" of society (see, for example, Beck, Giddens, and Lash 1994; for application to the contestation of discourses in international

---

[5] Similarly, Anthony Giddens's structuration theory treats social structures as simultaneously enabling and constraining.

politics, see Dryzek (2006: 20–5)). The traditions that can be called into question include those that once took economic growth and technological change as inevitable and benign, as well as older traditions of deference and religious authority. Indeed, for Beck the possibility of such choices becomes the defining feature of modernity proper (as opposed to the semi-modernity of industrial society), which ought to augur well for the prospects for deliberative democracy.

Dryzek (2000) argues for a conception of discursive democracy in terms of the contestation of discourses in the public sphere on the grounds that it constitutes the only effective reply to two sets of critics of deliberation. The first set is composed of social choice theorists inspired by Riker (1982), who argue that the very conditions of structurelessness favored by deliberative democrats are exactly the conditions most conducive to arbitrariness, instability, and so manipulation in collective choice (e.g., Van Mill 1996). This critique has force so long as deliberation is a prelude to aggregation of opinion, usually by voting. However, if we reconceptualize public opinion in terms of the provisional outcome of the contestation of discourses as transmitted to the state, the Riker-inspired critique dissolves. Such transmission from the public sphere can come about through a number of means. These include the deployment of rhetoric, through alteration of the terms of political discourse in ways that come to change the understandings of state actors (as Habermas (1996: 486) puts it, "Communicative power is exercised in the manner of a siege. It influences the premises of judgment and decision making in the political system without intending to conquer the system itself."), through creating worries about political instability, and sometimes even through arguments being heard by public officials. In short, there are many non-electoral and nonvoting avenues of influence that bypass the social choice critique (in this light, it is hard to see why Habermas (1996) is at times insistent on stressing elections as the main channel of influence from the public sphere to the state).

Now, this re-specification of discursive democracy and public opinion is not the only way to reply to the social choice critique.[6] However, it has the

---

[6] For example, Miller (1992) argues that social choice theory highlights some problems that deliberation can solve by disaggregating the dimensions of collective choice. Dryzek and List (2003) show further that deliberation can induce truthfulness in the presentation of individual views and preferences, narrow the domain of preference profiles present in a collective choice situation, produce agreement on the set of relevant alternatives, and yield agreement on an interpersonally comparable evaluation variable. All of these effects enable avoidance of the impossibility results that social choice theorists can invoke in criticizing democracy. Thus, properly interpreted, social choice theory shows exactly why deliberation is necessary in any political situation.

benefit of also responding to a set of critics who arrive from precisely the opposite direction: difference democrats who charge deliberative democrats with perpetuating an exclusive gentlemen's club (e.g., Young 1996, 1998; Sanders 1997; similar concerns were raised by Mansbridge (1990)). Where social choice theorists fear unmanageable diversity, difference democrats see stifling uniformity, under which deliberation is dominated by well-educated white males well versed in the niceties of rational argument. In this light, seemingly neutral deliberative procedures are systematically biased precisely because they traffic in unitary notions of public reason.

Taking difference seriously means attending to different identities and the different kinds of communication that accompany them, refusing to erase them in the name of a unitary public reason. This does not mean that "anything goes" in terms of the kinds of communication that deliberative democrats ought to welcome, as well as argument. According to Dryzek (2000: 68), anything goes (even gossips, jokes, and performances) provided it is (*a*) capable of inducing reflection, (*b*) noncoercive, and (*c*) capable of connecting the particular experience of an individual, group, or category with some more general principle (on applying the third of these to testimony, see also Miller (1999)). It would be possible here to add the idea of reciprocity developed by Gutmann and Thompson (1996): communication should be in terms that others who do not share the speaker's frame of reference can accept. Chapter 4 will contain an analysis that goes beyond this kind of categorical test for particular communications in order to judge their implications for construction of an effective deliberative system.

Identity differences should not be allowed to warrant a relativism in which deliberation is impossible and identities are only asserted dogmatically (as feared, for example, by Connolly (1991)). Rather, we should remember that any identity is tightly bound up with a discourse. The possibility for deliberation is retained to the extent that reflective interchange is possible across the boundaries of different discourses – which, to repeat, is the defining feature of a reflexive modernity.

Deliberation as the contestation of discourses in the public sphere lies somewhere in the middle of a triangle whose points are defined by Habermas, Foucault, and Beck. This account remains faithful to the core idea of deliberative democracy, which, as noted at the outset of this chapter, requires that claims made on behalf of or opposing collective decisions require justification to those subject to these decisions in terms that, on reflection, these individuals can accept. At the same time, conceiving of deliberation as the contestation of discourses enables effective response to the criticisms leveled by some social choice theorists and difference democrats. How then can the connection to legitimation be made in a way that respects the constraint of deliberative economy?

## DISCURSIVE LEGITIMACY

*Discursive legitimacy* is achieved to the extent a collective decision is consistent with the constellation of discourses present in the public sphere, in the degree to which this constellation is subject to the reflective control of competent actors. This conception accompanies a definition of *public opinion* as the provisional outcome of the contestation of discourses in the public sphere as transmitted to a public authority. In the language of the deliberative system sketched in chapter 1, this transmission is from public space to empowered space. The public authority in question need not be a state. Any number of the forms of transmission and accountability described in the discussion of the deliberative system in chapter 1 can play parts in the process of legitimation.

Clearly, it is impossible for any decision fully to meet the claims of all competing discourses. That would only be possible if one could envisage full consensus in collective choice, defined as agreement on both a course of action and the reasons for it. In a world of competing discourses, one can imagine such consensus only if the discourses were themselves either merged or dissolved – a prospect that is both unlikely and undesirable, inasmuch as it would erase the differences that make deliberation both possible and necessary. The ideal of consensus has long been rejected by most deliberative democrats, even those sympathetic to the Habermasian tradition where consensus once played a central role in the counterfactual standard of the ideal speech situation (see, for example, Gould 1988: 18, 126–7; Benhabib 1990; Dryzek 1990: 16–17; Bohman 1995; Mackie 1995), though their opponents have not always noticed. Working agreements (or what Sunstein (1997) calls "incompletely theorized agreements") in which assent can be secured for courses of action for different reasons are far more plausible (Eriksen 2006). Such agreements will vary in their degree of resonance with the prevailing constellation of discourses. More resonance means more discursive legitimacy. Working agreements in turn are facilitated by the kind of meta-consensus discussed in chapter 5.

Such possibilities for reasoned agreement resonating with the prevailing constellation of discourses notwithstanding, there inevitably will be times when particular discourses lose out in the contest for influence. Those attuned to an individualistic ontology would probably ask why partisans of losing discourses should accept outcomes.[7] For surely, these individualists would say, we still have to ask this question, because discourses as supra-individual entities are not in a position to confer or withdraw legitimacy, because they lack agency. The resonance of discourses with collective outcomes is something that can be discerned by an observer, but not felt by discourses – because discourses cannot feel.

It is important here to resist reducing discourses to an individualistic ontology in such fashion, because though discourses do not possess agency, they do possess the capacity to underwrite or destabilize collective outcomes – which, from the point of view of legitimacy, is the most important aspect of agency to begin with.[8] This resistance to reductionism does not mean that reflecting individuals need to be purged from the account. It is simply to imply that these individuals are not required to pass competent judgment on every collective outcome to which they are subject (this would of course run headlong into the economy constraint). They can, however, still engage the contestation of discourses as they see fit.

Indeed, it is important that such engagement be possible. For particular discourses might of course be slaves to tradition or religion, or subject to manipulation by spin doctors, advertisers, and propagandists. Such is the very antithesis of deliberative democracy. Crucially, then, the constellation of discourses must itself be open to dispersed and communicatively competent popular control – which returns us to the idea of a reflexive modernity.

Having established what discursive legitimacy means, what now remains to be shown is how it meets the constraint of deliberative economy. To restate the challenge: deliberative democracy requires that for a collective decision to

---

[7] In standard individualistic accounts of democracy, legitimacy is granted to collective outcomes by people who disagree with them either as a result of instrumental calculation that they have a good chance of winning at some future point under the prevailing system of rules, or through recognition that procedures were transparent and fair. The latter principles can be applied in a deliberative context. As Cohen (1989: 21) puts it, "Because the members of a democratic association regard deliberative procedures as the source of *legitimacy*, it is important to them that the terms of their association not merely *be* the results of their deliberation, but that it be *manifest* to them as such" [emphasis in original].

[8] An additional reason why an individualistic ontology is inappropriate is that discourses are not like parties or clubs or groups, for they do not have members, and so are not reducible to a well-defined set of members. It is quite possible for any individual to have simultaneous leanings toward multiple, perhaps incompatible, discourses. Or, to put it another way, subjectivity can be multidimensional (Elster 1986b). For example, part of me may subscribe to a radical green critique of industrial society; another part of me may evaluate government according to how well it is promoting economic growth and a positive investment climate. Different (discursive) situations may invoke these different aspects of subjectivity, which can be latent or manifest at any given time, or indeed not exist until the situation is such as to invoke the aspect in question. This issue and its implications for representation are addressed at length in chapter 3.

be legitimate, it must be subject to reflective acceptance of those subject to it, who should be able to participate in consequential deliberation concerning the production of the decision. But reflective acceptance must be attained in a way that does not impose impossible burdens on the deliberative capacities of individuals or the polity they constitute. As already noted, the most plausible existing approaches respond to the challenge by somehow restricting the number of participants to representatives or to experts in discerning the opinions and interests of others.

The approach proposed here solves the problem, because the number of participants in deliberation is indeterminate. That is, it does not *require* any exclusions – not even exclusions based on not being selected at random for a citizen's jury, or not being elected to parliament, or on apathy, or on a choice not to exercise deliberative citizenship rights. At any given time, the contestation of discourses can be engaged by the many or the few, or indeed by none. Typically, that number will fluctuate widely over time for any given issue area. Think, for example, of the upsurges in environmental concern in most developed countries around 1970, again around 1990, and then again with the explosion of concern for climate change beginning around 2006. Such upsurges might lead to dramatic shifts in the prevailing balance of discourses – which might then remain settled for a while, and receive less public attention. Who can engage such contestation? Pretty much everybody. If Jacobs, Cook, and Delli Carpini (2009) are right, around two-thirds of the U.S. citizenry already does so at some time or another. In addition, the contestation of discourses overlaps with cultural change. Consider, for example, the life and times of feminism over the past three decades in its contest with patriarchy, or environmentalism's rise in a (continuing) contest with industrialism. These discursive advances cannot just be measured in terms of legislation or policy decisions, but also in everyday practice, in challenges made and resisted in households, in workplaces, in classrooms, and elsewhere.

This indeterminacy in numbers of participants in the contestation of discourses solves the seeming incompatible demands of deliberative economy and the need for collective decisions to secure actual popular reflective acceptance. A Schumpeterian might argue here that all that has been done is to substitute packages in the form of discourses for individuals – paralleling the way Schumpeterians substitute the platforms of competing party elites for the will of the people. But there is a crucial difference, because Schumpeterians require that ordinary people do no more than vote, and then sleep between elections. In contrast, discursive contestation can accept, even welcome, the participation of the many at any time. Moreover, party platforms are crafted by elites, whereas discourses can be made and remade by anybody.

This argument does not imply that the deliberative democrat can sit back and accept society's prevailing constellation of discourses, their changes over time, and the many ways in which these discourses can pervade policy making. There are still insistently critical roles to be played. First, deliberative democrats can expose occasions where imperatives emanating from non-democratic sources (related, for example, to the need to maintain the confidence of financial markets) override the constellation of discourses in determining the content of public policy or other collective choices (see, for example, Dryzek 1996a). Second, they can expose the degree to which popular discourses themselves are ideological in the pejorative sense of specifying false necessities, perhaps even the necessity of always having to please financial markets. (Discourses are inescapably ideological in a more neutral sense of "ideology.") Third, they can criticize the degree to which the contestation of discourses is manipulated by strategy and power, by spin doctors and propagandists, and not subject to reflexive control. Fourth, they can be alert to the problem of self-selection by those who engage discourses most enthusiastically. Self-selection may mean that discourses advanced by "the incensed and the articulate" (Carson and Martin 1999: 57) get the most play. Remedies for this problem will be addressed in the discussion of discursive representation in chapter 3.

## FORMATIONS IN PUBLIC SPACE

Beyond these critical tasks, deliberative democrats might also think about the way that particular formations in public space can facilitate the dispersed and competent engagement of discourses in the terms laid out in this chapter. For example, the role that networks can play in the public sphere has been investigated by Schlosberg (1999) in a study of the U.S. environmental justice movement (see also Torgerson 1999: 148–54). A network begins from the bottom up, and is especially interesting from the point of view of the contestation of discourses when it brings together actors with quite different backgrounds. Such is certainly the case for the U.S. environmental justice movement. This began in 1978 in Love Canal, where working-class whites were upset at the toxic chemicals found buried beneath their homes – one of whom, Lois Gibbs, became a key figure in the development of the network. The movement grew to encompass groups from very different racial, ethnic, and class backgrounds, and very different kinds of experiences – though of course they share the experience of exposure and resistance to environmental hazards. With the possible exception of an informational clearing house (the most famous of which is perhaps the Citizen's Clearinghouse for Hazardous Waste, which in 1997 changed its name to the Center for Health, Environment and Justice), a network does not have any central organization, still less an organizational hierarchy.

Social movement networks of this sort can also extend across national boundaries – as is the case for international networks concerned with, for example, biopiracy, human rights, pollution from oil refineries, or landmines. One of the more prominent international social movement networks has been the antiglobalization movement that began in 1999, which brings together activists from many different countries, backgrounds, and with many different initial agendas. This movement was initially scorned by mainstream media and politicians for its negativism and seemingly contradictory goals (such as protectionism for workers in developed countries and a better deal for workers in developing countries). Yet, these very contradictions and differences eventually proved a source of strength, as common positions had to be deliberated to cope with them. The result was the construction of a powerful counter-discourse to market liberal globalization that eventually forced international institutions such as the World Bank and World Trade Organization (WTO) to change at least some of their ways (Stiglitz 2002). In the terms established in this chapter, the World Bank and WTO sought to make their activities more legitimate by making them responsive to a broader array of discourses – beyond the narrow discourse of market liberalism which after 1999 proved increasingly inadequate as a basis for legitimacy.

From the point of view of the democratic contestation of discourses in the public sphere, networks are especially interesting because, to the degree they engage truly diverse participants, networks just have to work according to principles of equality, openness, respect, and reciprocity – standard deliberative virtues. These principles do not just happen to describe particular networks; they are necessary for the network form, so long as it has to produce coordinated social movement activism. (Governance networks as discussed in chapter 6, in particular financial networks as described by Castells (1996), often do not abide by these principles, and are democratically problematic as a result.) There is no centralized hierarchy or leadership promulgating goals, norms, and strategies to bring diverse participants into line.[9] Networks do engage in discursive contests, but the positions they take grow out of the experiences of network participants. For example, the very concept of environmental justice emerges from what began as a collection of local antitoxics

---

[9] The norms that a social movement network develops can, however, sometimes be formalized as constitutive principles. For an example from the Southwest Network for Environmental and Economic Justice in the United States, see Schlosberg (1999: 128).

struggles. The idea that environmental risks are systematically maldistributed across lines of race, ethnicity, and class came later, the product of a variety of local but eventually interconnected experiences. The discourse of environmental justice could then contest, engage, and change other kinds of environmentalism – as well as join them in a larger contest against the discourse of industrialism.

Social movement networks do not merit uncritical celebration. In particular, they raise the specter of what Parkinson (2006a: 167) calls "thorubocracy" – the rule of those who can shout loudest and longest. And as Chambers and Kopstein (2001) remind us, civil society – and so public space – can also be home to, for example, networks of racist hate groups (just as electoral systems can be home to racist voters). Networks in public space, no less than other components of a deliberative system, always merit careful critical scrutiny.

Oppositional discourses such as environmental justice and antiglobalization join other discourses in pressing claims on collective decisions. It would obviously be wrong to say that a collective decision is legitimate only to the degree of its consistency with a relevant oppositional discourse. As pointed out earlier, no decision can ever fully meet the claims of all competing discourses, for simple consensus is in reality neither possible nor desirable. Working agreements that can secure assent for different reasons are more plausible. Discursive legitimacy is achieved to the extent of the resonance of such an agreement with the prevailing constellation of discourses in the degree to which this constellation is subject to dispersed and competent control – to which networks in public space, among other things, can contribute.


## CONCLUSION

Democracy does not have to be a matter of counting heads – even deliberating heads. Nor does it have to be confined to the formal institutions of a state, or the constitutional surface of political life. Accepting such confinement means accepting a needlessly thin conception of democracy, and a needlessly tenuous account of deliberative legitimacy. Legitimacy can be sought instead in the resonance of collective decisions with public opinion, defined in terms of the provisional outcome of the engagement and contestation of discourses in the public sphere as transmitted to public authority in empowered space. Legitimacy so defined can be sought (if never perfectly achieved) in a way that meets the basic constraint of deliberative economy and so solves the scale problem bedeviling deliberative democracy. But we should speak of *discursive* legitimacy only to the extent that engagement and contestation can be joined by a broad variety of competent actors in public space. Unlike other approaches to deliberative legitimacy, in the end it does not matter whether at any one time the number of such actors is large or small.

Legitimacy in a deliberative system is still going to require the making, acceptance, or rejection of claims to representation and representativeness. However, in a deliberative democracy, such representations can have multiple meanings, origins, and targets. And in the approach to legitimacy sketched in this chapter, highlighting the engagement of discourses and the transmission of public opinion to public authority, the representation of discourses will necessarily loom large. Chapter 3 explores exactly what discursive representation can mean and how it can be enacted.

# 3

## Representation

*John S. Dryzek and Simon Niemeyer*

For better or worse, contemporary democracies are mostly representative democracies, at least in the sense that citizens rarely govern themselves collectively and directly. However, representation in the familiar sense of elected representatives governing a geographically bounded demos of citizens does not do justice to a world in which geographical constituencies are only one of the many kinds of entity that now demand representation. Today's world witnesses a proliferation of representation claims made on behalf of dispersed categories, such as citizens or noncitizens, future generations, nonhuman nature, and a wide variety of interests, values, and perspectives. As Urbinati and Warren (2008: 403) put it, "practices of representation increasingly go beyond electoral venues, a phenomenon that testifies to the expansion and pluralization of spaces of political judgment in today's democracies."

Chapter 2 argued that legitimacy in a deliberative democracy depends crucially on the resonance of collective decisions with the prevailing constellation of discourses, requiring too that the contestation of discourses be subject to dispersed and competent control. This means that discourses will often need to be represented, especially when it comes to making claims upon empowered space on behalf of discourses in public space, to use the terminology of the deliberative system established in chapter 1. Discursive representation is therefore central to the solution of the scale problem that animated the discussion of legitimacy.[1]

Discursive representation is actually something that already occurs, though it is not always recognized as such, even by those who do it. In his survey of

---

[1] We believe the term "discursive representation" was first used by Keck (2003) for whom in international politics it means representing perspectives or positions, not discourses as we define them.

the legitimacy claims of unelected representatives, Saward (2009: 1) opens with a quote from the rock star Bono:[2]

I represent a lot of people [in Africa] who have no voice at all. . . . They haven't asked me to represent them.

Nobody elected Bono, he is not formally accountable to anybody, and most of the people he claims to represent have no idea who he is or what he proposes. Nevertheless, his representation claim makes some sense. It makes most sense not in terms of representing African people, nor in terms of representing a place called Africa, but rather in terms of representing a discourse of Africa. "Africa" as constructed in this discourse may bear some relation to people and their places, but more important is that it constructs these people in a particular kind of way: as victims of an unjust world and the caprice of nature, lacking much in the way of agency themselves, with claims upon the conscience of the wealthy.[3] These claims stop at a better deal within the existing world system, falling short of structural transformation. A cynic might also see a place for celebrity and conspicuous charity in the discourse. This discourse is transnational, may be only weakly present in Africa itself, and is generally only one among several or many discourses that particular individuals who engage it (be it at G8 meetings or Live 8 concerts) subscribe to. Discursive representation does, then, already happen, though as our invocation of Bono suggests, it is not necessarily done without controversy. Bono himself might insist he is representing real people, not a discourse. His critics might accept that he is indeed representing a discourse – but not one that actually benefits people in Africa.

Democracy, then, can entail the representation of discourses as well as persons, interests, or groups. In this chapter, we justify discursive representation, and show how it can be accomplished in practice. For those who ponder the design of deliberative institutions as part of the architecture of government, we show how to organize representation in a "Chamber of Discourses." The number of discourses that need representing on any issue is generally much smaller than, for example, the number of representatives in general-purpose legislatures, so it ought to be feasible to constitute relatively small issue-specific deliberating groups that contain representatives of all relevant discourses. For those more attuned to deliberation in the larger public sphere, we show how to evaluate representation practices in the more informal interplay of discourses. We draw contrasts with more conventional notions

---

[2] Sophisticated and wide ranging, Saward's treatment remains wedded to the representation of people rather than discourses.
[3] On social constructions of "Africa," see Ferguson (2006).

about representing individuals and groups, and identify discursive counterparts to concepts of authorization and accountability that figure in most accounts of representation. Discursive representation is one way to redeem the promise of deliberative democracy when the deliberative participation of all affected by a collective decision is infeasible. The idea is especially applicable to settings such as the international system lacking a well-defined demos, though a full discussion of the transnational application is left until chapter 9.

## REPRESENTING DISCOURSES

Representation is conventionally defined as "substantive acting for others," in Pitkin's terms (1967). "Others" may be captured in terms of the discourses to which they subscribe. Whether or not discourses are represented *by* particular persons is an open question. We show how to designate discursive representatives, but also demonstrate less-tangible ways in which discourses can find representation. We do not claim that representation of discourses is always preferable to that of individuals, just that it is different, sometimes feasible when the representation of persons is not so feasible (especially in transnational settings lacking a well-defined demos), and on some criteria and in some settings may do better. Deliberative democracy ought to be less wedded to conventional notions of representing persons than is the aggregative kind of democracy to which it is often contrasted, because it puts talk and communication at the center of democracy (Chambers 2003: 308). There are times when it may be more important for the quality of deliberation that all relevant discourses get represented, rather than that all individuals get represented. And as Mansbridge (2003: 524) points out, in deliberative democracy there is no requirement that perspectives get "presented by a number of legislators proportional to the numbers of citizens who hold those perspectives." Weaver et al. (2007) show experimentally that the "weight" of a message in the forum depends more on the frequency with which it is repeated than on the number of people who present it, a finding that further undermines any argument for proportionality in representation in communicative settings.

Exactly what is meant by a discourse was defined in chapter 2. Further to that definition, any political discourse will normally feature an ontology of entities recognized as existing or relevant. Among these entities, some (e.g., individuals, social classes, groups, or states) will be ascribed agency, the capacity to act, while in competing discourses the same entities will be denied agency (e.g., liberal individualists deny the agency of classes). For those entities recognized as agents, some motives will be recognized, others denied. So, for example, administrative discourses recognize the agency of managers motivated by public interest values, while market liberal discourses ascribe to administrators only rational egoism. Any discourse will also contain an account of the relationships taken to prevail between agents and others. So economistic discourses see competition as natural, while feminist discourses would see the possibility of cooperation while recognizing pervasive patriarchy. Finally, discourses rely on metaphors and other rhetorical devices. So a "spaceship earth" metaphor is central to some environmental discourses, while horror stories about "welfare queens" and the like are central to individualistic conservative discourses on social policy. (For details on the logical content of political discourses, see Alker and Sylvan (1994) and Dryzek and Berejikian (1993).)

Discourses do not constitute the entirety of nonindividual political phenomena that may demand representation. In particular, discourses should not be confused with groups defined by ascriptive characteristics, such as race, class, or gender; coalitions of actors who may favor a policy for different reasons; interests, which though they may be constituted by discourses, can also exist independent of discourse; interest groups, which have a tangible organization that discourses lack; or opinions on particular issues, which may be embedded in particular discourses – but need not be.

## WHY REPRESENT DISCOURSES?

Given that other modes of representation already exist, why might discursive representation be attractive? We begin our argument through reference to the rationality of systematically involving multiple discourses in collective decision. We then turn to an ontological justification of the priority of discourses, grounded in the discursive psychology of a world of fractured individual commitments. This account enables an ethical argument that even the individual autonomy prized by liberals can be promoted by representing the multiple discourses each individual inhabits. We then show that discursive representation is especially appropriate when a well-bounded demos is hard to locate.

## Rationality

In a long tradition encompassing among others Mill, Dewey, Popper (1966), and Charles Lindblom (1965), democracy is seen as more rational in the production of collective outcomes than are its alternatives. For democracy provides opportunities for policy proposals to be criticized from a variety of directions, both before and after their implementation, thus providing the ideal setting for systematic trial and error in policy making. Democracy is, in Mill's terms, a "Congress of Opinions." The key consideration here is that all the vantage points for criticizing policy get represented – *not* that these vantage points get represented in proportion to the number of people who subscribe to them. When it comes to representing arguments, proportionality may actually be undesirable – for it can pave the way to groupthink and the silencing of uncomfortable voices from the margins or across divides. Sunstein's deployment of social psychological findings (2000) on group polarization shows that if members of a group (such as a jury) start with an inclination in one direction, deliberation will have the effect of moving the average position in the group toward an extreme version of that inclination. If a substantial majority of the population leans in one direction, proportionality in their representation in the forum may produce this movement to an extreme. Thus, it is important from the point of view of responsiveness to the initial distribution of positions, let alone collective rationality, to have countervailing discourses well represented in the forum at the outset to check this polarizing effect.

For policy-making rationality, then, all relevant discourses should get represented – no matter how many people subscribe to each. Rationality may even benefit from the presence of a vantage point to which *nobody* subscribes; such was presumably the rationale for the use of a "Devil's Advocate" when evaluating cases for sainthood in the Catholic Church (which is of course not a paragon of democracy in most other senses).[4]

Now, it is one thing to ask that for the sake of rationality all vantage points, perspectives, or viewpoints get represented more or less equally in a forum, quite another to ask that all relevant *discourses* get represented. Our justification here is that discourses have a solidity that "perspectives" do not. Further, discourses can be measured and described (we will explore methods in the sections on selection below), while "perspectives" can be more elusive. In contemplating the representation of perspectives, Young (2000: 143–4) solves this elusiveness problem by assuming that "to the extent that persons are positioned similarly in those [social] structures, then they have similar perspectives," such that analysis of social structure can guide the selection of representatives. In contrast, we are open to discourses having a force independent of, and possibly prior to, social structure. Discursive representation is a conceptually simpler matter than the complex representations of perspectives, interests, opinions, and groups that are the ingredients of what Young calls "communicative democracy."

---

[4] The Devil's Advocate was abolished by Pope John Paul II, leading to an irrational proliferation of saints.

## An ontological justification

What are the key entities that populate the political world and merit representation? In the liberal tradition, the answer would be "individuals." However, as Castiglione and Warren (2006: 13) point out:

> ...from the perspective of those who are represented, what is represented are not persons as such, but some of the interests, identities, and values that persons have or hold. Representative relationships select for specific aspects of persons, by framing wants, desires, discontents, values and judgments in ways that they become publicly visible, articulated in language and symbols, and thus politically salient.

Thus, the whole person cannot be represented (see also Young 2000: 133). Which "aspects of persons" merit representation, and what happens when they point in different directions? This question has received a number of analytical treatments. Sagoff (1988) distinguished between the "consumer" and "citizen" preferences of individuals; so (to use one of his examples) the same individuals who would as consumers love to use a ski resort will as citizens oppose its construction in a wilderness area. Sagoff resolves the problem by asserting the superiority of politics and citizen preferences over markets and consumer preferences; economists wedded to contingent valuation would disagree, as would market liberals. Goodin (1986) speaks of "laundering preferences" before they are ready to be put into collective choice processes. When it comes to elections, Brennan and Lomasky (1993) argue that the very fact that any one person's vote is almost always inconsequential releases voters' "expressive preferences" as opposed to their material self-interest in deciding whom to vote for. Thus, in choosing whether to emphasize voting systems or markets, we also choose the relative weight of individuals' expressive preferences and their material interests. Expressive preferences might involve ethics or identity politics.

We prefer a less analytical and more empirical treatment of what Elster (1986*b*) calls the "multiple self." Speaking in terms of "preferences" is unduly restrictive, for aspects of the multiple self may not be reducible to preferences (and the instrumental form of rationality it implies). This question can be illuminated by discursive psychology (Edwards and Potter 1992). Discursive psychology takes seriously the Wittgensteinian notion of language games as the framework in which cognition is possible. The mind itself lies at the intersection of such games: "I inhabit many different discourses each of which has its own cluster of significations" (Harré and Gillett 1994: 25). Subjectivity is, then, multifaceted: "most of us will fashion a complex subjectivity from participation in many different discourses" (Harré and Gillett 1994: 25). This is not a matter of an autonomous self picking and choosing across discourses, for the multifaceted self is constituted by discourses; we cannot think outside discourses, for they also enter and help constitute the mind. However, the very fact that each individual engages multiple discourses provides some freedom for maneuver, such that "fluid positionings instead of fixed roles" are possible (Harré and Gillett 1994: 36) – which is crucial when it comes to the possibilities for the reflection that is central to deliberative and democratic interaction. Thus, persons are not simply bundles of discourses; autonomous individuals can reflect across the discourses they engage, even as these individuals can never fully escape their constraints. This feature fits nicely with deliberative democracy, for the reflective agents who populate a deliberative democracy can be seen as negotiating the field of discourses in which they necessarily participate, with more or less competence.

The individual selves prized by liberals can, then, be quite fractured by the discourses that the individual engages. Group representation is no less problematic in this light. It is normally tied to descriptive representation, where "blacks represent blacks and women represent women," as Mansbridge (1999) puts it. There may be more than one discourse relevant to black interests or women's interests, which a unitary framing of that group's interests will not capture. Some of its advocates recognize the need to "pluralize group representation," but then face indeterminacy in how far to go in representing different subgroups (Dovi 2002: 741). This indeterminacy can be ameliorated (though not eliminated) if we can show how the range of relevant discourses can be described.

### Ethics

The liberal argument for the representation of individuals has an ethical as well as an ontological aspect, on the grounds that individuals are capable of self-government, and the repositories of moral worth. There are non-liberal arguments in which groups, social classes, and communities have similar moral standing; but what about discourses? There is actually no need to give discourses any moral standing that is not reducible to that of the individuals who subscribe to them. Yet there is still a moral (as opposed to ontological) argument for discursive representation. Once we accept the insight from discursive psychology that any individual may engage multiple discourses, it is important that all these discourses get represented. For otherwise, the individual in his or her entirety is not represented. Discursive representation may, then, do a morally superior and a more comprehensive job of representing persons than theories that treat individuals as unproblematic wholes. Liberals might reply that each individual should manage the demands of competing discourses himself or herself prior to seeking representation, because an autonomous person is one who chooses not just among options, but also among reasons for that choice (Watson 1975). Yet, demanding this management prior to representation may paradoxically disrespect individual autonomy, if it requires the individual to repress some aspect of his or her self. For example, a government employee may choose to vote for party X because they fear that party Y, whose platform they otherwise prefer on moral grounds, will undertake budget cuts that endanger their job. Their moral preferences are repressed in their voting choice. Discursive representation would ensure both aspects of the self of this government employee get represented in subsequent deliberations.

## The decline of the demos

Rationality, ontology, and ethics can justify discursive representation in any time or place. We now introduce some developments in contemporary politics that reinforce the case. Democratic theory has traditionally been tied closely to the idea of a well-bounded demos: no demos, no democracy. Correspondingly, in Pitkin's classic statement (1967) about representation, the definition of the people is logically prior to contemplation of their representation. Representative democracy in this light requires a precisely bounded citizenry, normally defined by membership of a political unit organized on a territorial basis, which then elects representatives. However, today's world is increasingly unlike this. It is in politics beyond the demos that key features of deliberative democracy are now being tested (Scheuerman 2006).

Authority increasingly escapes the sovereign state, to be located in, or diffused throughout, the global system. Sometimes, authority is transferred to an international governmental organization, such as the World Trade Organization (WTO). When a tangible organization like the WTO exists, it is possible to imagine global elections to its board – but impossible to institute them in any feasible future. The most that can be hoped for is the representation of states – which entails representation of peoples at one very considerable remove (and of course not all states are internally democratic). Currently, the WTO runs according to a single discourse, that of market-oriented neoliberalism. A more democratic WTO would be responsive to a broader range of discourses, such as the counter-discourses constructed by antiglobalization activists (see chapter 9 for a more detailed treatment of global politics in these terms).

Political authority is also increasingly diffused into informal networks made up of governmental and nongovernmental actors, be they businesses, professional associations, unions, nongovernmental organizations (NGOs), social movements, or individual activists (Rhodes 1997). Networked governance is almost impossible to render accountable in standard democratic terms, for there is often no unique demos associated with a network. This is especially true when networks cross national boundaries. If networks cannot be held formally accountable to any well-defined demos, we have to look in other directions to render them accountable. One way of doing this is to try to ensure that a network is not dominated by a single discourse whose terms are accepted uncritically by all involved actors in a way that marginalizes other discourses that could claim relevance. For example, the international networks of finance and capital described by Castells (1996) have generally been dominated by economistic discourses to the exclusion of social justice discourses. International environmental networks have often been dominated by a moderate discourse of sustainable development that by the lights of more radical green discourses is too easily accommodated to economic growth rather than effective environmental conservation. The democratization of governance networks will be addressed at greater length in chapter 6.

If the demos is in decline, then Ankersmit's contention (2002) that the process of representation itself constitutes any "people" gains in plausibility. This kind of indeterminacy can be embraced by discursive representation, under which different discourses can constitute the relevant people in different ways. So, for example, in a cosmopolitan discourse, "the people" is global; in a nationalist discourse, it is always more particular.

We now ask how small groups might be constituted formally in order to combine effective deliberation with discursive representation. Then, we will turn to more informal ways of securing discursive representation that resonate with accounts of deliberative democracy emphasizing engagement of discourses in a broad public sphere.


## FORMALLY CONSTITUTING THE CHAMBER OF DISCOURSES

It is possible to imagine a Chamber of Discourses corresponding to more familiar assemblies based on the representation of individuals. Existing parliamentary chambers do of course feature discourses, but only unsystematically, as a by-product of electoral representation.

We have already argued that there is no need for proportionality in discursive representation. However, it is important to ensure that each relevant discourse gets articulate representation, and we should be wary of the "lottery of talent" introducing inequalities across discursive representatives. Having multiple representatives for each discourse ought to ameliorate at least chance factors here. It may also be true that the nature of a discourse is associated with the capacity of its adherents to articulate its content. Here, deliberative democrats would stress the need for forum design to bring out the "communicative competence" of representatives. Experience with deliberative mini-publics shows that ordinary citizens can become capable deliberators.

In thinking about the Chamber of Discourses, we must allow that in deliberation individuals reflect upon the discourses they engage and can change their minds. Mansbridge (2003: 524) suggests that when "deliberative mechanisms work well" they should select against "the least informed political positions in the polity." It is entirely possible that particular discourses initially identified for representation in the forum will not survive deliberation unscathed, but that may not be so bad if the transformation renders the constellation of discourses more publicly defensible. Niemeyer (2004) demonstrates this process empirically. On an environmental issue deliberated in a citizen's jury, he shows that a discourse that tried to assuage anxieties on both sides of the issue was transformed for its adherents toward a more clearly preservationist discourse. The possibility that discourses get transformed once represented does mean that discursive representation is inconsistent with a "delegate" model of representation, under which representatives simply follow the instructions of their constituents.

We should also recognize that discourses can be transformed, or even constituted, by the very fact of their representation. Representing a previously marginalized discourse may mean that a particular category of people gets constituted as agents within the discourse. For example, the fact that the discourse of environmental justice became heard in policy-making processes in the United States in the late 1980s validated the agency in environmental affairs of low-income ethnic minority victims of pollution. And the discourse of Africa associated with Bono perhaps exists mainly in the fact of its representation at high-profile international events. But this last feature is by no means unique to discourses. As Ankersmit (2002: 115) puts it, perhaps overstating the point, "without political representation we are without a conception of what reality – the represented – is like; without it, political reality has neither face nor contours. Without representation there is no represented."

To constitute formally a Chamber of Discourses would require to begin a way of identifying and describing the array of relevant discourses on an issue.

We would then need a way to designate representatives of each discourse (or of positions in the array of discourses). Members of the Chamber of Discourses could not be elected, for then they would represent constituencies of individuals. Another option would be through random selection, as discussed in chapter 2. The problem with random selection is that large numbers are needed to guard against the possibility that a relevant discourse might be missed. But the larger the number of representatives, the harder it becomes for them to deliberate together. This is why large-scale processes, such as deliberative opinion polls, citizens' assemblies, and our own Australian Citizens' Parliament subdivide their participants into smaller deliberative groups of no more than twenty or so each. Thus, we need a procedure better than random chance to ensure that all discourses are effectively represented in each group.

A more economical alternative would involve constituting a deliberative mini-public of around fifteen to twenty citizens, the kind of number now used extensively in institutions such as citizens' juries, consensus conferences, and planning cells. The standard procedure is to begin with an initial random sample of citizens, then target individuals with particular social characteristics – age, education, place of residence, income, ethnicity, and so forth. This is essentially a "politics of presence" kind of approach to representation (Phillips 1995). However, discursive representation involves (in Phillips's terms) a "politics of ideas." There is no guarantee or even strong likelihood that people with different social characteristics will in fact represent different discourses; or that a reasonably full range of social characteristics will guarantee a reasonably full range of discourses is present in the forum. Discursive representation can improve the deliberative capacities of institutional designs featuring random selection by ensuring that a comprehensive range of discourses is present. Fortunately, there are methods available to both (*a*) map the constellation of discourses relevant to an issue and (*b*) determine which individuals best represent each discourse. We now describe some methods. These methods illustrate what is possible. Our basic argument for discursive representation does not depend on commitment to any or all of them.

## SYSTEMATIC SELECTION OF DISCURSIVE REPRESENTATIVES

Davies, Sherlock, and Rauschmayer (2005) show how Q methodology can be used to recruit individuals who best represent particular arguments to deliberative mini-publics. Q methodology involves measuring an individual's subjective orientation to an issue area in terms of his/her ranking of a set of thirty-five to sixty statements about the issue in a "Q sort." These statements can be keyed to the five features of discourses listed earlier: ontology, agency, motives of agents, relationships, and metaphors (though this is not done by Davies, Sherlock, and Rauschmayer). For example, in a study of discourses surrounding local sustainability issues in the United Kingdom, Barry and Proops (1999: 342) deploy thirty-six statements. One of their statements about ontology is "LETS [local employment and trading systems] is a new type of economy in which sustainability is a key aspect." A statement referring to agency is "We all have to take responsibility for environmental problems." A statement on motives is "People are taking a short-term view: they're not thinking about the long term." One about relationships is "You can't look at one part of the planet, because all the parts interact."[5]

The ranking process is itself reflective, so consistent with the notion that discourses can be transformed and winnowed in the process of their representation. Individuals from the subject population are asked to order the statements into a manageable number of categories from "most agree" to "most disagree." The subject population could be several hundred individuals selected at random (Q methodologists are happy working with much smaller numbers of subjects, but the link we are trying to make here to representation means that a larger number might be required to help us to find particularly good representatives of each discourse). The Q sorts so produced can then be factor analyzed; factor analysis is essentially a summary procedure that produces a manageable number of (in this case) discourses. And we can

---

[5] Though Barry and Proops do not have a "metaphors" category, an example of a relevant metaphor statement about sustainability is "If we continue with activities which destroy our environment and undermine the conditions for our survival, we are a virus" (speech by UK Environment Minister Michael Meacher, 2003). Many (but not all) Q methodologists describe what they do as a form of discourse analysis. The justification for using principles of political discourse analysis to select the statements that are the grist for the Q analysis (Q sample) is established by Dryzek and Berejikian (1993). We can begin by generating several hundred statements relevant to an issue (which can be done by holding discussion groups and transcribing what is said, or surveying sources such as newspaper letters columns, talkback radio, political speeches, weblogs, etc.). We then apply a sampling frame to select around thirty-five to sixty statements for the Q sort itself. The frame can be based on the five categories we introduced earlier in defining the concept of discourse: ontology (entities whose existence is affirmed or denied), agency (who or what has the capacity to act, and who or what does not), motives ascribed to agents, relationships (such as hierarchies on the basis of expertise, age, wealth, or gender; or their corresponding equalities), metaphors, and other rhetorical devices. Once the statements are classified, the required numbers of statements can be selected from each category. Dryzek and Berejikian and Barry and Proops also use a second dimension for statement categorization based on the kind of claim made in the statement (definitive, designative, evaluative, and advocative).

compute a loading (correlation coefficient) between each discourse and each individual. Those individuals loading highest on a particular discourse will make particularly good discursive representatives – at least in the sense that they are characteristic of the discourse in question, though of course they can vary in how articulate they are when it comes to deliberation itself. There may, however, be circumstances in which it is desirable to select more complex individuals who load on more than one discourse (as we will see in the section on "Different sorts of discursive representatives").

To take an example, consider the study of political discourses in Russia in the late 1990s reported in Dryzek and Holmes (2002: 92–113). This study identified three discourses. The first, chastened democracy, remained committed to democracy despite current political disasters. The second, reactionary antiliberalism, regretted the demise of the Soviet Union and opposed the postcommunist status quo. The third, authoritarian development, disapproved of both the Soviet Union and the postcommunist present, seeking a better economic future under a disciplined autocracy. Among the Russians interviewed, the person with the highest loading on chastened democracy (70, where 100 would indicate perfect agreement) is a public relations manager who describes herself as a liberal. The person with the highest loading (59) on reactionary antiliberalism is a teacher who describes himself as a Russian nationalist. The two people with the equal highest loading (60) on authoritarian development are a student who describes herself as a nonpartisan atheist, and a construction worker who claims not to care about politics. Assuming they are articulate, these individuals would on the face of it make particularly good representatives for any forum in which representation of the discourse in question is required – within Russia, or even internationally. (At meetings of international economic organizations, it could be instructive to have somebody representing authoritarian development.)

Most Q studies seek only to map discourses present. Davies, Sherlock, and Rauschmayer (2005) use Q to select participants for deliberative forums. We can designate those participants as representatives of discourses. In most theories of representation, those represented somehow authorize the representation. The method we have described seems to substitute social science for political process, with the risk of empowering an unaccountable social scientific elite. We address procedures for countering this hazard in the section on "Authorization and accountability"; but one check might be to expand the range of methods used, to which we now turn.

## OTHER METHODS FOR SELECTING DISCURSIVE
## REPRESENTATIVES

While we have discussed Q methodology as a particularly systematic way to identify relevant discourses and choose discursive representatives, there are other ways. When it comes to discourse identification, there exist in many issue areas enumerations of relevant discourses based on historical analysis. So, for example, for U.S. environmental politics, Brulle (2000) describes seven discourses on the environmental side: wildlife management, conservation, preservation, reform environmentalism, deep ecology, environmental justice, and ecofeminism, along with an antienvironmental discourse of "manifest destiny." In criminal justice policy, at least four discourses can be enumerated, as we noted in chapter 2. One stresses the psychopathology of criminals, a second treats crime as a matter of rational choice, a third emphasizes the social causes of crime, and a fourth the social dislocation of individual offenders. Each discourse comes with a range of treatments: respectively, retribution, deterrence, social policy, and restorative justice. In the criminal justice policy area, one could imagine constituting a Chamber with representatives from these different discourses. In these environmental and criminal justice examples, it is not hard to identify individual activists, publicists, or politicians associated with each discourse, who could serve as discursive representatives.

Q is an interpretive methodology that happens to be quantitative, but other interpretive methods for discourse analysis are qualitative or ethnographic. Both in-depth interviews with individuals and focus groups could be used to map relevant discourses in an issue area. Hochschild (1981) analyzes twenty-eight depth interviews of rich and poor Americans in order to map different beliefs about distributive justice, and the sorts of distributive rules that should be applied to different policy areas. Despite considerable ambiguity and inconsistency among her subjects, Hochschild's analysis could be mined for discourses and their representatives. Notably, she finds six kinds of distributive rule applied by her subjects – though their application is issue-area specific. But (for example) when it comes to policy for financing schools, it would be possible to identify using her analysis an individual who subscribes to a discourse of need, one that stresses performance, and so forth. An ethnographic study that began with the intent of identifying discourses and their representatives would enable a much sharper focus.

Opinion surveys too could inform the identification of relevant discourses, though their lack of interpretive depth may mean they have to be supplemented by other sorts of analysis. So, for example, Kempton, Boster, and Hartley (1995) combine surveys and semi-structured interviews. They find a vernacular environmental discourse that appears to be shared by most ordinary people in the United States (including categories of people they targeted for explicit antienvironmental sentiments), though for some individuals in-depth interviews reveal that it is overridden by discourses that stress either employment and social justice or cynicism about the way environmental values get deployed (Kempton, Boster, and Hartley 1995: 215). Discursive representation here would mean identifying individuals who prioritized the latter two discourses, as well as those who did not.

There are, then, a number of methods that could be deployed to select discursive representatives. Different methods might yield different representations, just as different electoral systems produce different configurations of political parties. Triangulation across different methods might increase our confidence in the validity of any particular representation, thought it would be of little help should representations differ. But in the latter case, there would be no problem in using different methods to pick different discursive representatives. One method might simply pick up on a discourse that another method missed. For example, opinion surveys would miss subjugated or marginal discourses that were not preconceived by the survey designer; it might take depth interviews or Q methodology to reveal these. We should also allow that particular discourses may only crystallize in the process of selection of their representatives. Depth interviews might well have such an effect, especially if they have the salutary effects psychotherapists claim.

Among alternative methods for the selection of discursive representatives, Q methodology or depth interviews should be used when the content and configuration of relevant discourses is weakly understood. Depth interviews should be used to tease out discourses that have yet to crystallize fully in the understandings of any actor. Opinion surveys can be used when the content of relevant discourses is well understood and/or financial constraints suggest a low-cost method. Historical methods are appropriate when conducting interviews is impossible, too expensive, or the population from which one might select discursive representatives is highly dispersed (as in transnational affairs).

## DIFFERENT SORTS OF DISCURSIVE REPRESENTATIVES

Choosing as representatives for participation in deliberation only those individuals who are strongly identified with particular discourses is not necessarily the most defensible procedure. Discursive psychology suggests that the typical individual actually has access to more than one discourse. In this light, choosing individuals who identify strongly with a single discourse might look a bit like selecting for extremism. One solution here might be to constitute two deliberating sub-chambers: one made up of individuals initially identifying strongly with single discourses, the other made up of individuals identified with two or more discourses. The first group might then be best at opening up the relevant range of issues, the second better at reaching reflective judgment across discourses. Alternatively, we might decide what we actually want the deliberating group to do, and select for extremism and moderation accordingly. If the deliberating forum is akin to a jury delivering a verdict (say, a health-care committee deciding whether or not an expensive lifesaving treatment is warranted in a particular case), we might want to select for moderation across discourses. If we want the forum to generate ideas (e.g., on a novel policy problem), we might want to select for extremism in discursive representation.[6] But in light of the possibility of deliberation-induced change in individuals' commitments to particular discourses, and even the content of discourses, these suggestions remain speculative. Designing empirical studies to test the effects of different forum compositions along these lines would actually be quite straightforward.

It might even be useful to have a "Chamber of Extremism" and a "Chamber of Moderation" sitting in parallel. This would be analogous to the way lower and upper houses currently operate in bicameral parliaments, with the upper house expected to be a moderate house of review controlling the partisan excesses of the lower house. In practice, lower houses are themselves vulnerable to excessive moderation as parties converge on the position of the median voter in their efforts to win elections, so an explicit "Chamber of Extremism" might actually improve the quality of debate by sharpening differences.

Another possible institutional design might involve a "Chamber of Moderation adjudicating the presentations made to it by individuals strongly associated with particular discourses. Such a design would resemble the way mini-publics such as citizens' juries and consensus conferences already operate, though citizen adjudicators in these forums are currently selected on the basis of their lack of any prior partisanship, rather than sympathy with multiple discourses.

In thinking about discursive representation, it is important to stress that discourses are not necessarily reducible to the opinions of a well-defined set of subscribers. Discursive psychology accepts, and Q methodological studies

---

[6] Discursive representatives could reflexively help constitute the "we" here.

typically confirm, that any given individual may subscribe partially to several different, perhaps competing, discourses, each of which resonates with a particular aspect of the "self." For this individual, different situations may then invoke different discourses. Discursive representation then involves representing discourses, not selves, even when we need to identify individuals to articulate the discourse in question. It is even possible that a particular discourse may find no complete resonance with any individual, though partial resonance with many, attracting minor aspects of a number of "divided selves." How exactly might the representation of any such discourse be organized? One solution might be to find the individual or set of individuals loading most highly on this discourse – even if they load more highly on another discourse. The likelihood of any such fugitive discourse on any issue is an empirical question. But such a discourse could conceivably represent a new understanding currently at the margins of public opinion – with the potential to become more significant in future. It might, of course, also represent an understanding on the way out, or one that is destined to remain marginal. But from the point of view of problem-solving rationality discussed earlier, marginal discourses may still be important. Representation of marginal discourses is especially important from the point of view of democratic equality to the degree dominant discourses embody privilege and power.

## DECISION AND POWER

How should decisions be reached in any formal Chamber of Discourses? One can imagine a variety of decision mechanisms, including voting. Consensus may be a plausible rule if the Chamber is composed of a small number of individuals, each of whom can be associated with more than one discourse (so featuring moderation as defined earlier), though undesirable conformity pressures may accompany small size. Consensus is less plausible as numbers increase, or to the degree each participant is strongly associated with a particular discourse, though even here we should not assume that discourses are necessarily incommensurable. "Working agreements" may still be possible in which participants agree of a course of action for different reasons, but understand as morally legitimate the reasons of others (Eriksen 2006). And even if they cannot agree on major issues, participants might still practice the "economy of moral disagreement" advocated by Gutmann and Thompson (1996), what we could style an economy of discourse disagreement, searching for aspects of issues representatives can agree upon. There is no justification for giving discursive representatives veto power over decisions that affect their discourse, of the sort that Young (1990) believes should be possessed by representatives of oppressed groups.

How much power should any Chamber of Discourses possess in relation to other sorts of representative institutions, such as legislatures? Discursive representation might complement the work of familiar institutions, rather than replace them. A formal Chamber of Discourses could take its place in existing institutional architecture in a variety of ways. Mini-publics deployed so far have generally been issue specific, authorized by legislatures or political executives, constituted for one occasion, then dissolved immediately afterward. This is the normal procedure when it comes to consensus conferences, planning cells, citizen's juries, and the citizens' assemblies used to frame referendum questions on constitutional reform in British Columbia, Ontario, and the Netherlands. If (in contrast to the Canadian Citizens' Assemblies, which had a specified role in decision making), the Chamber of Discourses is advisory, then it needs an audience, which may be found in the broader public sphere, as well as the legislature. Taking the idea of a Chamber of Discourses very literally would suggest that it could begin with several hundred citizens serving a term as members of the upper house of a bicameral legislature (a proposal of this sort was made by the Demos think tank in the context of debates about reform of the House of Lords in the United Kingdom). Subsets of the house could then be chosen along the lines we have specified to deliberate particular issues. Alternatively, these citizens could constitute Leib's proposed fourth "popular" branch of government (2004), reviewing policy proposals generated in executive or legislative branches, or generating proposals for review by the other three branches. In non-state and transnational contexts, it is easier to imagine granting more substantial and perhaps even final authority to a Chamber of Discourses, if other sorts of representative institutions are not available. Within more familiar governmental contexts, legislative mandates for public consultation and participation present opportunities for experimentation, especially in cases where established forms of consultation are recognized as ineffective. Liberal democratic governments are occasionally willing to experiment, as, for example, in UK Prime Minister Gordon Brown's 2007 "big idea" for citizens' juries on major policy issues, plus a citizens' summit to deliberate basic national values.

## AUTHORIZATION AND ACCOUNTABILITY

Theories of representation from Pitkin (1967) to Young (1990: 128–33) require not just the selection of representatives, but also their authorization by and accountability to those represented. Issues concerning authorization and accountability become pressing to the degree a Chamber of Discourses has an explicit share in decision-making authority. Authorization is, on the face of it, problematic in the methods we have described for the selection of discursive representatives, which would involve social science rather than political process. Such use of social science is already practiced when it comes to the constitution of familiar mini-publics, such as deliberative polls, citizens' juries, consensus conferences, and citizens' assemblies. Random selection itself is a social scientific technique that often makes little sense to those not versed in social science. And the use of social characteristics to narrow down an initial random sample into a smaller deliberating group is again soaked in social science theories about what individual characteristics matter, as well as assumed links between social characteristics and points of view. Further, when it comes to the engineering of electoral systems, social scientific theories inform the selection of alternative systems (Reilly 2001) (though as the British Columbia Citizens' Assembly shows, such theories can be made intelligible to lay citizens). Yet the authorization problem remains.

There are several ways to ameliorate this problem. To begin, the social science itself can be done as democratically as possible. In the case of Q methodology, this principle would entail using only statements that appear in ordinary political language, not ones contrived by the analyst. The initial set of statements should be as comprehensive as possible in capturing the variety of things that could be said about the issue at hand, so as to enable capture of the extant variety of discourses. For all methods, data should be analyzed in ways that minimize the observer's discretion in interpreting results. Multiple methods can be used to ensure no discourse is missed. Once results are produced, they can be presented in plain language for validation by citizen participants. In Q methodology, it is easy to summarize an identified discourse in narrative form (Dryzek and Holmes 2002), and those designated as representatives of a discourse can be asked if the narrative really does describe them.

Once we have identified a set of individuals loading highly on a discourse, we could ask them to select a representative. This would require informing this set about both the content of the discourse and the way it was delineated. Further, it may be possible to involve citizens themselves in doing the social science. Social scientists could still be technical consultants, but defer to citizens when it comes to judgments about (say) the items to be included in a Q sort or survey, or the interpretation of depth interview transcripts. Whatever use is made of social science, it is important to make it transparent to nonexperts involved in the forum in question. Analysts could then be accountable before hearings – just as executive officials can be called before hearings of nonexpert representatives in an elected legislature. Those conducting the hearings could not, however, be discursive representatives, as they would have been selected by the procedure they are assessing. Instead, they could be drawn from the larger pool from which discursive representatives are selected. As a final check, validation of the configuration of discursive representatives could be sought from actors in the broader public sphere by inviting their comments on forum composition.

Accountability cannot in discursive representation be induced by the representative's fear of sanction; for there is no subsequent election at which the representative might be punished. Discursive accountability must be understood instead in communicative fashion. To be accountable to the discourse (or discourses) they represent, representatives must continue to communicate in terms that make sense within that discourse (or discourses), even as they encounter different others in the Chamber of Discourses, and even as they reflect and change their minds in such encounters. If, in the limiting case, representatives seem to be abandoning their discourse and adopting another (as happened in the environmental citizens' jury we discussed earlier), then discursive accountability requires that any shift make sense in the terms established by the original discourse.[7] This requirement is not necessarily met when, for example, social justice advocates get drawn into the language of stability, security, and efficiency; when environmentalists abandon the language of intrinsic value in nature, and start speaking in terms of how preserving nature has economic benefits; or when advocates of an ethical foreign policy slip into the language of realism. Discursive accountability can be facilitated by publicity, such that representatives are always mindful of how what they say will be received in the terms of the discourse(s) that validate their representation. Discursive representatives do not have to be "delegates" of discourses, unable to reflect and change their minds. But if they do change their minds, they must justify the change in terms set by the discourse(s) they represent.

---

[7] This requirement was in fact met in the citizens' jury. The two discourses were not mutually exclusive (orthogonal), enabling those who shifted to reason their way from the original discourse on which they loaded to a more exclusive association with "preservationism" in a way that could make sense to those outside the jury who subscribed to the original discourse.

## A MORE INFORMAL CHAMBER OF DISCOURSES
## IN PUBLIC SPACE

We noted at the outset that discourses currently get represented in mostly informal fashion (e.g., by high-profile activists such as Bono). Conceptualizations of deliberative democracy that emphasize the engagement of discourses in a broad public sphere can welcome this kind of activity. Discourses are generated within and populate the public sphere, and so a more informal Chamber of Discourses could be grounded in this public sphere. Historically, new discourses have been brought onto the democratic agenda from oppositional public spheres, outside the formal institutions of the state. Think, for example, of how environmentalism and feminism arrived in the 1960s. In some cases, these discourses were brought very quickly into governing processes – environmentalism in the United States in 1970, and feminism in Scandinavian countries around the same time. (The result in these countries was, however, rapid attenuation of any radical critique associated with the discourse.) This informal Chamber could coexist with the formal Chamber we have described, and they could be linked as elements in what Hendriks (2006: 499–502) calls an "integrated deliberative system." Within that system, representatives in the informal Chamber could present discourses for validation in the formal Chamber. These informal representatives could also exercise critical oversight over the constellation of discourses identified for the formal Chamber (as indicated in our earlier discussion of discursive accountability).

If we think of a Chamber of Discourses in these informal terms, then it would seem at first sight that all that needs to be done is leave it alone. In Habermas's terms, the public sphere is a "wild" zone that can be protected by, for example, a standard range of liberal rights to free belief, expression, assembly, and association. Beyond that, critics might need to expose and counter agents of distortion in the public sphere, such as the influence exercised by large media corporations, lack of material resources meaning that some sorts of voices do not get heard, hegemonic discourses that serve the interests of the powerful, and so forth.

In this light, discourses get represented by the normal array of actors present in the public sphere. However, the idea of discursive representation enables and provides criteria for reevaluation of some standard normative treatments of civil society. Putnam (2000) disparages "checkbook" groups such as the Sierra Club that demand nothing more than money from their members, and have little in the way of internal participation of the sort that might help build social capital in the larger society in which the Sierra Club operates. In light of discursive representation, Putnam's criticism misses the point. Checkbook groups may build discursive capital (in the sense of facilitating the articulation of discourses), if not social capital. The Sierra Club exists to represent a particular discourse of environmental preservation, and contributors to the Sierra Club express solidarity with that discourse. Discursive accountability can be sought by these leaders continuing to communicate in terms that make sense within the discourse of preservation (even as they engage other discourses). If leaders could not justify their actions in these terms, contributors can back other groups instead.

Discourses engaging in the broad public sphere get represented to more authoritative political structures (such as states) through a variety of mechanisms. Public opinion defined in the engagement of discourses can reach the state or other public authority – and so find representation. In his "two-track" model of deliberation in the public sphere influencing deliberation in the legislature, Habermas (1996) (very conventionally) eventually stresses elections. In this light, we might evaluate electoral systems by how well they represent discourses. For example, preferential voting as practiced in Australia almost guarantees a two-party system in parliament. However, minor discourses get represented even when nobody in parliament is formally associated with them, because the two major parties need to cultivate minor parties in order to receive their voters' second preferences, so preferential voting may at least be better than first-past-the-post plurality voting in representing discourses (though they may be worse than proportional representation). But elections are not the only transmission mechanisms. Others include the use of rhetoric by activists, influence upon the terms of political discussion that can change the understandings of government actors, and arguments that are heard by public officials (Dryzek 2000). Conceptualizing such transmission mechanisms as forms of discursive representation drives home the need to subject them to critical scrutiny. Rhetoric in particular is often treated with suspicion by democratic theorists, on the grounds of its capacity for emotional manipulation and coercion (e.g., Chambers 1996: 151), by racist and nationalist and other kinds of demagogues. But rhetoric may be vital in representing a discourse to those in positions of political authority not initially subscribing to it. The solution here would be to hold rhetoric to standards such as those developed in chapter 4. The latter could, for example, curb the racist or ethnic nationalist rhetoric of demagogues.

In addition, all forms of transmission need to be held to the discursive accountability standard introduced earlier. Anyone claiming to represent a discourse or discourses should always communicate in terms that make sense within the discourse or discourses in question, even when they contemplate shifting in relation to the constellation of discourses they subsequently encounter. This standard is probably met more easily to the degree representatives keep their distance from explicit participation in collective decision making in, for example, corporatist arrangements.

In the case of networked governance, discursive accountability could be facilitated by specifying that a network does not require as the price of entry that participants commit to the hegemonic discourse of the network and renounce other relevant discourses. This kind of accountability would be hard to secure in transnational financial networks that currently exclude discourses of sustainability and social justice.

Informal discursive representation may currently be found directed toward familiar and conventional authority structures, such as states and international organizations. This kind of representation is especially appropriate to global politics, an application developed at length in chapter 9. Informal representation could also mesh with any formal Chamber of Discourses. In this context, public sphere activism could provide a check on the degree to which the formal Chamber features a comprehensive and accurate set of the relevant discourses, and promote discursive accountability by calling changes of language in the formal Chamber to account.

## CONCLUSION

Once the basic idea of discursive representation is accepted, choices need to be made on several dimensions. Should discursive representation be formal, informal, or an integrated combination of both? It could be formalized, especially in connection with growing enthusiasm for the constitution of mini-publics to deliberate complex and controversial policy issues, and as a way for governments to meet mandated requirements for public consultation. If it is formal, what method should we use to select representatives? How much authority should any "Chamber of Discourses" possess in relation to other representative institutions? There is no universal answer to any of these questions, though we have provided guidance about how each might be answered in particular contexts.

We have argued that discursive representation already occurs, though it is not always recognized as such. Whether formal, informal, or an integrated mix of both, it can help render policy making more rational, respect individual autonomy by more fully representing diverse aspects of the self, and make deliberative democracy more applicable to a world where the consequences of decisions are felt across organizational boundaries.

Especially in its informal aspects, discursive representation confirms the need to allow rhetoric into deliberative democracy. Good discursive representatives are often effective rhetoricians. The ideas we have developed in this chapter about discursive representation and its place in deliberative systems enable renewed consideration of the old question of what kinds of communication belong in a deliberative democracy, and that is the subject of chapter 4.

# 4

---

# Communication and Rhetoric

The deliberative turn in democratic theory confirmed the place of communication at the very center of democracy. But not just any kind will do, because deliberation is a particular type of communication. Different analysts draw the line between deliberative and non-deliberative forms in different places. In particular, they dispute the degree to which *rhetorical* communication belongs in a deliberative democracy – and if so how, where, when, and to what effect. This dispute is actually just the latest twist in a disagreement that extends back 2,400 years, to the days when Plato criticized rhetoric and Aristotle appreciated its multiple forms. The concepts of discursive legitimacy, deliberative system, and discursive representation developed in previous chapters can shed new light on this ancient dispute, if not resolve it once and for all. This chapter reexamines the roles that rhetoric can play in a deliberative democracy, and proposes innovative ways to distinguish between desirable and undesirable uses of rhetoric.

The idea of a deliberative system begins with the recognition that a deliberative democracy cannot easily be sought in a single forum. Instead, it should be sought in the contributions of multiple sites. Rhetoric is essential when it comes to communication between different elements in a deliberative system, because those elements will often feature differently situated actors with different perspectives, subscribing to different discourses. Rhetoric is in part the art of reaching and persuading different others. Sometimes, those others will be in positions of public authority. Thus, rhetoric is required by the account of democratic legitimacy developed in chapter 2. This account characterized legitimacy in terms of the resonance of collective decisions with public opinion defined as the outcome of the engagement of discourses in the public sphere, in the degree to which this engagement is under the dispersed control of competent actors. Public opinion so defined needs somehow to be transmitted to public authority in empowered space – and rhetoric can be a crucial means of transmission. The concept of a deliberative system also enables a systemic (as opposed to more familiar categorical) test for distinguishing between desirable and undesirable uses of rhetoric. The systemic test developed in this chapter involves asking whether or not a particular deployment of rhetoric contributes to the construction or maintenance of a deliberative system linking competent and reflective actors.

In chapter 3, we noted the contemporary pluralization of representation claims that characterizes a world of dispersed political authority, with multi-level and networked governance. Discursive representation is part of the response to such pluralization. Discursive representatives will endeavor to persuade their audiences to invoke discourses conducive to the representative's claims, and suppress competing discourses. Thus, tests are necessary to distinguish between desirable and undesirable rhetorical invocation and suppression of particular discourses.

This chapter stresses not the source of representation claims, but the target audience of claims. This audience is not necessarily some authoritative public body (such as a legislature, executive, or international governmental organization) – though it can be. The audience can also be made up of (for example) other members of a governance network, a broad public capable of exerting influence on many formal decision-making bodies, an international organization, people in other political jurisdictions, or a corporation. Good understanding of the discursive psychology of an audience proves essential to the effective deployment of rhetoric in representation.

## RHETORIC AND REASON

Rhetoric involves persuasion in the variety of its forms. For Aristotle, those forms were *logos*, *ethos*, and *pathos*: respectively, argument, the virtue of the speaker, and emotion. Rhetoric can also involve vivid metaphors, creative interpretation of evidence, arresting figures of speech, irony, humor, exaggeration, gestures, performance, and dramaturgy, not all of which fit neatly into the Aristotelian categories. Crucially, rhetoric recognizes the situated character of its audience (Young 1996: 130). It follows that the effective rhetorician needs some knowledge of the particular dispositions of that audience (Yack 2006: 427), analyzed here in the language of discursive psychology.

Rhetoric's association with reason is complex and contested. For Plato, rhetoric was everything reason is not: persuasion on nonrational and therefore undesirable grounds. To this day, those who dismiss "mere rhetoric" echo Plato. It was Plato who, as Eberly (2003: 47) says, originally put the "ick" in rhetoric on the basis that it obstructs the pursuit of truth, in politics no less than elsewhere. Yet if rhetoric encompasses the argument of *logos*, its relationship to and contrast with reason giving is not so clear-cut. Some believe that reason cannot escape rhetoric. For example, "post-structuralists treat rhetoricality as an internal part of all reason-giving" (Norval 2007: 59). One does not have to be a post-structuralist to see that justifications for political arrangements and public policies that appeal to the rational grounds on which they are constructed become less solid to the degree the grounds for persuasion are expanded and rational argument loses its distinction and primacy. An appreciation of rhetoric therefore calls into question the efforts of those who try to establish public reason as the guide for political arguments: most notably, John Rawls (1993).

If public reason is defined as justification in terms that all can accept, then it does not have to rule out appeals that recognize the situated and particular character of the political community in question. But if public reason is defined as justification in terms that all can accept solely by virtue of their own reasonableness, then public reason seems to exclude any elements of rhetoric not reducible to *logos*. Public reason of this Rawlsian sort does not allow for the situatedness of an audience – except by calling it a comprehensive doctrine that presents a problem to be overcome.

One other major school of thought challenged by rhetoric would be rational choice theory. If they do accept that it is more than epiphenomenal cheap talk, rational choice theorists would treat rhetoric like all other communication: as either signaling that indicates the preferences and intentions of the speaker, or selective disclosure of information relevant to choice among options on the part of the audience. Riker's distinction between heresthetic and rhetoric (1996) is relevant here. Heresthetic, grounded in rational choice theory, manipulates the choice set of others, while rhetoric attempts to persuade them. (If they turn to behavioral economics, rational choice theorists might recognize that rhetoric could play a role in framing that affects individual decision.)

While rhetoric is essential for a number of reasons, its hazards are also well known. Thus, we need to figure out how to take advantage of its positive contributions to democracy while avoiding the hazards. Before turning to the positive argument, attention needs to be paid to the suspicion of and hostility toward rhetoric that can be found in democratic theory, which are not to be dismissed lightly.

## DEMOCRATIC SUSPICION OF RHETORIC

Though Plato was no democrat (partly because he thought democracy had to involve rhetoric, just to cope with large numbers of listeners), his contemporary influence extends to democratic political philosophers. The suspicion is that effective rhetoric can involve emotional manipulation of an audience's mood (*pathos*) and so is a kind of coercion (Bessette 1994). This is dangerous when done by demagogues. Chambers (2009) suggests, however, that Plato's main reason for antipathy to rhetoric is not that it invokes emotion or passion over reason, but that its communication is one-way or monological, prompting no reflection, and anticipating no questioning response from those to whom it is addressed. Applying this point to contemporary politics, Chambers argues that vote-seeking politicians can use rhetoric that panders to the audience (speaking in a way that appeals to the existing preferences of the audience, without challenging those preferences). Further, they can highlight issues on which the politician is likely to get the most support (crafting), and invoke symbols that will prime bias and prejudice in the audience, rather than reason (e.g., by stigmatizing proposals for public health insurance as socialist, and so unacceptable in the United States). Chambers does, however, believe that more truly deliberative rhetoric is both possible and desirable (see the section on "Evaluating rhetoric").

Rhetoricians can select, highlight, downplay, or interpret facts so as to make them consistent with a self-serving story. Think, for example, of clever lawyers who introduce creative explanations that can account for the observed facts. Effective rhetoric persuades rather than proves. Premises are therefore not taken as given and fixed, but rather can be invoked selectively by the speaker in support of his or her position. However, the need to deploy rhetoric (rather than command) means that the audience does have substantial freedom of choice when it comes to whether or not to accept the position of the speaker, and so in this respect at least rhetoric has some affinities with the kind of freedom of choice that helps define liberal democracy.

On one account, suspicion of rhetoric extends to contemporary deliberative democrats. O'Neill (2002: 251–4) traces this suspicion to the common Kantian roots of both Rawls and Habermas, who in turn have influenced the contemporary theory of deliberative democracy. Kant believed that oratory propagated appealing illusions, and so sought to violate the autonomy of the rational agent. If public reason requires justifications that others can accept solely by virtue of their own reasonableness, then rhetoric only gets in the way. In rhetoric, the speaker needs to invoke premises that are either held by or can be made to appear plausible to a particular audience. So its currency is particular rather than universal appeals, such that those who believe political communication ought to emphasize Rawlsian public reason will therefore not like it. For Habermas (1988), communicative rationality is oriented by a quest for consensus based on reason giving. So when Habermas (1996) turns to thinking about deliberative democracy, reasoned argument is central, and rhetoric is nowhere. Yet even Rawls and Habermas do not *explicitly* dismiss rhetoric; the dismissal is just implicit in their overarching emphasis on reason and its requirements. Still, for Rawls and Habermas alike, rhetoric stops at reason's door. Rawlsians and Habermasians can and do allow that rhetoric may be useful in stimulating reasoned reflection and interchange, but they are reluctant to allow that its non-*logos* aspects can ever substitute for reason. The systemic view developed here shows that such substitution can sometimes be fruitful.

Fontana, Nederman, and Remer (2004: 8–19) charge deliberative democracy in its entirety with a Platonic commitment to truth seeking and concomitant abhorrence of rhetoric (see also Yack 2006). But this charge is false. While links from Plato to Kant to Rawls and Habermas to contemporary deliberative theory are easy to trace, when deliberative democrats think for very long about rhetoric they mostly come down on the side of allowing that it does have roles to play. The lineup here includes Bohman (1996), Gutmann and Thompson (1996), Rehg (1997), Dryzek (2000: 52–4), O'Neill (2002), Baber and Bartlett (2005: 143–63) and Chambers (2009). The reasons are varied. For Bohman (1996: 205), "irony, jokes, metaphors and other jarring ways of expressing something" may be necessary to penetrate the misconceptions of those who are systematically deceived, capable of reaching the latter when reasoned argument is blocked by the very structure of misconception. For Gutmann and Thompson (1996: 135–6), rhetoric enables issues to get onto the agenda from the margins, thereafter to be subject to reasoned deliberation. For Young (who styles herself a communicative rather than deliberative democrat, but by the time of her 2000 book is edging close to deliberative democracy), it is because rhetoric is one of the communication styles that can be employed by marginalized individuals who are disadvantaged when it comes to rational argument. Hauser and Benoit-Barne (2002) expand this point to argue that rhetoric is what makes possible the participation in a deliberative democracy of civil society in all its variety. Similarly, for Chambers (2009), rhetoric is necessary as we scale up from a small face-to-face forum to communication in the larger public sphere. For Dryzek (2000: 54), rhetoric is one possible transmission mechanism from public sphere to state. For O'Neill (2002), complexity in many contemporary policy issues means lay audiences have to make judgments based on the *ethos* of multiple and sometimes opposing experts (see also Baber and Bartlett 2005). We may, for example, choose not to believe the claims of scientists about the efficacy of a drug if their research is financed by a pharmaceutical company that stands to benefit if the drug is widely prescribed. Even Benhabib (1996: 83) tempers her hostility to the idea that rhetoric belongs in democratic institutions with an acceptance that it can be allowed in "the informally structured processes of

everyday communication among individuals who share a cultural and historical life world."

In short, the opposite of rhetoric is not deliberation. Rhetoric's opposites
are Rawlsian public reason, heresthetic, and command. However, existing
deliberative treatments of rhetoric are inadequate inasmuch as they have not
come to grips with the ideas about representation and the deliberative system
dealt with in the previous chapters.


## RHETORIC IN (DISCURSIVE) REPRESENTATION

Representative claims in a democracy are made by representatives on behalf of
some subject or subjects to some audience. Thus, representatives often need
to bridge differently situated actors. In chapter 3, we argued that the multiplicity of discourses that a single individual engages means that discourses
themselves merit representation, and subjects when seeking representation
should not be forced to repress any particular discourse to which they
partially subscribe. Instead, if the individual is to be represented in his or
her entirety, *all* the discourses to which he or she subscribes generally merit
representation in the forum. Discursive representatives should then be able to
deliberate across discourses and judge the relative merits of claims coming
from each of them.

I now stress that the kind of discursive psychology addressed in chapter 3
also applies to the *audience* of representation claims: those whom the representative (be he or she representing persons, discourses, interests, opinions,
groups, perspectives, or whatever) is trying to reach. That audience may itself
be fractured in its commitments, and open to persuasion as to which of its
commitments it ought to invoke. And it is rhetoric which can affect that
decision. The most interesting kind of situation exists when the intended
audience subscribes in part to a particular discourse – but is not initially
inclined to act upon that subscription.

Consider, for example, that brilliant rhetorician and representative Dr. Martin
Luther King, Jr. While being seen as a representative of African-American
people, King also represented a discourse of civil rights, which he was careful
to distinguish from the discourse of black liberation also current at the time.
His white audience was fractured in its commitments. While it is too late for
direct empirical studies of the discursive psychology of this audience, it seems
that at least two relevant competing discourses were present in the white
population of the United States in the 1960s. One was racist. Another was
liberal-universal. Most whites probably subscribed partially to both of these

discourses – though the proportions could vary substantially across different individuals. His task was to invoke the liberal-universal discursive commitments of his white audience, and convince its members to suppress racist discursive positions. He did this by appealing to and deploying the language of the Declaration of Independence and U.S. Constitution – to which many whites had an emotional attachment. Of course, white racist rhetoricians tried to do exactly the opposite, which points to the need for ethical tests of the kind developed below.

To take another example from an exemplary rhetorician, consider the televised speech of Nelson Mandela after the assassination of Chris Hani in 1993 as analyzed by Zagacki (2003). Hani, one of the leaders of the African National Congress, had been killed by white extremists who wanted to provoke a race war that would end the transition then under way from apartheid to multiracial government in South Africa. Mandela's key audience was composed of radicals on his own side who believed the assassination should be met with violence. He invoked his own past suffering and imprisonment (*ethos*), but then praised Hani as a "soldier for peace." In so doing, he demonstrated an understanding of the discursive psychology of his more radical audience (though, of course, he would not have put it quite like that). He effectively separated the discourse of struggle from the discourse of violence, validating the former while seeking to marginalize the latter. In this speech, he was both representing a particular discourse (struggle) and trying to affect the relative weight of different discourses in his audience.

In keeping with the pluralization of representation claims noted at the outset of chapter 3 and this chapter, recent discussions of representation in democratic theory have paid close attention to the roles played by nonelected representatives (Saward 2009), many of whom are self-appointed (Montanero 2008). Given the absence of conventional electoral means of authorization and accountability, the legitimacy of such representatives can be a thorny question. Saward suggests contemplating the degree of connectedness of the representative to the larger political system, the existence of any constituency (which need not be territorial) that might be called upon to validate a claim, independence from strategic advantage, and independence from the structural imperatives of the state. Montanero suggests we ask whether the representative contributes to the empowerment of those he/she claims to represent, is accountable to their voice, attends to public reputation, and is accepted by peers. Thinking about rhetoric suggests an additional criterion. This criterion, though insufficient in itself, is the capacity of the representative to identify the configuration of discourses in the intended audience, and to appeal successfully to and so raise the standing of one (or more) of the discourses in question. For that capacity helps make the representation effective (though of course that leaves open other aspects of its ethical standing). And in this task, rhetoric is obviously crucial. Sometimes, a speaker can strive to enable an audience to take up an unfamiliar discourse – think, for example, of feminism in the 1960s – though even here it is hard to see how rhetoric could work with *tabula rasa* in its audience.

## RHETORIC IN THE DELIBERATIVE SYSTEM

In light of the systemic turn outlined in chapter 1, deliberative democracy can be sought in the production of collective outcomes in the interactions between different elements, actors, and locations in deliberative systems that span public space and empowered space. To the extent different elements of a deliberative system feature different sorts of people subject to different structural constraints and opportunities and different kinds of perspectives, rhetoric is often going to be necessary in reaching across these different elements. There is a link here to the prior discussion of representation: representations will need to be made between different locations in the deliberative system.

Consider in this light the international governance of the ozone layer, which in 1987 received a boost with the signing of the Montreal Protocol. Scientists and environmental activists had long constituted a transnational public sphere that stressed the damage caused by chlorofluorocarbons (CFCs) and other chemicals to the ozone layer. The international negotiations leading up to Montreal moved at a glacial pace as countries and blocks such as the European Union (EU) sought to consolidate their own economic interests. What changed, on Litfin's account (1994), was the promulgation by the community of scientists and activists of the idea of an "ozone hole" over Antarctica and the Southern Hemisphere. A "hole" in the atmosphere does have some physical referents in seasonally and geographically variable concentrations of stratospheric ozone. But the idea of a hole has particular rhetorical force that previous representations had failed to convey. Thus, the problem could be communicated simply and effectively in the way masses of scientific data could not. If we think of the transnational public sphere and the intergovernmental negotiations as two components in a global deliberative system, rhetoric was crucial in linking the two – and so enabling effective global action that generated a high degree of legitimacy for coordinated international action on the ozone issue.

To take another example of how rhetoric can be used to link components of a deliberative system, consider the impact of deliberative citizen forums. These forums often feature high-quality and inclusive deliberation. However, the frequent fate of the recommendations of these forums is to be ignored or lost in the give-and-take of larger political interaction. Often there is little reason for politicians and bureaucrats to take much notice of the forum and its recommendations (unless it provides them with some ammunition to be used in strategic struggles). High-quality deliberation in such forums is relatively easy to obtain, but that does not guarantee the forum will have any impact. Many such forums, such as citizens' juries and consensus con-ferences, involve fewer than twenty citizen deliberators – which, provided they are selected to ensure diversity, can do a pretty good job of simulating what would happen with larger numbers of deliberators. The America-*Speaks* Foundation, in contrast, advertises the forums it sponsors as involving "thousands of voices." This is true enough; though those thousands probably produce results little different from the smaller forums. But in terms of getting politicians to sit up and take notice, the rhetoric associated with "thousands" is much more effective. America*Speaks* has had some notable successes in securing wide public attention and substantial policy impact for its events, most famously the Listening to the City forum it sponsored in New York in 2002 on plans for the redevelopment of the World Trade Center site after the attacks of 9/11. Absent any constitutional role, to achieve any impact in a wider deliberative system, citizen forums (whatever their size) need to be accompanied by performance (Hajer and Versteeg 2008).

The upshot of this contemplation of communication in the deliberative system is that rhetoric can play an essential part in communicating across and so linking differently situated and differently disposed actors, forums, and institutions.

## EVALUATING RHETORIC

Democratic representation and the deliberative system make rhetoric neces-sary. But its well-documented hazards remain. So we still need some way to sort defensible uses of rhetoric from undesirable uses.

Having stressed the role of rhetoric in enabling representation, we might begin by asking whether the standards of authorization and accountability that appear in conventional accounts of representation can have any bearing on rhetoric. Authorization may have bearing on the selection of who can claim to be a representative – but not on the kind of communication they subsequently employ. Accountability is more promising. As demonstrated in chapter 3, discursive accountability may be defined in terms of a representa-tive continuing to communicate in terms that make sense in the discourse being represented, even as he or she makes representations to other actors, institutions, or discourses. This is especially important in situations of deep division, and again the examples of King and Mandela stand out. In their rhetoric, both had to maintain the mobilization of their own side in the struggle, while convincing the other side of the justice of their cause and the peacefulness of their intentions, simultaneously to validate struggle and seek reconciliation. So they always had two very different audiences. Discursive accountability is lost when the representative can no longer give an account in terms that make sense to the side he/she represents. This happens (for example) when environmentalist leaders begin to speak in the language of economic efficiency and cost–benefit analysis rather than the intrinsic value of species and ecosystems.

When encountering adversaries, representatives may in a deliberative democracy reflect and change their minds (indeed, this reflective feature helps define deliberative democracy). But if they do so, representatives should still be able to give an account as to why they did so in terms that make sense to those they are representing. This is a common problem for representatives of social movements as they eventually receive invitations to participate in more conventional kinds of political exchange (including, of course, thoroughly non-deliberative ones). But an environmentalist representative might (for example) justify this on the grounds that it is the only feasible way to secure structural transformations in the industrial political economy that will provide a space for nature preservation. Of course, accountability is only part of the story when it comes to evaluating rhetoric (just as it is only part of the story in electoral representation). For example, ethnic nationalist demagogues might very well pass the test of discursive accountability. So further standards are needed.

Within the literature on communication and democracy, some categorical standards have been advanced for the evaluation of communications that include rhetoric. So Spragens (1990: 249) believes "healthy rhetoric" stresses general interests rather than particular interests in disguise, appeals to "morally defensible or praiseworthy emotions" as opposed to "darker passions," is "forthright and open to correction" rather than "mendacious and dogmatic." Young (2000: 77–9) suggests we ask whether the communication in question is "respectful, publicly assertable, and does it stand up to public challenge?" Dryzek (2000: 68–70) believes we should admit only communications that are noncoercive and capable of inducing reflection on the part of the audience, and that when claims are made on behalf of some specific interests (such as the material interest of a group), they be linked to some more general principle (e.g., social justice). Christian Kock (2007) suggests we apply as standards some "norms of legitimate dissensus," such as good faith, respect for opponent, and the avoidance of accusations of prejudice, delusion, and the like. Chambers (2009) distinguishes "plebiscitary" rhetoric suffering from pandering, crafting, and priming (see above) from "deliberative" rhetoric. "Deliberative rhetoric makes people think, it makes people see things in new ways, it conveys information and knowledge, and it makes people more reflective" (Chambers 2009: 335).

There are, however, limits to these tests, because one speech or one speaker does not take effect in isolation, and so cannot be judged in isolation. Rhetoric normally takes effect within some communicative system, and so we should always look at the consequences for the deliberative qualities of the system in which it is occurring. So, for example, if a speaker is trying to develop the identity of an audience sharing an incipient interest, identity, or set of values, it makes a great deal of difference whether that audience is a poorly organized category seeking greater equality within a liberal democracy, or a well-defined set of people with potential access to means of coercion and violence in an unstable political setting. In passing, it should be noted that those such as Norval (2007: 56–104) who celebrate the disruptive aspects of rhetoric in creating new political understandings and subjectivities are also in need of some way to assess the systemic consequences of the kinds of subjectivities generated.

## BONDING AND BRIDGING RHETORIC

We can begin contemplation of systemic aspects by distinguishing between two sorts of rhetoric, *bonding* and *bridging*. This section looks at reasons for valuing bridging over bonding. The next section discusses important exceptions to this generalization, such that any priority for bridging is downgraded to a presumption that can be overridden by still larger systemic considerations. The terminology is taken from Robert Putnam's treatment of social capital (2000): bonding is associating with people who are similar in social background, bridging is associating with people with different social characteristics. We can adopt these terms with no commitment at all to any of Putnam's views on social capital. In this light, bonding rhetoric is the kind generally feared by democrats, because it is likely to deepen divisions with out-groups, to invoke dangerous emotions, to mobilize passions, and to move groups to extremes. As Miller (2000: 216) puts it, rhetoric is "a powerful force when people are united in their aims, [but] it is equally clearly a divisive force in situations of conflict." And as Sunstein (2000) points out, people who communicate only with like-minded others are likely to move to extremes, as they reinforce each others' initial dispositions. In contrast, bridging rhetoric takes seriously the outlooks (ideally, the discursive psychology) of an intended audience that is different in key respects from the speaker – and from the kind of people or discourses the speaker represents. For example, Martin Luther King, Jr. deployed bridging rhetoric when trying to reach a white audience, though at the same time he was trying to bond his African-American supporters around the discourse of civil rights.

Bridging rhetoric is hard work for the speaker, because he or she must strive to understand an audience whose dispositions are different, as well as hold on to his or her own side. The idea of discursive representation shows how this can be done. The trick here is *not* to represent a group in its entirety to an audience in its entirety (as, say, an ambassador might represent a nation). Instead, the idea is to represent a discourse on one's own side that has some compatibility with a discourse on the other side. So Martin Luther King, Jr. could build a bridge between civil rights (on his side) and liberal-universalism in his white audience. Building this bridge meant marginalizing both black liberation and white racism. Similarly, Nelson Mandela could build a bridge from a discourse of struggle on his own side to one of nation building among white South Africans, which meant marginalizing discourses of violence on his side and apartheid on the other side.

The bonding rhetorician, in contrast, has the relatively easy task of energizing similarly disposed people. This very difference in cognitive demands may invoke greater reflection and reflexivity on the part of the bridging speaker, and these are key deliberative virtues. Bridging rhetoric can also be connected to the other essential deliberative virtue of reciprocity stressed by Gutmann and Thompson (1996). Reciprocity means arguing in terms that others can accept. So, for example, if a person argues for a position on the grounds it is required by their religion, there is no reason why others with different religious beliefs or no religious beliefs can accept the argument. So the person in question must find arguments that do translate; and this is in fact how (for example) Catholic opponents of abortion in the United States often strive to argue. Bridging rhetoric is, however, different from reciprocity as presented by Gutmann and Thompson in two ways. The first is that it is indeed rhetoric, and not just argument. The second is that reciprocity works with an image of a unitary other. In contrast, bridging rhetoric as characterized here works with a conception of the other that lies potentially at the intersection of multiple discourses.

The case of Martin Luther King, Jr. shows that it can (with skill) prove possible to combine bonding and bridging rhetoric to good effect. But it is equally easy to find examples where an emphasis on bonding rhetoric drives out a bridging rhetoric that is available but scorned by key players. The consequences can be disastrous. Consider for example divided societies at the edge of violence. It is not hard to find "bonding" demagogues, who interpret every violent act perpetrated by members of the "other" ethnic, racial, or religious group as evidence of the irredeemable perfidy of the group as a whole – as opposed to an isolated instance of criminality, or a violation of universal human rights principles. This was, for example, how Serb and Croat leaders stoked the fires of conflict as Yugoslavia disintegrated in the 1990s. Contrast such rhetoric with that adopted by Nelson Mandela and his associates in the equally divided society of South Africa, which bridged across the racial divide in order to welcome whites into the new multiracial "rainbow nation" under construction in the 1990s.

The international system provides another example where a choice of bonding over bridging rhetoric can prove disastrous. In the wake of the terrorist attacks of 9/11, President George W. Bush and his senior officials chose a bonding rhetoric that emphasized solidarity, accompanying a Manichean division of the world. As Bush put it in his speech to Congress on September 20, 2001, referring to all nations in the world, "Either you are with us, or you are with the terrorists." To accompany the more material "war on terror," the United States declared a "war of ideas" (proclaimed, for example, in the September 2002 *National Security Strategy of the United States of America*). There was only scorn and ridicule for those not completely in support of U.S. policy positions. The rhetoric worked well at home in uniting most Americans behind the Bush administration. The effects internationally were very different, as the United States squandered the worldwide goodwill it had received in the immediate wake of the 2001 attacks.

Bridging rhetoric is available and sometimes deployed in the international system. Think, for example, of Mikhail Gorbachev's frequent invocation in the 1980s of a "common European home" that hosted both the North Atlantic Treaty Organization (NATO) and Warsaw Pact countries, and the part this and similar symbols played in defusing the Cold War in Europe. (Gorbachev did perhaps neglect the bonding rhetoric that might have been conducive to his leadership surviving at home.)

Bridging rhetoric can also be important when it comes to expanding the audience that might be sympathetic to a position. In the United States, environmentalists have since the early 1970s been associated with the left-liberal wing of conventional politics. Evangelical Christians for their part have found a home in the conservative wing of the Republican Party, and have traditionally been hostile to environmentalists. How can this gap be bridged? Simply by using the rhetoric of "creation" rather than "environment." As the web site 'Creation Care for Pastors' puts it, "We like the word 'creation' even better than the word 'environment' because it includes all that makes the earth a wonderful place, and it reminds us it's a gift, a sacred trust from the hands of the creator" (www.creationcareforpastors.com). This is a (rare?) example of an audience telling a set of advocates exactly what kind of bridging rhetoric to use. Religious discourses are more easily reached by rhetoric than by public reason, because the very demand that believers set aside their commitments in favor of public reason can create an angry reaction, and even drive believers toward bonding extremists (Garsten 2006: 184–5).

## THE LIMITS OF THE BONDING–BRIDGING DISTINCTION

It would be tempting to conclude here that bridging rhetoric is desirable, while bonding rhetoric is undesirable. However, while the contrast is useful, its normative force does not always hold. A first limitation arises because the distinction itself only applies when divisions between entities (be they interest groups, races, ethnic groups, nations, religions, states, institutions, social classes, or discourses) are well defined, problematic, and persistent. If the divisions are not well defined, it is not clear exactly what is being bridged. If they are not problematic, there is no situation that calls for rhetoric. If they are not persistent, what starts as bridging may become bonding as a common identity encompassing the two sides is forged.

Even when situations do possess these three features, bridging is not necessarily more desirable than bonding. Bonding rhetoric may enable an oppressed group to generate a degree of solidarity that will enable it subsequently to enter with confidence into a larger public sphere where its representatives can make claims to other actors, audiences, and institutions (as well as solve their own collective action problem). In this light, the group polarization feared by Sunstein (2000) may actually be desirable. Fraser (1992) conceives of the role played by what she calls "subaltern counter-publics" in these terms; it is within these enclaves that individuals can craft their identities and develop their competence. Eventually, the larger delibera-tive public sphere can benefit from this competence. And sometimes a bridge is simply not available. So, for example, the exclusive corporatist character of the West German state that lasted until the mid-1980s meant that any rhetoric from the emerging green movement fell on deaf ears in government (Dryzek et al. 2003). Thus, the green public sphere featured instead bonding that both developed green identities and justified strategic confrontation with the state. When the state did eventually become less exclusive, the radical green critique of the political economy could be taken into a deliberative system encompassing state actors, meaning environmental concerns could be taken more seriously in public policy in Germany than just about anywhere else.

Bridging rhetoric for its part is undesirable when deployed by dominant actors to co-opt and neutralize potential troublemakers. This is (for example) how an upper class might try to neutralize a working class, by using rhetoric that stresses they are both part of "one nation." The term, and the strategy, are associated with Benjamin Disraeli, the nineteenth-century British Conservative leader who tried to forge an alliance between the landed upper classes and the workers against the liberal urban capitalist class – but the alliance would be under Tory control. What this suggests is that bridging rhetoric is more clearly defensible when it comes from those representing a historically subordinate position (like Martin Luther King, Jr.) or an equal partner (like Gorbachev in international relations in the 1980s) rather than a historically dominant position (Disraeli). Even across equals, there may be times when bridging rhetoric forges a coalition – but not a deliberative relationship. The "creation care" pastors just mentioned might join environmentalists in an effective lobbying operation, but democracy will not necessarily be any more deliberative as a result.

Thus, while it highlights some morally relevant issues, the bonding–bridging distinction does *not* produce a sufficiently clear evaluative standard. Yet the distinction should not be jettisoned unless it can be replaced by something better. The bridging–bonding contrast does provide some useful vocabulary that can be put to service in a systemic test that recognizes and moves beyond its limitations.

## SYSTEMIC EVALUATION OF RHETORIC

The bonding–bridging distinction is ultimately limited because while it pays some attention to the systemic aspects of rhetoric, it does not pay enough attention to the consequences for the larger deliberative system in which the communication in question is occurring.

Now, there are many things we might want a deliberative system to do, and so want rhetoric to contribute toward. The relevant desiderata might include generation of legitimacy for collective decisions (see chapter 2), effective resolution of complex social problems (Hajer and Wagenaar 2003), promotion of social justice (Young 2000), tractability in social choice (see chapter 5), positive freedom (Rostbøll 2008), promotion of individual and collective political competences, healing of deep social divisions (Dryzek 2005), and facilitation of reflexivity in the steering capacity of society. Specifying and weighting these desiderata is a task for the normative theory of deliberative democracy in general, rather than a burden we should place on rhetoric in particular. But *whatever* we want a deliberative democracy to accomplish, we need an effective deliberative system. And this consideration reveals the key task for rhetoric, and so a means for evaluating its place in a democracy. We can take a step back and ask: does the rhetoric in question help create and constitute an effective deliberative system joining competent and reflective actors?

This question is always vital because a deliberative system is never just *there*, waiting to be called into use when a new issue arises. A deliberative system always needs to be constructed and performed when an issue arises. Such is especially the case in contemporary conditions of institutionally fluid governance, where public authority has to be performed as dramaturgy before multiple audiences to be accepted as legitimate (Hajer 2009). In this sense, a deliberative system is quite unlike (say) a political system operating under constitutional rules. Deliberation is a particular kind of reflection-inducing communication that can never be assumed to exist; it is always going to require work to maintain and advance that kind of communication, and prevent it lapsing into other modes such as bargaining, command, routine, deception, and ritual.

In this light, we can see that bridging rhetoric will often contribute directly to the building of a deliberative system (as the examples of King and Mandela introduced earlier illustrate). Bridging rhetoric may be able to work here when public reason cannot, as the earlier example of religious discourses that react against demands to frame arguments in terms of public reason illustrates. But it may sometimes be suspect in these terms, if it involves co-option and neutralization of a potentially troublesome group, thus diminishing the capacity of that group to participate effectively in, and so contribute to the construction of, a deliberative system. Disraeli's "one nation" rhetoric was designed to induce working-class support for his aristocratic party – not to engage the working class under conditions of deliberative equality. Bonding rhetoric for its part will often look suspicious in the terms we have established – but not if it imbues the bonded group with a capacity subsequently to go forth and help constitute a larger deliberative system, as in the case of Fraser's "subaltern counterpublics," and in the history of the green public sphere in Germany discussed earlier.

Returning to some of the other cases discussed earlier, we can see how this systemic consideration applies. In the ozone case, the "ozone hole" rhetoric did help create an effective and productive deliberative system joining environmental activists, scientists, corporations, state negotiators, and international organizations. Gorbachev's "common European home" rhetoric facilitated the creation of a transnational deliberative system in Europe. This system was activated in a number of settings: for example, in talks involving the Soviet Union, United States, and NATO on the reunification of Germany, which as Risse (2000) demonstrates involved substantial communicative action in which participants were open to argument and persuasion, not just bargaining. In the case of George W. Bush's rhetoric in the "war on terror" and international security, any hopes for a transnational deliberative system on security affairs were dashed by the denigration directed at any actor not totally aligned with the Bush administration's position. Examples of sectarian demagoguery precluding any deliberative system are easily found (e.g., as the former Yugoslavia fell apart).

## WHEN CATEGORICAL AND SYSTEMIC TESTS COLLIDE

Categorical and systemic tests vie for our attention. Appreciation of the systemic aspect implies that categorical tests will sometimes give misleading answers, so if the two tests point in different directions, the systemic test should take priority. There may even be occasions when categorically ugly rhetoric produces good systemic results.

One such case would be when a speaker's rhetoric galvanizes a deliberative system composed largely of people who find the speaker's position abhorrent. Consider, for example, the populist Australian politician Pauline Hanson, who in the 1990s appealed to white working-class Australians anxious about multiculturalism, free trade, and immigration. At one level, Hanson crystallized from these anxieties a previously marginalized discourse, thus creating a possible ingredient for a deliberative system. At another level, her activities provoked countermobilization of liberal and multicultural discourses. She had little in the way of commitment to any categorical deliberative norms, and was not averse to racial stereotyping. Yet the net result of her activities was a more deliberative polity, at least in the sense that a number of discourses that were either taken for granted or had yet to crystallize or had been marginalized took shape in a way that *could* have allowed for their engagement in the public sphere (though the *actual* interchange that occurred was not always salutary). The general point here is that we cannot read off the systemic effects of rhetoric from the intentions of the speaker. The best that can be said here is that especially in the absence of compelling evidence about actual systemic effects, the intentions of the speaker in trying to create or undermine a deliberative system remain morally relevant.

It is harder to prioritize the positive systemic effects of categorically ugly rhetoric when they are delayed. For example, with the benefit of hindsight, we might perceive that sectarian rhetoric on the part of skeptics of the 1998 Good Friday Agreement was in the long run instrumental in facilitating eventual dialogue between the two sides in the divided society of Northern Ireland. Only when the extremists on both sides (Sinn Fein and the Democratic Unionist Party) had disposed of their more moderate opponents (Social Democratic Labour Party and "official" Ulster Unionist Party, respectively) could dialogue across the two sides be effective, and eventually a power-sharing government formed. For neither leadership then had to look over its shoulder at anyone more extreme on their own side. If we were applying a categorical test to their earlier rhetoric, we would condemn it as plebiscitary and divisive. Only in the long run did it help create a more deliberative system. Now, there may have been other routes to the creation of such a system to which categorically defensible rhetoric could have contributed. But in this case, the long history of failed attempts involving moderate rhetoric indicates such routes were not available.

Northern Ireland may offer a highly unusual case from which it would be unwise to draw any generalizations; but it does drive home the importance of a systemic test, for a categorical condemnation of the earlier rhetoric would, with the benefit of hindsight, have provided the wrong answer. Yet it can be hard to apply systemic tests prospectively. Be they categorical or systemic, tests for admissible rhetoric cannot solve all the riddles of history.

These two sorts of hard case do not suggest categorical tests would do any better than systemic ones. If in the surely more common kinds of cases discussed in this chapter, systemic tests are more clearly preferable, then the argument for the priority of systemic tests remains.

## CONCLUSION

Contemplation of the communicative aspects of democracy, especially when it comes to contemporary patterns of representation and deliberation, reveals the necessity of rhetoric. This necessity applies to both the stimulation of reasoned interchange, and continued rhetorical presence within deliberative systems. Yet the hazards highlighted by Plato and his successors remain. Categorical tests for the admissibility of rhetoric have been developed by a number of theorists of communication and democracy, and while they can inform judgments, they are limited by their inattention to the larger systemic context in which rhetoric takes effect. Appreciation of this systemic aspect leads to presumption in favor of bridging and against bonding rhetoric, but this distinction is capable of producing some misleading results. A better test involves asking whether or not the rhetoric in question contributes to the construction of an effective deliberative system joining competent and reflective actors on the issue at hand. The intentions of the speaker can provide useful information when it comes to applying these tests, especially when evidence about actual systemic effects is thin, even though we cannot read off these effects from intentions.

Sometimes, it is only with the benefit of hindsight that positive and negative systemic effects can be revealed. But we should not let history have the last laugh. All the tests examined in this chapter have their contingent and contextual aspects. They can and should inform judgment about what constitutes defensible and useful rhetoric, even when they provide no conclusive way to determine in advance what is right and wrong. We can state some strong presumptions. In general, actors should abjure categorically ugly rhetoric. In general, bridging rhetoric is preferable to bonding rhetoric. Only when the larger deliberative system is clearly served by violating these two presumptions should such violation be applauded. In the end, it is systemic considerations that merit priority.

This chapter has argued that *whatever* we want a deliberative system to accomplish, rhetoric can assist in the building of that system. In chapter 5, we will show how pursuit of many of the goals of democracy and deliberation can be facilitated to the degree deliberative systems are capable of generating meta-consensus spanning values, beliefs, preferences, and discourses.

# 5

## Pluralism and Meta-Consensus

*John S. Dryzek and Simon Niemeyer*

Previous chapters discussed (or at least mentioned) the many things we might want deliberative democracy to accomplish. These include legitimacy for collective decisions, conflict resolution, healing deep social divisions, solving collective policy problems, providing public goods, securing tractability in social choice, promoting the competence of citizens, freedom, and social justice. This chapter argues that whatever we want deliberative democracy to do, the task will be facilitated by the degree to which a deliberative system can generate free and reasoned meta-consensus. Meta-consensus is therefore a key concept in deliberative theory. We explain the various forms of meta-consensus (normative, epistemic, preference, and discursive), and the work that each can do. But first we need to clear up some of the confusion surrounding the part that consensus plays in deliberative democracy, and how it relates to pluralism of values, beliefs, and discourses.

Some early accounts of deliberative democracy were taken by the idea that deliberation can yield consensus (e.g., Elster 1986*a*). Even more recent treatments (e.g., Knops 2007) retain the idea that deliberation should be oriented by the search for consensus, without necessarily expecting to find it. Throughout, deliberative democrats influenced by Habermas's ideas about communicative action have had to come to terms with his view that ideal deliberation converges on consensus. Any stress on consensus provided a soft target for pluralist critics, who charge deliberative democracy with attempting to eliminate the multiplicity of positions on which politics thrives. These arguments have often involved substantial confusion on the part of deliberative democrats and some of their most severe critics alike. The source of the confusion is that there is actually no consensus on what consensus means, so protagonists end up talking past each other, and criticize positions which nobody actually holds. Thus, the field stands in need of an analysis that tries to cut through this confusion and elucidate the variety of meanings of consensus and their proper place (if any) in a deliberative democracy. That is what we try to do in this chapter, in the context of a seeming opposition between pluralism and consensus.

We conclude that deliberation should strive for meta-consensus on values, beliefs, preferences, and discourses (yielding what Kock (2007) calls some "norms of legitimate dissensus"). This conclusion means that deliberation can thrive on the ineliminable pluralism of viewpoints, perspectives, values, judgments, and (especially) discourses that among other things provide the grist for the kind of democratic legitimacy discussed in chapter 2, and discursive representation as developed in chapter 3. In this way, the seeming conflict between competing ideals of consensus and pluralism can be resolved. This resolution will involve pluralism in values, beliefs, preferences, and discourses in the context of a meta-consensus on one or more of these four aspects, though both the content of meta-consensus and the way it is produced turn out to require critical scrutiny.

We begin by asking why deliberative democrats should have been attracted by the idea of consensus to begin with. Next, we look at liberal pluralism, whose celebration of diversity is immediately qualified by recognition of the need to manage diversity – which often means consensus at some level. We pay special attention to John Rawls's idea of an overlapping consensus, which turns out not to be up to the task of managing diversity of any depth. We move then to more radical critical pluralists (agonists and difference democrats), who scorn deliberative consensus and ambiguous liberal celebrations of diversity alike. However, even critical pluralists turn out to require some test for the substance of contributions to political dispute, which opens the door to a meta-consensus concerning this substance. In this tour of existing arguments, we find no adequate resolution of the tension between pluralism and consensus, but we do find a number of pointers to what such a resolution would require. We build upon these to develop some ideas about simple pluralism combined with consensus at the meta level.

## ARGUMENTS FOR CONSENSUS

The deliberative turn in democratic theory meant that the legitimacy of political arrangements came to be seen in terms of the right, capacity, and opportunity of those subject to a collective decision to participate in deliberation about its content. To some deliberative democrats (e.g., Manin 1987), deliberation was just a prelude to voting and majority rule, though legitimacy was sought in the procedures of the prior deliberation, not in voting itself. Others scorned the thin "aggregative" model of democracy to which voting seemed to belong, and instead endorsed consensus as an alternative (e.g., Elster 1986a), conferring legitimacy to the extent it is informed, uncoerced, and reflective. The appeal of consensus in this context echoes the argument of Rousseau from over 200 years ago. For Rousseau, consensus was the obvious way for individuals to remain free while being subject to collective decisions, for then those decisions embody only the desires of free people in what he called the "general will." For some deliberative democrats, consensus remained the gold standard of political justification, although they never sought the degree of homogeneity in points of view that Rousseau wanted. As Cohen (1989: 22) put it in his classic statement, "outcomes are democratically legitimate if and only if they could be the object of free and reasoned agreement among equals," though what exactly constitutes free and reasoned agreement remains open to interpretation. Critics had no difficulty in identifying deliberative democracy with the pursuit of consensus; as Young (1996: 122) put it, "the goal of deliberation is to arrive at consensus." Similarly, Norval (2007: 34) says that "there is no disputing the fact that the model of deliberative democracy does indeed privilege consensus over dissensus." Here, we will dispute exactly this "fact."

Habermas (1996: 110) acknowledges pluralism but also tries to cling to consensus: "The democratic principle states that only those statutes may claim legitimacy that can meet with the assent of all citizens in a discursive process of legislation that in turn has been legally constituted." Bohman (1998: 402) interprets this as a "procedural ideal for laws: the legitimacy of laws depends on the democratic character of the legislative process that makes possible a consensus of all citizens." But what exactly is the consensus about? That the law has been arrived at through proper procedures, or that it is an intrinsically good law? If it is the latter, then deliberative democracy is wide open to pluralist attack. If the former, the position of deliberative democracy looks little different to that of liberal pluralists, to whom we now turn.

## LIBERAL PLURALISM

Pluralism has been widely celebrated as a cornerstone of democracy, because it features multiple centers of power, counters authoritarianism, and provides the basic grist for political debate. In the 1950s, Robert Dahl and David Truman located pluralism in interest group politics and placed it at the heart of their explanation and positive evaluation of American liberal democracy. Interest group pluralism of this sort is an easy target for deliberative democrats, because the bargains reached by private interests bringing to bear their resources (money, expertise, commitment, and numbers of supporters) bear no necessary relation to the public interest. Deliberation could be seen as penetrating the fog of private interests to arrive at more truly public interests.

Stronger liberal justifications for pluralism are not tied to interest group politics. For John Stuart Mill, political disagreement was instrumental in the development of competent individuals, because only in disagreement could individuals come to know the basis for their own positions. The contemporary theory of liberal pluralism owes much to Isaiah Berlin (1969), who stressed the plurality and incommensurability of basic values. Berlin is known as a theorist of liberty as well as pluralism, and for him the kind that mattered was "negative liberty," in which individuals have rights to protect them against other individuals and against government. For Berlin, negative liberty is conducive to the flourishing of diversity and judgment across different values (Gray 1996). For Galston (2002: 4), pluralism is part of the basic justification of liberalism. Diversity for Galston is an "intrinsic value," not a problem to be overcome or managed as it is in the very different liberalism of Rawls (Galston 2002: 27). Popper (1966) justifies liberal pluralism in terms of political rationality: effective policy making consists of cautious interventions that are tested and criticized from a variety of directions so that their benefits and flaws may be revealed, and policy improved.

Liberal arguments do not end neatly with celebration of diversity, because diversity begs the question of how conflict is to be managed. Often, this search for conflict management means finding consensus at some level. The answer of James Madison, embedded in the U.S. Constitution, is that constitutions should be designed to channel conflict across "factions" in productive direction – and so we need consensus on the constitution. Dahl and Truman in their celebration of the U.S. political system almost two centuries on from Madison posited unproblematic background consensus on the rules of the political game, and received criticism for their failure to recognize inbuilt biases of those rules to the rich and powerful. Gray (1996) favors a *modus vivendi* across conflicting values – bargain practical agreements when you have to. Galston (2002) follows Berlin in stressing pragmatic judgment in particular contexts. But that judgment is itself constrained. Aside from constitutional constraint, Galston (2002: 65–78) also highlights "minimal conditions of public order" and "ethical presumption" in curbing pluralism's "centrifugal" tendencies. "Ethical presumption" consists of basic principles (e.g., never lie and do not target noncombatants in wartime) that may be overridden in extraordinary circumstances. Galston draws comfort from his experience in government, where, faced with diverse views coming from different departments, "I found it remarkable that we could reach deliberative closure in the face of this heterogeneity" (p. 7).

The conditions of dialogue in which reconciliation across competing values is sought matter enormously, and in Galston's hands they have a very substantively liberal tinge to them. They include "clear and stable property relations, the rule of law, a public authority with the capacity to enforce the law" (p. 65), "a suitably regulated market economy, a basic level of social provision" (p. 66). Liberal pluralism of the Berlin–Galston type is itself a pragmatic compromise that makes some liberals and some pluralists uneasy. Some liberals veer away from pluralism: most prominent among them is Rawls. Some pluralists veer away from liberalism: notably, agonists and difference democrats. Let us examine these two approaches.

## RAWLS'S OVERLAPPING CONSENSUS

One of the more high-profile attempts to reconcile pluralism and consensus is Rawls's "overlapping consensus" (1993) on the basic institutions of society; once this structure is established, pluralism can hold in particular policy issues. Rawls starts from the ineliminable plurality of what he calls "comprehensive doctrines" in contemporary societies (which are closely related to what we would call discourses). These doctrines might be religious, ideological, or moral, but their differences are incapable of being erased (in the way Rawls (1971) himself once thought possible in *A Theory of Justice*). How, then, are their partisans to agree on the basic structure of society? He rejects a *modus vivendi* as a temporary resolution sensitive to the relative power of supporters of different doctrines, which as that power shifts, is likely to come undone. For Rawls, *modus vivendi* involves a compromise based on whatever reasons seem expedient to each side. Real-world examples would include consociational democracies as characterized by Lijphart (1977), in which the leaders of each block in a deeply divided society negotiate a power-sharing settlement.

Rawls (1993: 134) argues that an overlapping consensus must be supported from each comprehensive doctrine by moral reasons,[1] yet "the reasonable doctrines endorse the political conception [ie, the principles of justice], each from its own point of view." Waldron (2004: 95) says that the overlapping consensus is "acceptable on moral grounds to the adherents of C1 . . . C2, and

---

[1] Rawls is not proposing meta-consensus; rather it is overlapping consensus at the simple level he seeks. As List (2002: 77) puts it, participants "agree at a substantive level, albeit with respect to a restricted realm of issues, without necessarily agreeing on any meta-theoretical foundations for their substantive agreement."

so on. The grounds of course would not be the same in each case." It is worth quoting Waldron's supporting example at length:

> ... the proposition that religious toleration is required as a matter of justice may be affirmed by Christians on Lockean grounds having to do with each person's individualized responsibility to God for his own religious beliefs, by secular Lockeans on the grounds of unamenability of belief to coercion, by Kantians on the grounds of the high ethical importance accorded to autonomy, by followers of John Stuart Mill on the basis of the importance of individuality and the free interplay of ideas, and so on. (pp. 95–6)

The problem is that the "so on" will not go very far. Lockean protestants, secular Lockeans, Kantians, and Millians are all species of liberal, and consent to the liberal principle of religious toleration for essentially liberal individualist reasons. Even within this restricted range, Waldron believes the kind of toleration reached by the four routes will actually be different, and back different courses of action precisely when the principle of toleration is needed to resolve key disputes (p. 96). This suggests overlapping consensus is stronger to the degree different doctrines muster *similar* reasons for subscribing to it. At an extreme, to make a truly secure overlapping consensus, they will be able to muster the *same* moral reasons. And these reasons ought to be basic ones for each doctrine. This drive to uniformity warrants Mouffe's skepticism (1996) of what Rawls calls a *reasonable* pluralism. For Rawls defines a "reasonable" individual as someone committed to basic liberal principles (Mouffe 1996: 249). Thus, it is no surprise that these individuals endorse a liberal conception of justice in their overlapping consensus. Setting aside any specifically liberal content of the overlapping consensus and focusing on its formal structure, the general point is that any overlapping consensus requires agreement on the priority of some set of substantive values.

The limits of Rawlsian overlapping consensus can be clarified through reference to MacIntyre's suggestion (1984) that theorists' worries about the centrifugal effects of conflicting values may often be misplaced. MacIntyre (1984: 500–1) points to examples where ethicists who disagree on fundamental principles of morality (pure ethics) often agree when it comes to practical issues (applied ethics), as context-specific reasoning overcomes abstract differences. But mainly he is talking about differences among ethicists in Western societies, trivial in comparison to some of the deeper divisions in the contemporary world. For MacIntyre, part of the key to resolution is a shared tradition, given his belief that conceptions of justice and rationality are tradition specific (MacIntyre 1988). Liberalism for MacIntyre is one such tradition – and most ethicists are liberals of one kind or another. So for all their differences, MacIntyre and Rawls end up with the same problem: neither offers a *general* solution here for the management of pluralism, because a shared tradition such as liberalism or a shared set of values may not always be available.[2]

## CRITICAL PLURALISM AND DIFFERENCE DEMOCRACY

A more radical contemporary pluralism is suspicious of liberal and communitarian devices for reconciling difference. Such a critical pluralism is associated with agonists such as Connolly (1991), Honig (1993), Mouffe (2000), and Schaap (2006) and difference democrats such as Young (2000). As Honig (1996: 60) puts it, "difference is just another word for what used to be called pluralism." Critical pluralists resemble liberals in that they begin from the variety of ways it is possible to experience the world, but stress that the experiences and perspectives of marginalized and oppressed groups are likely to be very different from dominant groups. They also have a strong suspicion of liberal theory that looks neutral but in practice supports and serves the powerful.

Difference democrats are hostile to consensus, partly because consensus decision making (of the sort popular in 1970's radical groups) conceals informal oppression under the guise of concern for all by disallowing dissent (Zablocki 1980). But the real target is political theory that deploys consensus, especially deliberative and liberal theory. Young (1996: 125–6) argues that the appeals to unity and the common good that deliberative theorists under sway of the consensus ideal stress as the proper forms of political communication can often be oppressive. For deliberation so oriented all too easily equates the common good with the interests of the more powerful, thus sidelining legitimate concerns of the marginalized. Asking the underprivileged to set aside their particularistic concerns also means marginalizing their favored forms of expression, especially the telling of personal stories (Young 1996: 126).[3] Speaking for an agonistic conception of democracy (to which Young (2000: 49–51) also subscribes), Mouffe (1996: 248) states:

To negate the ineradicable character of antagonism and aim at a universal rational consensus – that is the real threat to democracy. Indeed, this can lead to violence being

---

[2] If it is not, then MacIntyre (1988) believes reasoned discourse across traditions can still take place when one tradition reaches a crisis (in its own terms) that moves its adherents to look for resources for its resolution in other traditions.

[3] Correspondingly, Young (1996: 123) believes that deliberation privileges argument oriented to winning, a form of expression suited to well-educated and well-off men.

unrecognized and hidden behind appeals to "rationality", as is often the case in liberal thinking.

Mouffe (1996: 246) is a radical pluralist: "By pluralism I mean the end of a substantive idea of the good life." But neither Mouffe nor Young want to abolish communication in the name of pluralism and difference; much of their work advocates sustained attention to communication. Mouffe (1996: 247) also cautions against uncritical celebration of difference, for some differences imply "subordination and should therefore be challenged by a radical democratic politics." She raises the question of the terms in which engagement across difference might proceed. Participants should ideally accept that the positions of others are legitimate, though not as a result of being persuaded in argument. Instead, it is a matter of being open to conversion due to adoption of a particular kind of democratic attitude that converts antagonism into agonism, fighting into critical engagement, enemies into adversaries who are treated with respect. Respect here is not just (liberal) toleration, but positive validation of the position of others. For Young (1996: 126), a communicative democracy would be composed of people showing "equal respect," under "procedural rules of fair discussion and decision-making." Schlosberg (1999: 70) speaks of "agonistic respect" as "a critical pluralist ethos."

Mouffe and Young both want pluralism to be regulated by a particular kind of attitude, be it respectful, agonistic, or even in Young's case (2000: 16–51) reasonable. Thus, neither proposes unregulated pluralism as an alternative to (deliberative) consensus. This regulation cannot be just procedural, for that would imply "anything goes" in terms of the substance of positions. Recall that Mouffe rejects differences that imply subordination. Agonistic ideals demand judgments about what is worthy of respect and what is not. Connolly (1991: 211) worries about dogmatic assertions and denials of identity that fuel existential resentments that would have to be changed to make agonism possible. Young (2000: 51) seeks "transformation of private, self-regarding desires into public appeals to justice." Thus, for Mouffe, Connolly, and Young alike, regulative principles for democratic communication are not just attitudinal or procedural; they also refer to the substance of the kinds of claims that are worthy of respect. These authors would not want to legislate substance, and are suspicious of the content of any alleged consensus. But in retreating from "anything goes" relativism, they need principles to regulate the substance of what rightfully belongs in democratic debate – and consensus on those principles. Knops (2007) argues that for Mouffe, these principles are respect for the right of others to defend their beliefs, and opposition to domination and subordination. Knops points out that these principles are pretty much the same as those basic in deliberative democracy, so Mouffe is a deliberative democrat in disguise. Critical pluralists might want to recoil at this point and deny they have any standards for communication – asserting perhaps that they are "radical democrats in the post-structuralist tradition, who are concerned with the disruptive and dislocationary aspects of democracy" (Norval 2007: 39). But doing so would risk the heavy price of restricting their attention to some fragments of democratic theory, and associated irrelevance to central democratic concerns, because there just has to be more to democracy than disruption.

Whatever their differences, all the pluralist schools of thought canvassed so far agree that pluralism is a potentially problematic issue as well as a value. All see communication across difference as key to resolution (except for Rawlsian liberals who want to legislate basic structure for the resolution of differences). What we propose in the rest of this chapter is a way of thinking about what such communication ought to try to achieve, doing our best not to smuggle in substantive political commitments. We do not expect this approach to be accepted by all those we have discussed, but we try to make it sensitive to the issues they have raised.

## A TYPOLOGY OF CONSENSUS

Consensus first needs to be broken down into its constituents based on the processes at work when individuals arrive at policy preferences. Some conceptions of consensus proceed in terms of preference aggregation, such that consensus connotes agreement on what is to be done. However, consensus can also refer to the values and beliefs that help explain particular preferences. Preferences, values, and beliefs alike can be influenced by both decision procedures and political contexts. For the purposes of analytical tractability and ease of exposition, we proceed for the moment with a very conventional model of preference formation in which individual preferences result from the values the individuals hold combined with a set of beliefs about how particular causes map onto those values. In this exposition, we set aside for the moment the fact that values, beliefs, and preferences alike can be conditioned by particular discourses. We will eventually return to, and highlight, the idea of discursive meta-consensus.

In this light, building upon Elster (1998*b*: 100), three kinds of consensus can be identified (see Table 5.1). The first, *normative consensus* (or what Rescher (1993) calls *axiological* consensus), refers to agreement regarding

Table 5.1 Types of consensus

| | Element of preference construction | | |
| --- | --- | --- | --- |
| | Value | Belief | Expressed preference |
| **Type of consensus** | *Normative consensus* | *Epistemic consensus* | *Preference consensus* |
| | (Agreement on the values that should predominate) | (Agreement on belief about the impact of a policy) | (Agreement on expressed preference for a policy) |
| **Meta counterpart** | Recognition of legitimacy of disputed values | Acceptance of credibility of disputed beliefs | Agreement on the nature of disputed choices |

values driving the decision process. The second, *epistemic consensus*, refers to the judgmental aspect of preference formation, agreement about how particular actions map onto values in cause and effect terms. The third type, *preference consensus*, pertains to the degree of agreement about what should be done. (This is where, for example, social choice theory operates.[4]) Universal consensus in Femia's terms (1996: 368) would occur with agreement in all three aspects – normative, epistemic, and, consequently, preference. Much of the confusion in theoretical debates for and against consensus stems from the fact that the protagonists rarely specify which of these three types (four types, if we include discursive) they are referring to when they use the word "consensus." Each of the three kinds of consensus we have described has a "meta" counterpart, which we will outline in the next section.

The three basic types of consensus can be illustrated by a particular policy issue. Our example is a Niemeyer perennial, and concerns the Bloomfield Track, a road constructed through World Heritage Rainforest in the tropical far north of Australia, the future of which was a matter of public contention.[5] Three groups defined on the basis of their underlying point of view on this issue are shown in the first column of Table 5.2. The second column reflects the normative value that each group holds most dear; the third column reflects the beliefs about what means are most likely to satisfy that end. The final column shows the expressed preference that follows from the combination of values and beliefs.

---

[4] We use the concept of "preference" as is standard in economics – that is, as a ranking of alternatives by an individual.

[5] The track ostensibly services an isolated community, but is more commonly used by tourists. For an extended description, see Niemeyer (2002: ch. 6).

Table 5.2 Preference formation, the Bloomfield Track

|  | Value | Belief | Expressed preference |
|---|---|---|---|
|  | *Normative level* | *Epistemic level* | *Preference level* |
| *Pragmatists* | Needs of community most important | Road will benefit the community | ***Keep road*** |
| *Preservationists* | Needs of environment most important | Road will negatively impact the environment | ***Close road*** |
| *Optimists* | Needs of environment most important (community matters too) | Road will benefit the environment | ***Keep road*** |

The first group, the "pragmatists," believes that the most important consideration is the need of the local community for access (particularly in the absence of clear evidence of environmental damage). They believe that the road best serves this purpose. This leads them to conclude that the best option is to keep the road open. By contrast, "preservationists," who give primacy to potential ecological impacts, believe that the road is detrimental in these terms. They accordingly prefer closure. A third group, "optimists," similarly places a premium on environmental values, but also recognizes community interests. The potential dissonance of this normative position is reduced by a belief that the road can actually benefit both these values – for example, if tourism can increase the profile of the region, promoting more widespread concern for its environmental value.

An examination of Table 5.2 shows there is no universal consensus across all three groups, but there is agreement across elements of their positions. There are normative overlaps among the groups (optimism with preservation on the dominance of environmental concern, optimism with pragmatism on recognition of the community dimension). At the epistemic level, there is dissensus across the three groups, which is why it is possible for agreement on values to coincide with disagreement on policy preference (preservationists and optimists). The converse is also true: pragmatists and optimists disagree at the normative level but have similar preferences. The latter is an example of what Sunstein (1995) calls an incompletely theorized agreement. Preference consensus unites the pragmatists and optimists against the preservationists.

## A TYPOLOGY OF META-CONSENSUS

We now develop and highlight the idea that normative, epistemic, and preference consensus all have a "meta" counterpart (see Table 5.1), which can help structure the process of deliberation. *Normative meta-consensus* exists to the extent that there is agreement on recognition of the legitimacy of a value, though not extending to agreement on which of two or more values ought to receive priority in a given decision. The recognition that defines normative meta-consensus is facilitated to the degree that the values in question are not positioned in a necessary zero-sum trade-off, though this perception is not crucial, and will not always be available. Normative meta-consensus is consistent with the sort of recognition one could expect under Habermasian conditions of communicative rationality, which does not require normative uniformity at the substantive level, only recognition of the "generalizable" status of norms, which may end up informing different policy positions (Dryzek 1990: 17). The value pluralism of liberals such as Berlin (1969) and Galston (2002) must always be discriminating in the values it allows, so requiring normative meta-consensus (though they do not use this terminology). However, normative meta-consensus need not be tied to Galston's prescriptive and substantively liberal tests for admissible values. It can be forged in pragmatic and contextual fashion as suggested by Berlin, though this begs a number of questions about the conditions of any such process, which we will address later. It differs from Rawlsian overlapping consensus, because its recognition of values does not depend on their having counterparts in other "comprehensive doctrines."

In the example in Table 5.2, there are two normative dimensions, pertaining respectively to community and environmental interests. Normative meta-consensus extends across the three groups. While environmental issues are often portrayed in terms of a clash between two kinds of values, most individuals are actually likely to endorse both sets of values (cf. Rokeach 1979). That an individual privileges community needs over environment is not to say that they are hostile to environmental concern, and vice versa. It is just as unlikely that individuals given unconstrained choices would support environmental degradation as it would be for them to want the Bloomfield community to be worse off. In addition, following the discursive psychology we introduced in chapter 3, individuals may have multiple and sometimes contradictory commitments at the normative level (Elster 1986b), the analog of normative pluralism among groups, with different "selves" invoked by different circumstances. Normative meta-consensus would mean different sides (and different selves) should end up agreeing that the others have legitimate values. We note in passing that adversarial processes (such as Anglo-American legal systems) may weaken normative meta-consensus if they frame issues in ways that induce advocates to denigrate the legitimacy of the values of the other side.

One of the more robust findings of the psychology literature on values is that at the abstract level, there is a high degree of agreement on the legitimacy of basic values (Rokeach 1979). Individuals differ mainly on the relative priority of values, and how they apply in particular cases. In our terminology, normative meta-consensus is pervasive (and can indeed be found in our Bloomfield Track case). Our results are consistent with the psychology literature on this point: no normative positions held by participants were hostile to environmental or community values before or after deliberation. However, prior to their deliberation, community and environmental values were widely perceived to exist in zero-sum relationship, such that a trade-off would need to be made. After deliberation, appreciation of the potential complementarity of community and environmental values had grown. If the psychology literature is correct, one of the main tasks of deliberation could be to uncover existing normative meta-consensus obscured by the strategic actions of partisans who try to delegitimate the values held by their opponents. For example, former U.S. Secretary of the Interior James Watt once tried to distinguish between Americans and environmentalists, implying strong environmental values had no place in the normative meta-consensus of American society. Less strategically inept moves with similar intention are made against those whose commitment to human rights can be made to look unpatriotic in the context of the "war on terror." This kind of strategic positioning is very different from the kind of problem that preoccupies agonists and difference democrats, which features a visceral clash of identities that often find validation in denial of the identity of others.

Our Bloomfield Track case does not feature such deep difference in values and identities, so let us introduce a case that has these problematic features. The case is reported by Forester (1999*a*) and Hughes, Forester, and Weiser (1999), and concerns a dialogue on HIV-AIDS policy in Colorado designed to produce advice for the state government. The dialogue involved sixty to seventy participants in a series of monthly and then weekly meetings facilitated by a mediator (Hughes). Participants were selected to represent demographic diversity as well as the key interests active on this issue. They included gay activists (including members of ACT-UP, the AIDS Coalition to Unleash Power), people with AIDS, and fundamentalist Christians active in anti-gay rights campaigns. Conflicting values were in this case basic to the identity of gay activists and fundamentalists in particular (Forester 1999*a*: 462). The fact that the fundamentalists were active in anti-gay rights campaigns – especially a 1992 statewide ballot initiative that passed, prohibiting state and local governments in Colorado from explicitly protecting civil rights for gays and lesbians – showed that their identity in particular required validation through denial of gay identity. Thus, the initial conditions were deep normative meta-dissensus and an absence of recognition (stemming from meta-dissensus at the level of basic discourses).

The deep difference between the two sides was crystallized in a statement by a gay activist to the forum that "There is a need to shift the discussion of AIDS in Colorado from a moral issue to a public health issue, and I refuse to participate in moving this plan forward until we wrestle with that" (quoted in Hughes, Forester, and Weiser 1999: 1020). To the fundamentalist Christians, the issue was entirely moral: "If it isn't a moral issue, people will continue to behave in ways that put them in danger" (quoted in Hughes, Forester, and Weiser 1999: 1021). Each side rejected the way the issue was framed by the other.

As the dialogue proceeded, the two sides could, however, realize that they were not going to change the values of the other side. Their written agreement contained an explicit statement of the participants' recognition of a normative meta-consensus: "For communities that include members with a range of moral perspectives, HIV prevention methods need to be appropriate to that range of moral perspectives" (Hughes, Forester, and Weiser 1999: 1025). From the outset, the participants had a shared interest in reducing risk, suffering, and death, ingredients it might seem for a Rawlsian overlapping consensus. But any shared interests along these lines did not move them beyond impasse; only a normative meta-consensus following prolonged confrontation with the other side and its values could do that. The specific measures to which each side consented were not components of an overlapping consensus. These measures included moral education in schools and sexually explicit material targeted at the gay community, which remained objectionable to gay activists and fundamentalist Christians, respectively.

*Epistemic meta-consensus* is agreement on the credibility of disputed beliefs, and on their relevance to the norms that define the issue at hand. (Beliefs may be credible but irrelevant.) Credibility here means that it is accepted by others as reasonable to hold the belief in question. Epistemic meta-consensus can therefore accommodate the multiplicity of perspectives required by epistemic arguments for the political rationality of pluralism (e.g., Popper 1966). Complexity of a phenomenon and associated uncertainty can preclude definitive choice across competing explanations and their associated theories or perspectives. Competing explanations may then coexist. This coexistence can apply not just in politics, but also in natural science: for example, explanations of the behavior of light as both a wave and a particle in optical physics.

The opposite of meta-consensus occurs when scientific paradigms compete (Kuhn 1970). This kind of epistemic meta-dissensus can also be seen in some environmental issues, with genetic modification a particularly good example of a large gap between the kinds of knowledge claims regarded as legitimate by proponents and opponents of the technology. Yet there are situations where competing epistemic claims can both be accepted as valid. For example, local residents' experiences of the ill-effects of toxic pollution could be regarded as just as valid as the epidemiological studies that typically do not confirm these experiences (Tesh 2000). Any fault may lie in the demanding statistical requirements of epidemiological proof, as much as in residents' perceptions.

*Preference meta-consensus* consists of agreement on the nature of disputed choices across alternatives, and has two aspects. The first concerns the range of alternatives considered acceptable. For example, Dworkin (1977) wants to rule out "external" preferences that an individual has for harm to others. Goodin (1986) speaks of "laundering" preferences before they are taken into account in collective decision making. Most theorists who have contemplated the issue want the acceptable range to be limited by constitutional or legal means – so, for example, the German constitution rules out the option of choosing an extreme right party. However, deliberation itself could produce consensus on the range of acceptable alternatives.

The second aspect of preference meta-consensus concerns the validity of different ways that choices across alternatives can be structured. Several types of structure are available. List (2002) has suggested one such type, in terms of agreement on a single important issue-dimension along which preferences are to be structured.[6] This is demonstrated in Figure 5.1 using the Bloomfield Track case study. Five policy alternatives can be ordered according to the degree of access they would permit to the Bloomfield region. Bitumenization (sealing) leads to greatest access for vehicles; closure the least access. Intermediate policies of upgrading by covering with gravel, stabilizing steep slopes to reduce soil slippage, or leaving the road as a four-wheel drive track, each give decreasing degrees of access. If there is agreement that degree of access is the most important dimension, policy preferences should be "single peaked" along this dimension. Preference meta-consensus on this particular dimension would form if there is epistemic meta-consensus that the condition of the

---

[6] The "preference" is added by us; List refers simply to meta-consensus, and does not recognize our normative, epistemic, and discursive categories, or the aspect of preference meta-consensus that refers to the acceptable range of alternatives, or forms of structure other than single peakedness on an agreed dimension. Later, List (2007) contemplates epistemic aspects by expanding "meta-agreement" to cover judgments as well as preferences, but as with preferences, he is concerned only with agreement on a common structuring dimension, as opposed to the credibility of disputed beliefs.

track is the prime causal factor determining benefits to the community and/or damage to the environment, which in turn are recognized as the key values in a normative meta-consensus. Figure 5.1 shows four cases of single-peaked policy preference rankings along this dimension, illustrated by the solid lines. The broken line is not single peaked.

According to List (2002), agreement at the meta level exists to the degree preference orderings are single peaked on a dimension that is recognized as central by participants (because non-single peakedness can only be explained by the individuals in question having their preference ordering determined along a different but related dimension).

However, single peakedness is not the only type of structuration of choices. Say for example that there is normative meta-consensus on the Bloomfield Track that environment and community values are the important considerations, and epistemic consensus that the mere presence of the road will continually increase environmental damage by opening up new areas for development. Preferences may then be structured not along degree of access, but simply between closure and all other options where the road remains open. This sort of preference meta-consensus involving option reduction became observable and important at a key point in deliberation on this issue. Option reduction has the effect of restricting the number of alternatives that pass the relevance test, and so formally resembles restriction on the basis of acceptability (the first kind of preference meta-consensus we identified).

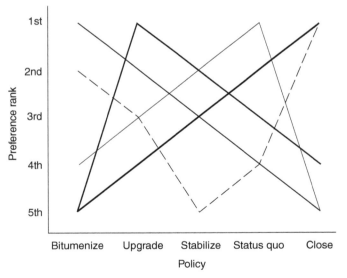

Figure 5.1 Single-peaked preference orderings of Bloomfield Track policies

## META-CONSENSUS AS THE KEY?

Our taxonomy of modes of consensus and meta-consensus points to the reconciliation of opposing ideals of consensus and pluralism. This reconciliation would involve normative, epistemic, and preference pluralism at the simple level (except in rare cases where simple consensus is unproblematic), together with consensus on one or more of these three aspects at the meta level. We now develop the positive side of this resolution, before moving to a consideration of discursive meta-consensus, and then a consideration of the circumstances in which meta-conensus of any sort gets produced. Pointing to the virtues of meta-consensus does not imply that *any* meta-consensus is defensible, or that it should strive to cover (say) Nazi values, crackpot science, and preferences for the suffering of others. Any meta-consensus is characterized by exclusions as well as inclusions.

The first argument to be made for this resolution is that at the simple level, consensus of any of our three types is likely to be elusive in any society with any degree of pluralism. Now, processes such as mediation (where parties to a dispute sit down under the auspices of a neutral third party and seek a resolution receiving the consent of all sides) often produce what at first looks like preference consensus in the sense of agreement about what is to be done. But such agreement will often represent only what each party can accept in comparison to what would happen otherwise. Indeed, partisans will generally enter into such a process only if they fear the outcome that will prevail otherwise. So in mediation over a development dispute, environmentalists and community groups may accept an outcome of "responsible development" if they think the likely alternative is irresponsible development. This acceptance does not mean that responsible development is now their first choice. Such an outcome can be achieved with continuing dissensus across environmentalists and developers at the normative, epistemic, and, indeed, preference levels. Mediation involves construction of a normative meta-consensus across initially hostile partisans, which then facilitates a search for mutually acceptable outcomes that are better than any mere compromise between the initial positions of partisans.

Meta-consensus makes fewer demands upon partisans than does simple consensus, and so ought to be available more often. In particular, it can still be available when partisans continue to disagree profoundly about what should be done. But meta-consensus will not always be available, and it may take hard work to discover or create. Sometimes, partisans will prefer to continue to fight with every means at their disposal. Yet because in comparison with simple consensus it makes fewer demands on partisans to compromise their first-order values, beliefs, and preferences, the achievement of meta-consensus is less dependent on the motivations of partisans to seek agreement. Even when disagreement can be resolved only by voting, meta-consensus can facilitate the generation of better outcomes – as we will show in a discussion of the benefits of preference meta-consensus.

Any rarity or elusiveness of simple consensus is not in the end a decisive argument against its pursuit. As we said at the outset, consensus of any kind can be a matter of degree. In the case of a citizen's jury convened to deliberate the Bloomfield Track issue,[7] the jury process did increase preference consensus. At the end of the jury, seven of twelve jurors favored closing the track, while at the outset of the process none of the five options was the first choice of more than four jurors. (So the product of deliberation was not a compromise, but rather a shift to one extreme. The Condorcet winner changed from stabilization of the existing condition of the track to closing the track.[8]) Yet, preference dissensus remained at the end of the process.

A more telling argument against an exclusive focus on simple consensus is that its content is hard to evaluate, except through reference to the procedure that produces it. So it is straightforward to condemn a procedure that involves threats and manipulation, or to praise procedures that involve relatively uncoerced dialogue. Though even here, warning bells are sounded by difference democrats who dispute the possibility of any neutral rules of debate, as well as by those such as Kuran (1998) and Femia (1996) who see conformity pressures at work in deliberation.

### On behalf of normative meta-consensus

Normative meta-consensus implies reciprocal understanding and recognition of the legitimacy of the values held by other participants in political interaction. Deliberative democrats who have taken deep moral disagreement seriously such as Gutmann and Thompson (1996: 52–3) prize reciprocity: "the capacity to seek fair terms of cooperation for their own sake." This means that citizens must provide reasons in terms that those with whom they disagree can accept – terms that go beyond their own particular interests in order to connect them with more general moral principles. In constructing justifications for their positions along these lines, individuals would in our language construct a normative meta-consensus. Gutmann and Thompson

---

[7] The jury is more extensively reported in Niemeyer (2002, 2004).

[8] A Condorcet winner by definition beats all others in pairwise comparisons.

are excessively prescriptive in specifying the content of normative meta-consensus as general moral principles. They lay out what their ideals of reasonableness require in the substantive resolution of particular policy disputes such as that over abortion. Thus, their normative meta-consensus is over-specified. From our point of view, normative meta-consensus not only promotes the ability of different groups in a plural society to coexist in civility and recognize their joint membership of a democratic polity, but also the likelihood that they will engage in a creative search for outcomes that respect the basic values of all parties, however different these values remain. Of course, this search will not necessarily prove successful; but collective choice does become more tractable.

We can further clarify the role of normative meta-consensus in making collective decisions more tractable by looking more closely at the practical literature on conflict resolution concerned with mediation and "consensus building" – essentially the same thing. Such approaches seek agreement across parties to a dispute, but not consensus in the sense usually used in political theory. In mediation and related approaches, agreement is sought on actions to be taken. Under the auspices of a neutral facilitator or mediator, participants strive for unanimity but do not necessarily achieve it. The agreement represents a course of action participants can live with; it is not necessarily their first preference, but they realize it is better than the best they are likely to get in the absence of any agreement. The agreement receives their reflective assent, partly in the knowledge that their concerns have been recognized and addressed, even if they are not shared by other participants. These approaches have been applied to disputes in many areas of life (environment and development, workplace disputes, divorce, planning, etc.). Their advocates point to the stability, efficiency, and fairness of the outcomes produced – especially in comparison with more adversarial legal processes.

Mediation and consensus building resemble the "incompletely theorized agreements" of which Sunstein (1995) speaks, and which were earlier described in Dryzek (1990: 16–17). Part of their lack of theorization is the absence of any attempt to ground them in shared principles, so actors can consent for completely different reasons. Less ambiguously than either MacIntyre or Rawls, Sunstein allows that agreements may be endorsed for truly different reasons from different sides. But beyond pointing to a practical possibility that may sometimes be available, Sunstein offers no general principles for political dialogue. Rawls would presumably object that an incompletely theorized agreement has no necessary moral content or backing from the moral principles of different partisans, and so provides an insecure basis for political arrangements in a plural society. Advocates of practical consensus building and mediation approaches such as Susskind, McKearnan, and

Thomas-Larmer (1999) would say that the lessons of experience contradict this theoretical worry; that such agreements do have staying power. But the whole point of consensus building and mediation is that such agreements require hard work on the part of both participants and the facilitator; they are not to be expected in the ordinary give-and-take of politics, still less in the legal system. Practitioners, advocates, and observers of these processes stress that they cannot be understood in strategic, game-theoretic terms. These processes are not oriented to simple compromise of the sort that could be achieved by strategic bargaining. Instead, the target is an outcome that is more responsive to the concerns of both sides than any bargained compromise could be, which in turn requires creativity in joint problem solving. Interactions are governed by a set of principles that might (say) forbid *ad hominem* attacks, stereotyping of adversaries, making threats, concealing information, delaying tactics, or statement of a bargaining position. Mediators regard it as crucial that participants come to recognize the legitimacy of the normative position of their adversaries, and are prepared to reflect upon their own positions. In our language, successful mediation requires construction of a normative meta-consensus.

We conclude that whatever the character of the issue at hand, some normative meta-consensus is desirable. This does not mean that *any* normative meta-consensus is defensible. Premature normative meta-consensus might blunt the force of moral crusades against (say) racial discrimination were activists to admit racist values into a meta-consensus. But even here efforts could be made to include some of the relevant values held by racists. Consider, for example, the frequent invocation by Dr. Martin Luther King, Jr. of the values embedded in the U.S. Declaration of Independence and Bill of Rights. These appeals were designed in part to remind white Southerners of their shared membership in a normative tradition within which claims for racial justice could then be processed peacefully. At issue here is not just the application of shared values to the particular case of African-American civil rights, but also the legitimate range of specific human rights that can be justified through reference to the basic idea of a rights-based political system and thus form part of a defensible meta-consensus.

We can distinguish between three types of issues. First, there are those that involve clashes of identity in a divided society. The key here is production of a discursive meta-consensus that remains contestable, which we will treat in the next section. Second, there are issues that involve deep moral conflicts. The key here is production of a stable normative meta-consensus. Third, there are issues that feature competing interests but no deep denials of identity or morality across participants. The key here is uncovering an existing normative meta-consensus that is obscured by the strategic machinations of partisans.

The HIV-AIDS case is an example of the second type of issue. While the conflict has its origins in contending discourses that produce incompatible identities, by processing the issue as one of competing values, a normative meta-consensus could be produced. The dialogue eventually produced agreement on a set of concrete policy measures. At the end of the process, the two sides still had fundamental differences in values and their identity differences were no different than when they began; the normative meta-consensus was specific to the HIV-AIDS issue under discussion. After the agreement had been reached, a discussion about whether being gay was a lifestyle choice threatened to explode; at this point, the mediator simply suggested that everyone go home (Hughes, Forester, and Weiser 1999: 1025). Thus, there was no normative consensus, no conversion of attitude to the other as sought by agonists, and no discursive meta-consensus (because each side still did not accept the identities inherent in the other's discourse). But there was a normative meta-consensus across deep difference produced by deliberation that made possible joint problem-solving progress, and a set of mutually acceptable policy recommendations. This example demonstrates that normative meta-consensus can be achieved much more easily than normative consensus.

## On behalf of epistemic meta-consensus

Epistemic meta-consensus for its part could be desirable on the grounds of deliberative economy. That is, to the extent a set of beliefs is accepted as credible and relevant, there is an understanding of what the main issues are, and so no need to debate fundamentals each time a claim is made. A parallel with paradigms in scientific communities can be drawn here. A paradigm by definition features strong epistemic meta-consensus, releasing practitioners from the sheer amount of time and effort it takes to get beyond debating basic assumptions and first principles. Of course, nothing as strong as a paradigm will normally be available (or necessarily desirable) in a political context. Epistemic meta-consensus permits the pluralism at the simple level required for complex issues to be scrutinized from a number of directions in the search for creative solutions that respond to different facets of issues (see our earlier discussion of Popper's argument for the rationality of simple pluralism in policy making).

In effect, epistemic meta-consensus creates a "problem-solving public" in the sense of pragmatist philosophers such as John Dewey (1927). To return to our toxic pollution example, government officials wielding epidemiological studies and local residents reporting particular experiences would not be stuck in ridiculing the methodological basis of each others' claims, but instead devote energy to joint problem solving. This effort might, for example, involve deploying some version of the "precautionary principle" in environmental policy, which is designed to inform policy making in situations of substantial uncertainty about the content and magnitude of risks. Such an outcome would not be in any sense a mere compromise between the epistemic positions of the two sides that would involve an assessment of risks somewhere between that of the epidemiologists and local residents, but rather a wholly new way of looking at decision in the context of risk.

Yet some differences of belief might resist incorporation in an epistemic meta-consensus; for example, when religious groups that deny the validity of modern science as an article of faith confront scientists who deny the validity of knowledge claims grounded in faith. Even here the impasse could be transcended to the extent the two sides could recognize that their conflict is in part about values rather than beliefs. Some joint problem solving might then be possible under a normative meta-consensus, as our HIV-AIDS example suggests.

Epistemic meta-consensus can also be instrumental to the creation of both normative and preference meta-consensus. If an issue is characterized by competing interests (but no deep denials of identity or morality – the third type mentioned in the previous subsection), then normative meta-consensus is facilitated to the degree values are not positioned in a necessary zero-sum relationship. To illustrate, in our Bloomfield Track example, deliberation reduced the credibility of claims about community access benefits of the track, which in turn led the jurors to recognize that community and environmental values were not necessarily diametrically opposed. Deliberation also enhanced the credibility of (still disputed) claims about the flow-on effects of development in the rainforest resulting from any option that left the track open, leading to a preference meta-consensus that the real choice was between closing the track and all other options.

## On behalf of preference meta-consensus

Preference meta-consensus is valuable because it makes social choice less vulnerable to arbitrariness, instability, and manipulation by clever strategists. The first type of preference meta-consensus we identified concerns the range of acceptable alternatives. In the language of Arrow's (1963) social choice theory, this kind of meta-consensus limits the capacity of individuals to manipulate outcomes by introducing irrelevant alternatives, as well as reducing the cognitive demands associated with multiple options. The second type of preference meta-consensus, concerning the validity of ways in which choices can be structured, operates to restrict the domain of admissible preference profiles (and would, for example, rule out the preference profile represented by the broken line in Figure 5.1), thus overcoming the problem that Arrow's "universal domain" condition causes for social choice. To the extent that the preferences of actors are single peaked along one dimension, the chances that there is a Condorcet winner across policy options – one that beats all others in pairwise comparisons – is increased (Knight and Johnson 1994: 282–3). And if there is a Condorcet winner, then the possibility of cycles across options disappears (Black 1948). It is the possibility of such cycles (where option A beats B beats C beats A in simple majority voting) that leads Riker (1982) to conclude that there is no such thing as the will of the people, which reflects only the aggregation (voting) mechanism used to measure it. Clever strategists realize this, and so attempt to manipulate procedures (e.g., the order in which votes are taken) to get their way.

We pointed out earlier that agreement on an issue dimension is not the only way choices can be structured. For example, in our Bloomfield Track case, structuration was eventually produced through meta-consensus that the real choice was between closure of the road and all other alternatives. Because this meta-consensus reduces the effective number of options to two, it would preclude manipulations such as introducing irrelevant alternatives, varying the order in which votes across multiple alternatives are taken, or proposing different voting systems. But whatever form it takes, preference meta-consensus helps banish social choice theory's dire prognostications about both the arbitrariness and instability of democracy and its vulnerability to manipulation (Dryzek and List 2003). Mackie (2003) demonstrates at length that real political actors often find ways to locate dimensions with single-peaked preference orderings.

## DISCURSIVE META-CONSENSUS

Having taken an extensive look at normative, epistemic, and preference meta-consensus in light of a simplified model of preference formation grounded in values and beliefs, we now return as promised to analysis of the ideas of discursive consensus and meta-consensus. This analysis is based on the discourses that can condition values, beliefs, and preferences alike. As sketched in chapter 2, discourses can generate and condition values, beliefs, and preferences. Any discourse conditions the way the world is apprehended. This will predispose adherents who subscribe in whole or in part to the discourse in question to particular story lines that involve opinions about both values that can go into normative meta-consensus, and the facts that can go into epistemic meta-consensus. These judgments or assumptions about values and facts, along with basic categories and dispositions, condition preferences that can be generated within the discourse, and so what can go into preference meta-consensus. So a more parsimonious treatment of many of the issues we have canvassed pertaining to pluralism, consensus, and meta-consensus could conceivably proceed in terms of discourses, subsuming normative, epistemic, and preference concerns. However, not all of the issues could be subsumed, because disputes about values, beliefs, and preferences can occur within discourses as well as across them. Not all disputes have their origins in disputes across discourses.

But some do. For example, the toxic pollution example we discussed earlier stems originally from a clash between scientific and experiential discourses that highlight, respectively, statistical analysis and personal experience. Sometimes, the differences between such systems are deep; consider, for example, differences between scientific and fundamentalist religious discourses when it comes to evolution and creation. The Colorado HIV-AIDS dispute involves conflicting values but it stems originally from identities produced by different discourses.

Simple discursive consensus would be agreement on the priority of a particular discourse (be it market liberalism, civil rights, sustainable development, counterterror, or whatever). This agreement can, however, also be described as hegemony: where all actors accept the terms set by the discourse in question. Hegemony is often castigated by critical pluralists as discussed earlier as a set of taken-for-granted understandings that in practice constitute and serve a particular set of power relations. Simple discursive consensus has all the problems we discussed earlier that pluralists identify in consensus – but writ especially large, because discursive consensus can be so encompassing as to go unrecognized, as it provides the concepts and categories that create meaning in the very language people use.

Discursive meta-consensus can be defined as agreement on the acceptable range of contested discourses. In the Bloomfield Track example, what we referred to as "groups" were actually discourses: pragmatism, preservationism, and optimism, which together were the ingredients of a discursive meta-consensus. The citizens' jury convened to deliberate the issue concluded that a fourth discourse, one which tried to assuage anxieties of both environmentalists and developers, did not belong in this meta-consensus (though it was present at the beginning of the jury).

Much of what we can say on behalf of discursive meta-consensus can be derived from our previous discussion of the other three types of meta-consensus. So, for example, in the Bloomfield Track case, the fact that in the course of deliberation one discourse dropped out of the discursive meta-consensus (the one that tried to assuage both sides) led to a preference meta-consensus that the real options boiled down to two: keeping the track open, or closing it. This in turn meant a simpler decision problem less vulnerable to strategic machinations.

In this light, discursive meta-consensus is instrumental to meta-consensus of the other three types, and so any argument on behalf of these three types can also be brought into the case for discursive meta-consensus. However, this instrumentality tells only part of the story when it comes to the desirability of discursive meta-consensus. For some kinds of conflicts are essentially about identities that are produced by discourses (Dryzek 2005), much more than they are about the values, beliefs, and preferences that the other three types of meta-consensus address.[9] Recognition of the identity of different others is prized by critical pluralists such as Schlosberg (1999), postmodern theorists of identity and difference such as Connolly (1991), and agonists such as Mouffe (2000). Discursive meta-consensus is consistent with the idea of "justice as recognition" that theorists of identity and difference promote. Even Mouffe (1999: 756) allows that "pluralist democracy requires a certain amount of consensus." This does not mean that difference democrats and critical pluralists would endorse *any* discursive meta-consensus, and they would be alive to the degree to which any particular meta-consensus unjustly excludes particular identities. Discursive meta-consensus might therefore have to be treated as provisional and itself contestable. As Mouffe (1999: 756) puts it, the "different and conflicting interpretations" of "ethico-political principles" means that "consensus is bound to be a 'conflictual consensus'." While allowing that (in our language) discursive meta-consensus is necessary for pluralist democratic communication, she believes its construction is inevitably political and so contestable. But, however under-specified its content in Mouffe's theory, her theory requires discursive meta-consensus – the basic agonistic distinction between "enemies" and "adversaries" implies that the latter are welcomed into a discursive meta-consensus, while the former are not. Under-specification may be fatal if we want democracy to be oriented to collective decision; but for agonists that is not the point of democracy, which is more about how to live together in open-ended conversation.

Our discussions of critical pluralism suggest the following tests for discursive meta-consensus, though as we have stressed, agonists would treat all these

---

[9] In Dryzek and Niemeyer (2006: 643–4), this discussion of identity conflicts was shoehorned into normative meta-consensus. Its rightful context is discursive meta-consensus, as it appears here.

tests as provisional and contestable. For critical pluralists, discourses are legitimate entrants into a discursive meta-consensus to the degree they

1. Are not dogmatic (Connolly)
2. Are not fueled by resentment (Connolly)
3. Do not deny the identity of others
4. Are not primarily about "private, self-regarding desires" (Young)
5. Do not entail the subordination of others (Mouffe)
6. Are not relativistic in a refusal to recognize a constitutive other (Mouffe)
7. Do not appeal to their own superior rationality (Mouffe)

These seven tests are quite demanding, and a discursive meta-consensus that falls short may still be valuable. In the Colorado HIV-AIDS case we introduced earlier, the discursive meta-consensus was extremely thin, approaching only recognition of "communities that include members with a range of moral perspectives" who should live together rather than seek to subordinate one another. While passing tests 2, 5, and 6, this particular meta-consensus did not reach the depth suggested by tests 1, 3, 4, and 7. This case is clearly one of normative meta-consensus, falling short of the kind of recognition that discursive meta-consensus would seek. The gay activists and fundamentalist Christians still rejected each others' (discourse-generated) identity at the end of their dialogue. This observation does not, however, detract from the desirability of discursive meta-consensus if it can be obtained.

In a deeply divided society, where the discourses generating identity might be religious, secular, national, or ethnic, each identity finds validation in rejection of the identity of the other side. So a discursive meta-consensus encompassing the two (or more) sides would almost by definition contribute to conflict resolution, because the clash of identities would no longer be so deadly. The generation of discursive meta-consensus can be found, for example, in the case of Northern Ireland, and is expressed in particular in the Good Friday Agreement of 1998 (though it took some years after 1998 to bring most significant actors into this meta-consensus). In the wake of that agreement, Protestant Unionists and Catholic Republicans still find their own identities in the rejection of that of the other side, and still oppose the core project of the other side (be it a republic encompassing all thirty-two counties of Ireland, or continued union with Britain). But each side's leadership has come to recognize the legitimacy of the discourse underlying the aspirations of the other side, even as both leaderships remain strenuously opposed to those aspirations.

## THE CONDITIONS OF META-CONSENSUS

At this point, we reach the tentative conclusion that ideals of consensus and pluralism in political interaction can be reconciled by the idea that consensus belongs at the meta level, while pluralism belongs at the simple level. Meta-consensus effectively reconciles theoretical arguments for pluralism on the one hand and consensus on the other. It is a set of standards that can be applied to the evaluation of deliberative forums and deliberative systems. An effective deliberative system should be able to produce meta-consensus. However, such a conclusion does not reach far enough. For meta-consensus might still be under the sway of ideological constriction. Elites can manipulate public opinion using arguments that invoke "symbolic" values and beliefs, as described by Edelman (1964). The idea here is to associate one's preferred outcomes with popular symbols (such as freedom) and undesired outcomes with unpopular symbols (e.g., communism or terrorism). The effect is to privilege particular norms invoked by symbolic arguments over others, so that normative meta-consensus is manipulated.

For the individuals following appealing cues, symbolic politics provides a simple and cognitively cheap solution to the problem of constructing preferences in relation to complex problems. In a plural society, different sides may compete in symbolic manipulation. Instead of beginning with a settlement on premises (values and beliefs) to arrive at conclusions (policy preferences), premises or perspectives are invoked by elites to support particular conclusions. These premises will often involve relations of cause and effect, and so influence the content of any epistemic meta-consensus. Particular factual claims can be deployed strategically in the interests of particular discourses or normative positions.

In itself this is not a problem, because such deployment is a staple of the unavoidably rhetorical character of democratic politics. What it does suggest though is that we need standards to distinguish desirable from undesirable uses of rhetoric in deliberative politics of the sort developed in chapter 4.

A comparison of two kinds of environmental dispute is instructive here. The first would be climate change, where oil companies can be found financing studies that point to the absence of serious climate change resulting from increased carbon dioxide emissions, while environmentalists will make claims about imminent catastrophe unless greenhouse gas emissions are curbed. Almost all scientists recognize the reality of climate change caused by increasing carbon dioxide levels in the atmosphere resulting from fossil fuel use. Yet, fossil fuel industry-financed scientists still try to extend the epistemic meta-consensus to cover thorough skepticism about anthropogenic climate change. Here, credibility judgments can be made based on the source of a claim (classically, the *ethos* in rhetoric, referring to the character of the speaker). If a claim is backed *only* by science funded or undertaken by partisans, then it should not be accepted into an epistemic meta-consensus. On the climate change issue, this standard would rule out the consistently alarmist science of the Worldwatch Institute as well as the skepticism financed by the fossil fuel industry. Localized hazardous pollution and global warming examples are instructive here. The second, contrasting, kind of environmental example would be that where local residents claim health damage from hazardous pollution. There is a big difference between individuals expending time and energy to publicize perceived risks based on actual individual cases of death and disease on the one hand; and corporations financing studies designed to enhance their own profitability on the other. The former begin with evidence (however much it might be disputed by epidemiologists); the latter begin with an interest and seek to manufacture evidence. The former can stimulate formation of a deliberative system; the latter try to undermine the conditions for such a system.

By influencing meta-consensus at the level of values and beliefs, the kind of polarization that ensues under symbolic politics can have the effect of increasing preference meta-consensus. In their study of preferences before and after a deliberative poll conducted on the issue of whether or not Australia should become a republic, McLean et al. (2000) show that the degree of preference meta-consensus (defined in List's terms as agreement on a single important dimension along which preferences are structured) was unchanged by deliberation. They attribute the prior preference meta-consensus to the high salience of the republic issue. However, an equally plausible explanation is that the prior meta-consensus was a function of manipulation by political leaders. A coalition of direct-election (for the presidency) republicans and monarchists successfully portrayed the indirect-election republic on offer as elitist, a "politician's republic." This coalition invoked a widely held belief that politicians cannot be trusted, which then became central in determining the content of epistemic meta-consensus. Consequently, the symbolically determined dimension along which preferences were structured was elitist to non-elitist. After deliberation, the dominant dimension changed to republican to monarchist.

Discursive meta-consensus for its part can be achieved in more or less deliberative fashion. Struggles can occur in the public sphere over the content of discursive meta-consensus that involve both attempts to delegitimize particular discourses, and to get marginal discourses accepted as legitimate. One can think of the rise of (for example) environmentalist and feminist discourses since the 1960s in these terms: they now have a place in a discursive meta-consensus that was once denied them. Racist discourses for their part have occasionally been expelled from discursive meta-consensus. The "culture wars" in the United States have often been a struggle not just between competing positions, but over the acceptable range of discourses. Each side wants to expel the discourse of the other – not just to disagree with it. That is what makes them "wars." So on university campuses, those on the cultural left have tried to restrict the range of admissible speech. Outside campuses, those on the cultural right have scorned (for example) discourses about alternative sexualities as unacceptable and un-American.

Our discussion of the conditions of meta-consensus suggests that meta-consensus can be the product of symbol manipulation and strategic action, as well as relatively uncoerced dialogue. What this might seem to suggest is that we need to introduce some procedural norms for the evaluation of particular instances of meta-consensus. One candidate would be Habermasian standards of communicative rationality.

Now, invoking Habermas might produce a negative response on the part of pluralists who associate him with consensus. But many of their objections to Habermasian procedural conditions of consensus at the simple level are attenuated (if not actually eliminated) by a move to the meta level. Meta-consensus by definition allows for diversity in values, beliefs, preferences, and discourses. We have shown that all pluralists, be they liberal or critical, must in the end appeal to some kind of meta-consensus to regulate pluralism. If so, pluralists cannot avoid contemplation of the conditions under which meta-consensus gets produced or discovered. Pluralists do not have to endorse Habermasian procedural standards at the meta level, but it should not be hard for them to accept that any meta-consensus reached under these conditions is preferable to one reached through symbolic manipulation as captured by Edelman. Agonists might still insist that any such meta-consensus remain provisional and contestable, and that is fair enough – especially when it comes to issues involving fundamental conflict of identity. But to agonists we say this: if you do not like the standards we have proposed, tell us what you will accept, and exactly how they differ from those of deliberative democracy. And if you refuse to specify any standards at all, and celebrate only disruption, then accept your diminished relevance to core questions of democratic theory and practice.

## CONCLUSION

It makes little sense to be for pluralism, against pluralism, for consensus, or against consensus, and unproductive disputes among political theorists on this score should now cease. We have argued that competing ideals of pluralism and consensus can be reconciled by pluralism at the simple level combined with meta-consensus on values, beliefs, preferences, and discourses. However, close attention must be paid to the content of meta-consensus, as well as its conditions of production.

When it comes to content, we should avoid both over-specification and under-specification. Over-specification of normative meta-consensus can be found, for example, in the lessons Gutmann and Thompson draw for the substance of moral principles and content of public policy from their principle of reciprocity. Other examples of over-specification might refer to the content of an issue dimension along which preferences should be arrayed, if it is specified by an observer rather than discovered by participants; or allowing competing scientific viewpoints into epistemic meta-consensus while scorning lay knowledge. Under-specification characterizes agonism in its keenness to make discursive meta-consensus itself contestable. However defensible this might be for some of the identity conflicts that preoccupy agonists, it is a poor general principle. Under-specification of epistemic meta-consensus could approach "anything goes" in knowledge claims. When it comes to the conditions of its production, meta-consensus produced by symbolic politics in the service of partisans, or (worse) hegemonic actors is much less defensible than meta-consensus produced by relatively uncoerced dialogue.

Our emphasis on meta-consensus might seem to leave open the question of how collective decisions get made. But whatever the mechanism used (short of dictatorship), be it majority rule, approval voting, unanimity, bargained resolution, working agreements that all sides support for different reasons, or agreements that majorities support and minorities can live with, meta-consensus makes collective choice more tractable. Sometimes, tractability will enable agreement on what is to be done, but other kinds of outcome are possible: for example, different rules for different parts of the community (as in the HIV-AIDS example), or a decision supported by majority vote. Enhanced tractability can occur in different ways, depending on the kind of meta-consensus secured. Discursive meta-consensus involves recognition across difference, and as such facilitates conflict resolution under conditions of deep identity difference. Normative meta-consensus enables cooperative search for mutually acceptable solutions to joint problems while respecting value differences that can remain deep and irreconcilable, as the Colorado HIV-AIDS case illustrates. Aside from facilitating normative and preference meta-consensus, epistemic meta-consensus for its part can enable creation of a problem-solving public, as the example of epidemiological and local experiences of risks from hazardous pollution illustrates. Preference meta-consensus renders collective choice less vulnerable to strategizing and manipulation, by either producing agreement on the dimension along which choice can be structured, or reducing the effective number of options, as our Bloomfield Track example illustrates. The benefits of preference meta-consensus can be demonstrated most straightforwardly in situations where some kind of voting determines social choices – but these kinds of effects are generalizable to any mechanism for making collective choices, whether or not formal votes are taken.

In terms of the practical implications of this analysis for deliberators and facilitators (in any institutional setting), we suggest that:

- Discursive meta-consensus is particularly urgent in situations featuring deep difference in identities, especially in divided societies, but is useful in many settings.
- Normative meta-consensus matters most when there are major conflicts between value commitments, whether or not these conflicts are rooted in different discourses.
- Attention to the bounds of epistemic meta-consensus is especially important in settings where powerful actors invoke questionable empirical claims in support of their material interests.
- Preference meta-consensus matters most in situations where one or more actors is in a position to manipulate decision processes (through, for example, the range of options on the agenda or the order in which votes are taken).

To recognize these benefits is not to imply that any meta-consensus should be applauded, and we have pointed to the possibility of symbolic distortion in its production. But to recognize this limit means only that we need to be on guard – not that the pursuit of meta-consensus should be shunned. Recall that for Cohen (1989), "outcomes are democratically legitimate if and only if they could be the object of free and reasoned agreement among individuals." A better way of putting this is now possible: "outcomes are democratically legitimate to the degree they are structured by free and reasoned meta-consensus among individuals subject to them." A still richer conception of democratic legitimacy is reached if we join this conclusion with that of chapter 2. In this light, democratic legitimacy is to be found in the resonance of collective decisions with the outcome of the engagement of discourses in the public sphere, to the extent that engagement is regulated by free and reasoned meta-consensus.

# Part III

# Frontiers

# 6

## Governance Networks

### FROM DEMOS TO NETWORK, FROM GOVERNMENT TO GOVERNANCE

Political theory in general has long proceeded on the assumption that the main locus of political authority demanding attention is the sovereign state. Democratic theorists have generally concurred, specifying in addition that the state be accompanied by a well-defined demos, the people in whose name rule is exercised. The state can be made democratic by having its leadership elected by the demos, or otherwise made responsive and accountable to the expressed preferences, opinions, and interests of the demos, thus fulfilling the key democratic quality of popular control. The demos in turn must feature political equality at some level – for example, in terms of the right to an equal vote. The state can be made a liberal democracy by placing its rulers under constitutional constraints, and giving its citizens a set of liberties and rights that protect their private and public lives against oppressive interference by other citizens and by government itself. The rights might specify freedom of expression, thought, assembly, and association, and possibly private property, or subsistence needs. The imagery here is of a state with no rivals when it comes to exercising legitimate authority over the people within its jurisdiction, with the authorization of that people – and nobody else.

Yet this imagery captures only a subset of politics in today's world. Arguably, the size of this subset is declining. Erosion comes from two directions. The first is in the growth of effective political authority that is not confined within national boundaries. The authority in question might be exercised by regional governments such as the European Union (EU), global bodies such as the World Trade Organization (WTO), by regional alliances such as the North Atlantic Treaty Organization (NATO), by hegemonic states exercising hard or soft power over other states, and by multinational corporations and banks. Sovereignty is not at all absolute, but conditional on abiding by a set of norms concerning (for example) what kinds of weapons can be stockpiled and used, or how individuals residing within the state's borders can be treated. Chapter 9 will consider how deliberative democrats might respond to such transnational challenges. This chapter addresses a different, though related, source of erosion of the authority of the sovereign state: the extent to which governance is exercised by and in networks.

Networks can include state actors – but they do not have to, and these public officials do not necessarily have standing very different to that of other participants in networks, be they corporations, bankers, interest groups, nongovernmental organizations (NGOs), research institutes, consultancy firms, charities, celebrities, academics, or social movement activists. Public officials involved in networks may come from a number of different agencies, levels of government, or jurisdictions. Thus, networked governance and internationalization of authority are connected, because the jurisdictions in question may be in different countries: governance networks can transcend national boundaries. Multilevel governance has long been a reality in federal systems, and in transnational unions such as the EU, but is becoming pervasive as traditionally centralized states (such as France) increasingly devolve functions to lower levels of government.

A distinction here is now often made between *government* and *governance*. Government is hierarchical, exercised in formal institutions, and backed by the sovereign authority of the state that applies in general fashion to all problems that arise within its jurisdiction. "Networks are the defining characteristic of governance" (Bevir and Rhodes 2003: 55–6). Governance is networked and informal, and collective outcomes are generated with no necessary reference to centralized authority. Particular networks are often issue specific. Outcomes are produced by interactive means. They can be endorsed by the sovereign authority; and indeed states sometimes set up networks, and try to steer them. However, governance networks can also produce outcomes that are not either validated or steered by public officials acting in the name of the state. This is the post-Westphalian world to which political theory, and democratic theory in particular, must adjust (Braithwaite 2007). (It was the Treaty of Westphalia that set up the modern system of sovereign states in 1648.)

The significance for dialogue across difference in a deliberative democracy of a particular kind of network, that found in social movements, has been recognized for some time. The landmark study here is Schlosberg's interpretation of the environmental justice movement in the United States (1999), whose networks entail building respect across different ethnic and racial groups as they confront environmental injustices that affect them jointly (see also Dryzek 2000: 77–8). But networks can engage in governance as well as oppositional action in the public sphere. This eventually became true of environmental justice, as it extended into government agencies and sometimes sought less -confrontational relationships with corporations and governments.

Governance networks now join markets and hierarchies as a recognized mode of interaction in the delivery of public outcomes. They differ from hierarchies in being relatively flat and in their lack of clear relations of domination and subordination (though they can feature substantial political inequalities). They differ from markets in that relationships between actors are generally a mix of collaboration, negotiation, persuasion, and mutual adjustment, rather than competition. They differ from more legalistic and old-fashioned pluralism in that these relations are also not fundamentally adversarial. A governance network can be defined as:

1. a relatively stable horizontal articulation of interdependent but operationally autonomous actors; 2. who interact through negotiations; 3. which take place within a normative, cognitive and imaginary framework; 4. that is self-regulating within limits set by external agencies; and 5. which contributes to the production of public purpose. (Sørensen and Torfing 2007: 9)

Defined in this way, networks may sometimes represent movement beyond the state, though governments can also be set up by government agencies and other state actors (Pierre and Peters 2000); so Bell and Hindmoor (2009*a*) speak of a "state-centered relational approach" to governance.

Governance networks now abound in all kinds of areas. These include:

- Criminal justice, especially in connection with restorative justice (Braith-waite 2007)
- Energy policy (Hendriks and Grin 2007)
- Urban governance (Häikiö 2007)
- Finance and economics (Castells 1996)
- Water resources (Innes and Booher 2003)
- Environmental policy (Sabel, Fung, and Karkainnen 1999)
- Regulation of all kinds (Braithwaite 2008)

Indeed, there seem to be few limits to the kinds of policy areas in which governance networks can be found. Rhodes (1994) speaks of a state "hollowing out" as its functions are contracted out, or undertaken by a mix of public and private sector actors. Several European countries (and the EU) emphasize government's "social partners" – professions, trade unions, and private businesses. Public–private partnerships are pervasive when it comes to service delivery in many jurisdictions (Rosenau 2000) – be it logistical support for the U.S. military, or sustainable development projects in Third World countries. In such projects, corporations bring money and experts, NGOs provide political will, and host governments enable access for innovation and advice (Frantzius

2004). Castells (1996) speaks confidently of an entire "network society" in which corporations, banks, and other organizations look like networks internally, and produce (for example) investment decisions in combination with other public and private actors. The old distinction between government and market therefore loses its force. Governance networks seem to offer substantial advantages when it comes to aggregating diverse perspectives in ways that are both relatively effective in problem-solving terms and also relatively low cost in terms of demands upon government budgets. If all the key actors are involved in a network, then implementing decisions becomes less of a problem; indeed, agreements can become self-implementing. As such governance networks can seem especially appropriate to complex societies generating complex sets of problems that need to be solved (Hendriks 2008: 1009).

Any such advantages are, however, bought at the cost of diminished capacity for central control on the part of elected leaders – or anyone else. Complex, self-regulating, and intersecting systems elude centralized steering, and leaders who believe it can be done will often come to grief. There are multiple points of leverage, not a single locus that can be controlled (Pierre and Peters 2000). What this means is that formal moments such as the passing of legislation or high-level executive decisions or the election of a new government decline in importance relative to the more continuous and often low-profile production of policy outcomes by the network.

## BAD NEWS FOR DEMOCRACY?

Networked governance provides some obvious challenges to democracy and democratic theory. Lowi's horrified reaction (1999) to the governance thinking of Sabel, Fung, and Karkainnen (1999) is instructive here. For Lowi, governance implies a complete loss of public authority. Authority becomes privatized, and members of the network will typically work for what is in their joint interest – but almost certainly not in the public interest. Lowi's critique of governance (1969) mirrors his earlier famous castigation of "interest group liberalism" in U.S. government, under which power is devolved to coteries of interest groups cooperating with government agencies. There are antidotes to this proclivity: so Hendriks (2008: 1012) describes a case where network participants are selected for their autonomy rather than their ties to particular interests. However, in practice this still meant that the network in question was dominated by traditional elites, especially business elites, because these were the people who seemed to have the requisite time, experience, and leadership skills (p. 1015). Governance is additionally problematic because often it renders power invisible. In governance, there are few moments such as a vote in a legislature or election where power holders display themselves and can be called to public account for their actions. Policy making is often a low-visibility affair, and it may be hard to determine where power actually lies.

Clearly, electoral democracy is in trouble when networked governance dominates. Networks do not hold elections; they do not have an electorate, a government, an opposition, or any obvious alternative set of power holders. Nor can public servants easily be called to account for their actions, because if they do participate in a network they do not bear any more responsibility for what it does than (say) participants from the private sector.

None of this means that governance is always and necessarily bad from a democratic point of view. For example, Sagoff (1999) describes a case in which local environmentalists, loggers, and a timber-dependent community's government seek a more collaborative relationship and sharing of power in forest policy making, which was previously dominated by agencies of the federal government influenced only by national political formations and their priorities. This attempt at local governance was eventually overruled by land managers in national government, backed by national environmental groups (who did not want local complications to their national strategies). But if this local arrangement had succeeded, the outcome might have been more inclusive access to decision making. What this case suggests is that networks do not have to be exclusive and invisible, they can be relatively inclusive and visible.

Empirical study of networks in terms of their inclusiveness ought to be quite straightfoward. So in her detailed analysis of networks established for energy transition management in the Netherlands, Hendriks (2008: 1016) finds that in practice they are dominated by business elites in particular. Other groups were invited, but simply lacked the personnel and resources to participate effectively (ordinary citizens were not invited).

Networks are additionally problematic from a specifically liberal democratic point of view. Liberals stress constitutions and the specification of rights. While networks might operate against the background of a liberal constitution, their internal workings are typically informal and resistant to constitutionalization. And it is hard to see how liberal rights can be instantiated within a network, because the idea of (in particular) rights against government are not easily operationalized when there is no identifiable and distinct government operating. The liberal idea that the essence of freedom is negative liberty secured by rights against arbitrary power exercised by the state makes little sense when there is no obvious government authority. Republican ideas about freedom as non-domination (Pettit 1997) do, however, travel more easily to a governance context (Braithwaite 2007; Dryzek 2007*a*: 264).

Networks can feature more or less in the way of domination of some actors by others and, correspondingly, the degree in which participants feel secure that nobody else in the network has the capacity to dominate them. Empirical analysis of networks along these lines should actually be quite straightforward (though governance scholars themselves, coming from a concern with public policy rather than political theory, have rarely been interested in empirical study of this particular sort).

Political theory tied to Westphalian notions of state sovereignty, liberal notions of constitutionalism and liberty, and electoral notions of authorization and accountability does, then, fare badly when applied to governance networks. What this suggests is the need for some post-Westphalian (Braithwaite 2007), post-liberal (Sørensen and Torfing 2007), and post-electoral thinking about democracy. Such thinking might begin by contemplating operationalization of the more general principles of democracy – notably, political equality and popular control, as applied in many countries as the basis for "democratic audits" (see Beetham (1999) for a justification of these two principles). But even at this more general level, there is a problem. Political equality within the state is justified in large measure because the state plays such a large and inescapable part in the life of everyone. In contrast, a particular issue-specific network may play quite a small role in the lives of many people (though a big part for some). Moreover, exit from a network may be quite easy; exit from the state (emigration) is very hard and costly. This ease of exit from networks makes equality somewhat less pressing. Popular control for its part is not easy to conceptualize when there is no demos associated with a network. Now, sometimes the policies produced by a network may apply to all members of a conventional demos (population of a state). Consider, for example, a network spanning financial institutions that determines lending policies. But sometimes, networks produce outcomes applying only to some members of the demos, or it may produce outcomes that apply across national boundaries (a transnational financial network) with differential effects in different places. In such cases, it is far from clear what would make control "popular," because the populace in question is ill-defined.

## APPLYING DELIBERATIVE PRINCIPLES

There are a number of reasons why deliberative democratic principles ought to be more applicable to networked governance than the more conventional ones just canvassed. Networks are polycentric, and their medium of coordination is language. While inequalities may exist within networks, they are not formally constituted as hierarchies. So compared to a hierarchy, communication, and the distribution of communicative capacity, can be relatively egalitarian. The implication is that governance networks may have some potential for promoting dialogue compared to their more hierarchical alternatives (Bevir 2006), because to exert influence, an actor has to persuade others in the network. With this consideration in mind, it is a straightforward matter to apply communicative principles developed by deliberative democrats to the content of communication within a network. Some of the standard options available would be those developed by Gutmann and Thompson (1996), who want communication to be public, those who contribute to be accountable for what they say and do, and for the content of arguments to be governed by the norm of reciprocity: arguing in terms that others who do not share one's framework can accept. Dryzek (2000: 68) suggests that communications pass the deliberative test if they are first, capable of inducing reflection; second, are noncoercive; and third, able to connect any particular statement of particular experiences (such as a personal story) to some more general point or principle. Following Chambers (2009), a distinction can be made between plebiscitary and deliberative types of rhetoric (see chapter 4), though given networks will generally not involve large numbers and mass audiences, rhetoric may not necessarily play the kind of role it does in larger public spheres. From Habermas might be taken the idea that communicative rationality demands the absence of domination (which resonates with the republican notion of freedom as non-domination discussed earlier), strategizing, deception, and self-deception. In these terms, a network could be evaluated according to how closely it involves a reflective quest for mutual understanding, as opposed to strategic bargaining among self-interested participants. Whatever standards are applied, it seems that governance networks are amenable to evaluation in deliberative terms (though there are few if any existing systematic empirical studies along these lines).

This kind of evaluation would, however, remain incomplete because a network may be deliberative without necessarily being especially democratic. Recall that in standard arguments for deliberative democracy, an outcome is legitimate to the extent that all affected by it have the right, opportunity, and capacity to participate in consequential deliberation concerning its content (but see the later subsection on "Internal differentiation and legitimacy" for a more nuanced treatment of legitimacy in networked governance). So governance networks can be more or less inclusive of those affected by a decision, as well as more or less deliberative when it comes to the terms of their inclusion. Here, governance networks can aspire to what Eckersley (2000) calls a "democracy of the affected" (see also Hansen 2007: 255–7). Those affected will not necessarily coincide with the membership of any demos; they may be quite dispersed in space (and indeed time). Thus, the standard democratic audit criterion of "popular control" can be interpreted in a governance context as meaning participation in deliberation about a decision on the part of all those affected by it. Actors' degree of affectedness may of course vary. So in an urban environmental policy network, local polluters and residents may experience immediate and substantial effects of decisions, while those far downstream or downwind may only be lightly affected. Political equality for its part can therefore be specified in terms of inclusion in deliberation in proportion to the extent an individual or category of people is affected by the decisions of the network in question. So those affected most ought to have the most say.

This operationalization of political equality might come to look a bit dubious if the network in question is set up and financed by a government – because then "all affected" includes all of the taxpayers who finance government operations. Including only those with a more immediate stake in the decision may mean the scenario feared by public choice scholars. In this scenario, a network maximizes return to its participants at the expense of the broader mass of taxpayers, for example, if participants in an educational policy network decide that the obvious solution to all their various concerns involves a large injection of public funds. But solving this particular kind of problem may not be too hard if the network includes state actors whose concern is with how tax revenues get spent.

## NETWORKS AS DELIBERATIVE SYSTEMS

Beyond the categorical application of deliberative criteria, as described in the previous section, it is also possible to engage in more systemic thinking about the deliberative and democratic qualities of governance networks. In the terms outlined in chapter 1, a governance network can be interpreted and evaluated as a potentially deliberative system. Recall that any such system logically requires public space, empowered space, transmission from public space to empowered space, accountability of empowered space to public space, meta-deliberation, and decisiveness in affecting collective outcomes. Further, public space ought to feature contestation across multiple discourses, ideally engaged by dispersed and competent actors. With this conception in mind, it is possible to develop some ideas about how networks in practice may succeed or fail in deliberative terms.

The basic distinction between public space and empowered space highlights the first problematic feature of governance: if all relevant actors are networked in, then public space and empowered space may merge and become coterminous. That is, all communications may be integrated into the production of collective outcomes. The very idea of collaborative governance in particular is that all relevant interests and stakeholders join together in making collective decisions. The kind of collaboration in water resource management described by Innes and Booher (2003) involves traditional adversaries (agribusiness, environmentalists, and others) tiring of stalemate as they have fought each other to a standstill in conventional political arenas (election campaigns, the media, courts, and legislative politics). Instead, they engage in a more cooperative joint search for mutually satisfactory outcomes, and all communications are channeled into this search. Similarly, the widely discussed transnational network that engages in "civil regulation" (without government) to certify to consumers that wood products have been produced in environmentally sustainable ways (Meidinger 2003) involves timber corporations and NGOs such as the Rainforest Alliance and Worldwide Fund for Nature working together in the Forest Stewardship Council.

In both these cases, there is little in the way of public space at any critical distance from the exercise of power (though in the case of the water forum, there is a strong memory of recent contestation). Does this matter? The danger here can be highlighted by the traditional criticism of interest group liberalism (Lowi 1969): that it enables stakeholders to produce outcomes in the joint interests of their active members, but at the expense of those not party to the arrangement. These others might include taxpayers in general, who are called upon to pay for the network's activities; other more diffuse interests (e.g., consumers of financial services) who find it difficult to organize to get a place at the table; those who live downstream or downwind, or somewhere else where externalities can be displaced. Applying an "inclusiveness" or "all-affected" principle as discussed above could in theory take care of these sorts of problems, whatever the practical obstacles in implementing such a principle.

More insidious is when a network is dominated by a single discourse. Central to discursive democracy is the idea of engagement and contestation across multiple discourses in the public sphere. But the normal or at least frequent case within a governance network may actually be domination by a single uncontested discourse. Transnational forest certification may, for example, feature only a discourse of sustainable development. Transnational financial networks were characterized (at least until 2008) by a discourse of market liberalism. If all the actors involved do subscribe to a common discourse then that is an effective means of coordination, which reduces decision costs because those involved need not address fundamentals every time they communicate; there are substantial shared understandings that can be taken for granted. Discourses enable as well as constrain communication. A common discourse can stabilize a network. It may also be the case that a stable network will with time generate a discourse, as those involved build shared understandings.

But any such stabilization is bought at a cost. Any discourse will generally serve some interests and marginalize others, highlight some concerns and downplay others. So, for example, if a discourse of sustainable development dominates an environmental policy network, this means that some critical questions do not get raised. Sustainable development rests on the ultimate compatibility and mutually reinforcing interaction of economic growth, environmental conservation, and social justice. Its history shows it being moved in an ever more business-friendly direction. This means that a range of critical questions get sidelined. These include the ultimate compatibility of capitalist economic growth with ecological limits and the interests of non-human nature and ecosystemic integrity of the sort that radical greens are likely to recognize. Now, defenders of sustainable development might well argue that all these critical questions can be addressed within the terms of what can be a fairly flexible discourse. But the sustainable development discourse is not infinitely elastic, and the concerns just listed lie outside its limits.

If a single discourse does dominate, then eventually it may get so taken for granted that any potential for critique dissipates. In narrowing the terms of communication, the sorts of differences and challenges that are grist for a deliberative conception of democracy get lost. What is also lost is the kind of reflexive capacity that underpins the notion of meta-deliberation. In Beck's terms (1992), domination by a single discourse moves us from a reflexive modernity back to semi-modernity, under which discourses such as that which assumed economic growth was necessarily desirable, or that technical change was always progressive and had to be accommodated, went unchallenged. Today's world is increasingly characterized by the presence of multiple and competing discourses (see Dryzek 2006: 8–21). In part this is a consequence of what Beck, Giddens, and Lash (1994) call "de-traditionalization," as accepted understandings grounded in (for example) cultural practices or discourses of long standing are called into question by competent actors. This kind of reflexive modernization has its counterpart in reflexive traditionalization, under which adherents of (say) a religion react to their awareness of challengers by retreating into fundamentalism. But that very retreat is likely to cause conflict, with both moderates within the tradition in question, and other traditions with which the world is shared.

If a network shuts out contending discourses, then it risks becoming progressively illegitimate with time, as well as ineffective in problem-solving terms. The fate of market liberalism is illustrative here. The domination of global financial networks by the single discourse of market liberalism prior to the 2008 crisis meant that the system had no capacity for critical reflection upon its own deficiencies – even in narrow financial terms, let alone in relation to social justice. The system had also escaped democratic oversight or monitoring from any direction (Keane 2009). Virtually, nobody involved in the system (be they bankers, investors, financial journalists, or government officials) saw the crash coming. The crash was accompanied by almost instant delegitimization of banks and other financial institutions, and the market-oriented discourse under which they operated, which could not recognize the possibility of systemic failure.

Networks are a kind of adaptation to complexity. But the more complex a system, the greater the number of plausible interpretations of it. Domination of a network by a single discourse means that alternative interpretations that can only be generated within other discourses are not heard. Thus, the network fails to deliver on its promise in problem-solving terms, let alone in terms of deliberative democratic capacity.

Every network does, then, need to allow for contestations and critics. For Braithwaite (2007: 167), "It is the contestatory ideal that accounts for the importance of democratic citizens joining together at a node of governance to contest networked power that they believe oppresses them. . . . Deliberative democracy is the ideal that can most fruitfully be deployed to enrich freedom as non-domination." The appropriate kind of contestation may vary. Social movement activism may be helpful. The problem is that it is much easier for a social movement to target high-profile events (such as G20 summits on the part of the antiglobalization/global justice movement) than it is to target low-profile and continuous network operations. In her discussion of networked governance designed to manage the transition to more sustainable energy in the Netherlands, Hendriks (2008: 1018) notes that Greenpeace did not seek to participate, but instead concentrated its limited resources on lobbying parliament and the EU.

Finally, networks may fail as deliberative systems when it comes to decisiveness. The international network for forest certification organized under the Forest Stewardship Council is widely celebrated as an exemplary success story for governance without government. But as Bell and Hindmoor (2009*b*) point out, only 2 percent of the world's commercial forests are actually covered by the council. Most of the forests that are covered are those least in need of regulation – such as state-run forests in the Nordic countries. Where regulation is truly needed, especially in most of the world's tropical forests, the regulatory network has little presence. Thus, however deliberative the regulatory network, it is not decisive in producing collective outcomes for the world's forests.

## TOWARD A NORMATIVE DEMOCRATIC THEORY OF NETWORKED GOVERNANCE

The normative theory of networked governance currently consists mainly of a set of tools for making networks effective in delivering services, solving problems, or achieving the ends of government policy (Salamon 2002). This chapter is silent on such issues, but based on the analysis to date some normative democratic principles for networks can be identified, as follows. Each corresponds to the theme of one of the chapters of Part II of this book. It can be taken as given that standard deliberative criteria for the content of communication as discussed in the section on "Applying deliberative principles" can also be brought to bear. It can also be taken as given that there are a number of measures available to promote the public visibility, openness, and inclusiveness of networks. These range from cultivating connections with elected officials to funding disadvantaged actors to participate at key nodes in a network (Hendriks 2008: 1022–5).

### Internal differentiation and legitimacy

In chapter 2, legitimacy was defined in discursive terms, achieved to the extent of the resonance of collective decisions with the provisional outcome of the engagement of discourses in the public sphere, to the degree this engagement features reflective and competent actors. This resonance can be promoted to the extent a network features internal differentiation in the situation of its component actors and institutions. Parkinson's account of how legitimacy gets generated in deliberative systems (2006*a*) is relevant here. For Parkinson, it is generally too much to expect any one forum to bear the entire burden of legitimating policy decisions. Instead, multiple forums and elements can and should contribute. Each features different kinds of interaction, is responsive to different representations of public opinion, different publics and constituencies, and different kinds of procedural values (legal, bureaucratic, and popular control in their various manifestations). So, if a network looks like a single forum it is likely to suffer a legitimacy deficit. The more it can feature internal differentiation in the kinds of actors and sites it can encompass, the more it ought to be able to piece together the legitimacy puzzle in satisfactory fashion. The deliberative system that Parkinson describes in British health policy making is in some ways a highly differentiated governance network featuring health service professionals and their associations, advocacy groups and activists, health charities, administrators, elected officials at various levels, local, regional, and national bureaucracies, and occasional exercises in public participation. While it has its limitations, exclusions, blind spots, and some communication that is very un-deliberative, this differentiation provides Parkinson's starting point for thinking about how an effective deliberative system for health policy might be constructed. Accountability in networked governance ought to run to different categories of actors, some of whom can claim to represent publics (Esmark 2007).

The idea of discursive legitimacy points to a particular kind of differentiation being desirable: that between public space and empowered space. Public space is where many voices can be raised and many different points of view advanced, and critiques and novel ideas generated. A lively public space is essential to deliberative democracy. Consider in this light Schlosberg's (1999) account of the environmental justice movement in the United States. Schlosberg is concerned with describing a network in public space only, one that joins very differently situated communities and individuals as they confront shared environmental hazards. The network, and the very discourse of environmental justice accompanying it, were constructed from the bottom up. At first, this network confronted the established power of government and corporations – and operated at a distance from more conventional environmental groups that had little concern for the distribution of environmental harms across ethnic and racial lines. But with the success of the movement came recognition of the legitimacy of its demands, and this meant the establishment within government of (for example) the Office of Environmental Justice within the Federal Environmental Protection Agency. Individual environmental justice activists could sometimes move into government positions. Corporate polluters had to engage with the government bodies set up. So with time, environmental justice began to look more like a governance network. However, the social movement activism remained highly visible and contestatory. So the result was networked governance that featured both empowered space and public space at a critical distance.

## Discursive representation

One way to ensure that a network is inclusive is to attend to effective discursive representation within it. Democratic legitimacy can then benefit to the extent the network is responsive to the variety of relevant political discourses. Discursive accountability, defined in chapter 3 as continuing to communicate in terms that make sense within the discourse that one represents, means that a network should not demand as the price of admission that participants – representatives – renounce their original discourse and adopt that of the network.

In the Dutch energy network described by Hendriks (2008), participants were ostensibly selected on the basis of their autonomy from established interests and capacity to think creatively (even if in reality there was an overabundance of participants from business corporations). This selection might look like the antithesis of discursive representation. But given that independence from any discourse is hard even to conceptualize, another way of looking at these individuals is that any autonomy they do possess is probably enabled by the fact that their subjectivity is constructed at the intersection of a number of different discourses. Thus, they are particular kinds of discursive representatives, as discussed in chapter 3. Whether they were the right kind of discursive representatives may be more problematic. It was argued in chapter 3 that if we want a forum – or in this case a network – to generate new ideas, it is probably best to select for extremism rather than moderation in discursive representatives. If we want the forum to render a judgment, selecting for moderation (subscription to several discourses) is more defensible. (In many networks, participants would be self-selecting so this may be an unusual case.)

Hendriks (2009) also points out the whole idea of representation seemed problematic to participants in the network she studied. If they thought about it at all, participants and observers of the network thought that representation belonged elsewhere – notably in parliament. She showed that on closer examination representation was enacted – based on a participant's knowledge, descriptive congruence with a set of characteristics, or connection to particular interests. Her analysis confirms that conventional electoral notions of representation do not fare well in a networked governance context. In her Dutch case, discursive representation fared no better. But in a network context, discursive representation is at least conceivable, whereas electoral representation is not.

## Rhetoric

At first sight, it might seem that rhetoric ought to play little role in a governance network. For rhetoric is generally associated with very public appeals to large audiences, whereas governance networks are often low visibility. But the more networks feature differentiation between public space and empowered space, and the more they feature representation of different discourses, then the more rhetoric is going to be necessary. Rhetoric may be instrumental in creating a network. And it may be especially important in enabling actors in public space to press their claims on empowered space, thus opening the network to discursive contestation of the sort just described. Consider, for example, the ozone issue analyzed by Litfin (1994), as discussed in chapter 4. The "ozone hole" rhetoric enabled the relatively closed negotiations involving states and the EU to be opened up to atmospheric scientists and environmental activists in public space, who could in the short run join in a productive deliberative system. After the Montreal Protocol was signed in 1987, these same actors were now well placed to join a transnational network concerned with implementation of the agreement.

A more important rhetorical consideration in networked governance is that judgments about *ethos* of the speaker (one of the components of classical rhetoric) can help when it comes to deciding whose voice belongs. The importance of contestation within networks has been emphasized in this chapter. But what if contestation means (for example) welcoming skeptics into governance dealing with climate change issues? If the speaker in question is financed by fossil fuel industries that have a financial stake in denial of climate change, then their advocacy is not credible, and deliberative democracy will not benefit from their inclusion in the network.

## Meta-consensus

All of the arguments on behalf of pluralism canvassed in chapter 5 apply to networked governance no less than any other kind of politics. This application is especially true to the extent networked governance is a response to complexity, for the more complex an issue, the more rationality can benefit from the productive integration of plural perspectives. Chapter 5 did of course also argue the virtues of free and reasoned meta-consensus. To the extent networks feature normative, epistemic, preference, or discursive pluralism, then they are going to need the corresponding form of meta-consensus. At the discursive level, this means that each actor has to recognize the legitimacy of the identity of all other actors. While this might sound undemanding to the degree a network is a low-visibility assemblage of like-minded actors, it becomes more demanding to the degree governance involves actors in public space at a critical distance from empowered space. But without meta-consensus, there is surely no network, and certainly no possibility for episodes of collaborative problem solving.

## CONCLUSION

Governance networks can be interpreted as deliberative systems. What this means is that deliberative democratic theory travels to networked governance much more readily than do more established sorts of democratic theory, especially those that see competitive elections as the sine qua non of democratic government. If the authority of the sovereign state is devolving into networks, what looks at first sight like bad news for democracy may not always be so bad after all, once networks are interpreted as potentially deliberative systems. Governance networks certainly do not merit uncritical celebration, but neither are they necessarily gravediggers of democracy. But whether the news is good or bad, the growing importance of networked governance means that democrats in general, and deliberative democrats in particular, need to devote sustained attention to the challenges and opportunities they present.

# 7

## The Democratization of Authoritarian States

### DELIBERATION AND DEMOCRATIZATION

The deliberative turn in democratic theory and practice can now be applied to an area of study and reform that has hitherto proven strangely resistant to any such treatment: the democratization of authoritarian states. This chapter therefore shifts the focus away from established democratic states (where, for example, networked governance as analyzed in chapter 6 was first identified), and toward societies emerging from authoritarianism. The deliberative approach proves highly applicable to such cases. Indeed, its application may be especially urgent here. In this light, it is remarkable that the massive and well-funded field of democratization and its comparative study have missed the deliberative aspect of democracy that is now so pervasive everywhere else in the theory, practice, and promotion of democracy. There are pressing questions concerning where, how, and to what effect deliberative capacity can be sought as states emerge from authoritarianism. This chapter will show how the concept of deliberative capacity can be deployed in comparative empirical analysis, enumerate its roles under authoritarian rule and in democratic transition and consolidation (while recognizing the problematic nature of these concepts), and canvass its determinants. This does not mean that state democracy and democratization are only a matter of deliberation; they are also about decision, voting, the rule of law, and uncorrupt administration, among other things. But democracy, and so democratization, cannot do without deliberation. An emphasis on deliberation reveals important causes of effective democratic transition and consolidation, providing substantial explanatory as well as evaluative and normative purchase.

Most democratization scholars have in the past defined democracy in terms of electoral competition and effective constitutional respect for basic civil liberties and human rights. In this light, their first taxonomic task has been to capture the degree to which ostensibly democratic political systems fall short of liberal electoralist ideals and ostensibly authoritarian regimes might embody some of them; many regime types have been conceptualized (Collier and Levitsky 1997; Armony and Schamis 2005). On the electoral or competitive side, shortfall comes, for example, where one party or leadership group effectively manipulates the system so that it cannot lose, what Carothers (2002: 12–13) calls "dominant-power systems," pervasive in post-Soviet countries, with African National Congress (ANC)-dominated South Africa coming close. On the liberal side, Zakaria's "illiberal democracy" (2003) and O'Donnell's "delegative democracy" (1994) feature competitive elections, but winners rule without any constitutional checks, accountability, or respect for the rights of their people. Some scholars prefer to call such systems "competitive authoritarianism" (Levitsky and Way 2002).

This chapter does not argue that liberal electoral definitions of democracy are wrong (still less try to get to grips with approaches that deploy these definitions in all their variety and subtlety), just that they miss the key deliberative aspect. This aspect is ubiquitous in the theory, analysis, and practice of democracy everywhere except comparative state democratization studies. Just as liberal electoral democratization studies have an applied counterpart in "democracy promotion" by the U.S. Agency for International Development and other public and private bodies, so does deliberative democracy find application in a global movement to introduce deliberative institutions into governance. Some democracy promoters have discovered deliberation, and financed deliberative exercises in countries such as China. Deliberative capacity does not have to be sought in any particular set of institutions (such as elections), but can be manifested in different ways in different systems.

## DELIBERATIVE CAPACITY REVISITED

Recall that communications are deliberative to the degree they can induce reflection about the preferences that individuals hold, are noncoercive, able to relate the particular interests of individuals and groups to more universal principles, and exhibit reciprocity, or communicating in terms others can accept. Political systems are deliberatively undemocratic to the extent they minimize opportunities for individuals to reflect freely upon their political preferences. Autocracies may be interested in individuals' preferences, but only to convince people to accept the regime's doctrine, backed by a threat of coercion. If demagogues appeal to ethnic nationalist values, then the criterion of connection to more universal principles is violated. Authoritarians might appeal to general principles: so, for example, the Soviet leadership would justify its actions in terms of Marxist principles generalizable to humanity. However, that kind of justification cannot reach those who do not share a well-defined ideological framework, thus violating reciprocity. The same might be said of those invoking economic efficiency as a nonnegotiable principle for marketizing government.

Applying deliberative principles to evaluate particular instances of communication in democratic terms does not automatically translate to a concept that is useful in analyzing and evaluating whole regimes or political systems. For that we need an account of deliberative capacity, defined in chapter 1 as the extent to which a political system possesses structures to host deliberation that is *authentic, inclusive,* and *consequential.* Political systems, states in particular, can be arrayed on a continuum according to the extent of their deliberative capacity. At the negative end of the continuum lie not just autocracies, but also routinized administrative systems, and those dominated by strategic machination or armed conflict.

Pursuit of deliberative capacity does not connote any particular institutional prescription (be it competitive elections, a constitution, or a set of forums), but may be secured in connection with different sorts of institutions and practices. Authenticity can be understood in light of the tests just mentioned (deliberation must induce reflection in noncoercive fashion, connect particular claims to more general principles, and exhibit reciprocity). Inclusiveness applies to the range of interests and discourses present in a political setting. Without inclusiveness, there may be deliberation, but not deliberative *democracy.* (Mutz (2006) worries that deliberation works against inclusion because "hearing the other side" induces people to participate less. But Mutz is referring only to unstructured talk in everyday life, not deliberation, still less deliberation tied to particular locations in a political system.) "Consequential" means that deliberative processes must have an impact upon collective decisions, or social outcomes. This impact need not be direct – deliberation need not involve the actual making of policy decisions. For example, public deliberation might have an influence on decision makers who are not themselves participants in deliberation. This might occur when an informal deliberative forum makes recommendations that are subsequently taken into account by policy makers. Nor need the outcomes in question be explicit policy decisions; they might (for example) be informal products of a governance network as discussed in chapter 6.

Analysis of democratization in terms of deliberative capacity building requires a way to account for the completeness and effectiveness of deliberative systems. In chapter 1, the logic of a deliberative system was set out as being composed of

1. Public space
2. Empowered space

3. Transmission from public space to empowered space
4. Accountability of empowered space to public space
5. Meta-deliberation (about the deliberative qualities of the system itself)
6. Decisiveness (in relation to other political forces)

A system will have deliberative capacity to the extent of authentic deliberation in elements 1–5, inclusiveness in elements 1–2, and the decisiveness of what the system as a whole produces. In the real world, large or small shortfalls are inevitable, and elements of the system may conceivably be missing completely. These six logical requirements constitute a starting point for the description and evaluation of all real-world deliberative systems, and their comparison across space and time. It is in this sense that deliberative capacity building provides the basis for a comprehensive approach to the study of democratization. Democratization requires the development of all six elements, but it does not necessitate any specific institutions, be they competitive elections or a constitutional separation of powers. Meta-deliberation is especially important because it captures the reflexive capacity of a system to deliberate its own shortcomings and consequently deepen its own deliberative and democratic capacities with time. Conventional approaches to state democratization that see democratization as solely a matter of adopting a conventional set of liberal democratic institutions completely miss this dynamic aspect.

## SOURCES OF DELIBERATIVE CAPACITY

Where then should we look for contributions to deliberative capacity? When it comes to empowered space, the obvious place to start would be with the central institutions of states, such as legislatures, cabinets, corporatist councils that empower representatives of labor and business federations as well as government executives, and constitutional courts.[1] When it comes to public space, the media, social movements, political activism, Internet exchanges, and everyday conversations can all play their parts. Designed forums such as citizens' juries, citizens' assemblies, deliberative polls, consensus conferences, and stakeholder dialogues can also contribute to deliberative systems. The nature of that contribution will be discussed at length in chapter 8. These sorts of forums have appeared in developing countries, so are not just an attribute of developed liberal democracies. For example, a widely praised and occasionally copied deliberative approach to participatory civic budgeting

---

[1] Rawls (1993: 231) believes the U.S. Supreme Court is an exemplary deliberative institution.

that joins public space and empowered space has been developed in Brazil, notably in Porto Alegre (Fung 2003: 360–2). Brazil has pioneered a range of participatory and deliberative innovations, also including participatory councils for health service management.

Designed forums can be expensive, and there must always be more to the broad public sphere in a deliberative democracy than any such forum or set of forums. Any proliferation of such forums should not be mistaken for more systemic democratization. The public sphere may play an especially important role in countries where deliberation in legislatures and other institutions of government is weak or absent. For example, Poland in the early 1980s featured no legislature with any deliberative capacity. But Poland did have a flourishing public sphere associated with the Solidarity movement in which deliberation was practiced and deliberative capacity built. Ekiert and Kubik (1999) argue that even after 1989 and the end of communism, the public sphere in Poland was a kind of remedial site that compensated for deliberative failure in state institutions. But the public sphere in any democracy is where perspectives and ideas are generated, policy decisions are questioned, and citizen competences are developed.

Different sites can contribute to deliberative capacity in different proportions in different societies and systems. We should not fixate on any one particular institutional contributor to this mix and assume it is *the* key to deliberative capacity. For example, we might dismiss contemporary China as thoroughly lacking in deliberative capacity if we focused on central state institutions and the public sphere, severely circumscribed by controls over the media and restrictions on association, advocacy, and expression. If China does have any deliberative capacity, it might be found in participatory innovations at the local level, designed in part to cope with the unwanted side effects of rapid economic growth. Those interested in the democratization of China could look for ways of building up from this localized capacity. Some members of the Communist Party leadership have seemed receptive to such possibilities. Li Junru, Vice President of the Central Party School, in 2005 called for the expansion of deliberative democracy in China (He and Leib 2006: 8). Skeptics can point to particular local assemblies that remain controlled by party officials. But cases do exist where forums have overruled the decisions of party officials. Deliberative democratization need not be top-down reform of central state institutions.

Recognition of the variable ways in which deliberative systems and so capacity can be constituted in democratizing states means that some of the problems democracy promotion has when it is tied to a particular liberal electoral blueprint can be avoided. As Carothers (2002) points out, democracy promoters are often perplexed when specific elements of the blueprint (such as truly competitive elections) seem unattainable; thinking in terms of deliberative capacity would give them more options.

Institutions can constitute, and interact within, a deliberative system in intricate and variable ways. Seemingly low deliberative quality in one location (say, corporatist state institutions) may be compensated by, or even inspire, higher deliberative quality in another location (say, a flourishing public sphere). Conversely, high deliberative quality in one location may undermine deliberative quality in another location. For example, if legislators know that their more dubious collective decisions will be overruled by a constitutional court, they are free to engage in irresponsible rhetoric. Thus, we should always keep our eye on whole systems, and indeed on their extensions across national boundaries. So, for example, when governance networks transcend state boundaries, they may contribute to the deliberative capacity of states. The fact that the transnational network monitoring social and ecological certification of forest products actively engages timber producers and government officials in developing countries may contribute to the deliberative capacity of those countries.

## STUDYING DELIBERATIVE CAPACITY

When it comes to assessing deliberative authenticity at different points within the deliberative system, there are some tools available for systematic comparative analysis. An empirical measure of deliberative authenticity especially applicable to the comparative assessment of government institutions has been developed by Steiner et al. (2004), in the form of a discourse quality index. Applying this index involves parsing the transcript of a debate and coding each intervention in the debate on multiple criteria. The criteria themselves are derived from Jürgen Habermas's account of communicative action, one of the wellsprings of deliberative democratic theory. The scores for each contribution are summed and averaged to give a quantitative measure of the quality of the debate as a whole. Steiner et al. then compare similar types of debates in similar institutions in different countries, finding that parliamentary discourse quality is facilitated by presidential, consensual, and bicameral features of state institutions. To date, Steiner et al. have compared only developed liberal democracies, but it would be a straightforward matter to extend their analysis to other systems in a research program on the institutional determinants of deliberative authenticity. However, a system featuring quality legislative deliberation may conceivably have poor deliberation when it comes to other parts of empowered space, or public space. Ideally, we would want to apply a discourse quality index to communication in all these locations. Empirical studies can be qualitative as well as quantitative. Histories of the development (or attenuation) of deliberative capacity with time can be investigated, and comparative case study may be especially useful in locating the aspects of capacity present in one society but not in another.

In tracking deliberative capacity over time, we can evaluate continuous and long-drawn-out processes of democratization, such as that which unfolded over several centuries in the United Kingdom. But the deliberative approach can also be applied to the kinds of cases that now preoccupy democratization scholars, involving a disruptive transition in which an authoritarian regime gives way to a more democratic one. The concepts of transition and subsequent consolidation have been problematized by democratization scholars (Schedler 1998; Carothers 2002). Many hybrid regimes, including successors to clearly authoritarian regimes, fall far short of liberal democratic ideals, and show few signs of moving closer with time. It is possible to assess and explain the democratic fortunes of these and other sorts of regimes using the notion of deliberative capacity without mentioning either transition or consolidation. However, these two concepts remain important touchstones, and so the discussion in the next two sections will be organized through reference to them.

## DELIBERATION IN TRANSITION

Breakdown of an authoritarian regime is more likely to yield a democratic replacement when there is deliberative capacity present under the old regime, because that capacity affects the background and capabilities that key actors bring to the political crisis. If opponents of the old regime come from a deliberative public space as opposed to (for example) a militarized resistance movement or a network of exiles involved in strategic machinations, then they can bring to the crisis some clear democratic commitments that stem from abiding by deliberative precepts. This was the sense in which civil society was idealized in pre-1989 East Central Europe. Democratic credentials are not easily established or developed in electoral or constitutional terms, because authoritarian regimes by definition lack free and fair elections under a constitution. Leaders with a background in deliberative public space are more likely to see transition in terms of establishing a democracy – rather than putting themselves in power. The public space in question need not involve large numbers of people, as the 1989 experience of Czechoslovakia shows. Deliberative participation in oppositional civil society comes with a self-limiting obligation that may be carried into the transitional crisis. This may also explain why figures with this background often subsequently prove no match for strategic power-seeking politicians more ruthless in seeking electoral advantage and building coalitions.

Deliberative capacity under authoritarian regimes may be found most straightforwardly in oppositional public spheres. But it is conceivable the old regime itself may develop some such capacity; in which case, those schooled in it may be more likely to talk to rather than repress opponents as crisis looms. Deliberative capacity may also develop within society at a distance from state power, not clearly oppositional but not part of the administrative structure. While participants in such processes are unlikely to play a part in peak political events in the transitional crisis, they may be more likely to support a new democratic regime. He and Warren (2008) have this hope for China.

Deliberation may also be found in the crisis itself. At the peak level, this can come in negotiations between old regime leaders and their opponents. It is possible to analyze such talks in purely strategic terms, as positional bargaining in which authoritarian leaders give up power in return for guarantees about their status in the new order. However, as Elster (1998*b*: 105) points out, roundtable talks in Poland and (especially) Hungary in 1989 involved deliberation as well as bargaining. Participants made warnings about what might happen (that had to be explained and justified), not threats about what they could do to the other side; and argued in terms of the public interest. While the latter could be seen as hypocrisy on the part of old regime participants, as Elster argues, if public interest justifications were transparently dishonest, they would persuade nobody and there would be no point in making them. One indicator of dishonesty is perfect correspondence between one's own interest and the alleged public interest, so this mode of arguing forces participants to shift away from pure self-interest. Threats and self-interested argument would, on Elster's account, have risked breakdown of the talks.

More widespread public deliberation may enter the crisis, as with "people power" in the Philippines in 1986, the "autumn of the people" in 1989 East Central Europe, or the "color revolutions" in Georgia (2003) and Ukraine (2004/5). To the extent that participants in such movements abide by deliberative precepts of noncoercive communication that induces reflection and connects particular demands to more general principles, they are a moral force for democracy – rather than a mob seeking revenge against oppressors. And this force is felt by elite negotiators.

## DELIBERATION IN CONSOLIDATION

Democratic consolidation is a concept with multiple meanings. Schedler (1998) argues we should restrict the concept to regime survival, entailing only avoidance of breakdown and erosion of democracy. He thinks we should not apply it to the building of democracy. For "the concepts of 'democratic quality' and 'democratic deepening' are still unclear and controversial," such that conceptualizing consolidation as deepening "amounts to a free-for-all" (Schedler 1998: 104). However, at the core of the idea of deliberation is a developed notion of democratic quality, such that the greater the deliberative capacity of a system, the higher the quality of its democracy. The deliberative effects enumerated below can contribute to regime survival. But in potentially making regimes more legitimate, more effective in coping with divisions and solving social problems, better able to solve the basic problems of social choice, and more reflexive in correcting their own deficiencies through meta-deliberation, they increase democratic quality.

### Legitimacy

Any new regime is faced with the challenge of securing legitimacy in the eyes of its people. Legitimacy can be achieved in many different ways, not all of them democratic. But in a democracy, reflective acceptance of collective decisions by actors who have had a chance to participate in consequential deliberation is an especially secure basis. This claim is at the heart of deliberative theory, which began as an account of legitimacy. Empirical study has lagged behind, but Parkinson (2006a) shows how deliberative legitimacy can be generated by a combination of multiple forums and practices in a deliberative system for health policy making. Deliberative legitimacy can either substitute for or supplement other sources of legitimacy (such as consistency of a process with constitutional rules or traditional practices).

### Coping with deep division

Democratization in many societies is challenged by deep division on ethnic, racial, national, religious, or linguistic lines. While a number of solutions have been proposed to this problem, notably consociational power sharing (Lijphart 1977), deliberation too can play a part in healing division. Quite where this might be accomplished is an open question. O'Flynn (2006) seeks more deliberation linked to consociational institutions themselves. Dryzek (2005) stresses interactive forums composed of individuals from different blocks at a distance from contests about the construction of sovereign authority, concerned more with particular needs and concrete problems. Examples include mixed-race discussion groups in post-apartheid South Africa, and District Policing Partnerships in Northern Ireland. A large literature in conflict resolution emphasizes the effectiveness of deliberation among key parties to a dispute in producing durable solutions to conflicts, especially in mediation and through "consensus-building" exercises (Susskind, McKearnan, and Thomas-Larmer 1999). These exercises yield not consensus interpreted as universal agreement on a course of action and the reasons for it, but rather an agreement to which all sides can reflectively assent – if for different reasons (including fear of what might otherwise happen). In this light, agonistic critics of deliberation across identity difference such as Mouffe (1999) who allege a deadening emphasis on consensus miss the point (as well as providing no alternative way to reach collective decisions in the more passionate encounters of agonism).

Deliberation can have a social learning aspect that helps determine how different segments live together, without necessarily being validated in explicit policy decisions. Kanra (2005) shows that in Turkey, there are in fact substantial possibilities for deliberative learning across Islamists and secular left-liberals that cannot easily be expressed in public policy because of the way polarization between military-nationalist Kemalists and Islamists has been entrenched in electoral politics. Such social learning could nevertheless have consequences for political reconfiguration and social peace.

Deliberation's particular contribution to conflict resolution comes with mutual recognition of the legitimacy of disputed identities – the kind of discursive meta-consensus described in chapter 5. The absence of such recognition means politics becomes not a contest in which some losses and compromises are acceptable, but a fight to eradicate the identity of the other side. This absence defines, for example, religious fundamentalisms that cannot tolerate in their societies what they see as sinners and heretics. Neither side in such a contest can accept the possibility of even temporary defeat, and collective outcomes will lack legitimacy in the eyes of whichever side they disadvantage. Functioning democracies, in contrast, feature substantial discursive meta-consensus on the legitimacy of disputed identities. Meta-consensus of any sort has force in structuring political interaction across division to the degree it is reflectively accepted by key political actors; for that, deliberation is needed.

## Tractability in collective choice

Deliberation offers one way – perhaps the most effective *democratic* way – to dispel the problems of instability and arbitrariness that some social choice theorists believe ought to plague democracies, as clever politicians wreak havoc in their strategic games by introducing new options and new dimensions of choice. Such problems may be especially acute in new democracies with unclear rules and contested procedural understandings.

Riker (1982) suggests that this is in fact the normal condition of democratic politics – and not just in new democracies. So, for example, he blames the outbreak of the U.S. Civil War on the machinations of elected politicians taking advantage of opportunities to manipulate agendas and votes. Van Mill (1996) argues that the conditions of free deliberation are exactly those likely to exacerbate the problems Riker identifies. The puzzle then becomes why we observe so little chaos in established liberal democracies (Mackie 2003). One answer is that mature democracies have developed mechanisms endogenous to deliberation that can structure interaction and so overcome the dire predictions of Riker's theory (Dryzek and List 2003). Deliberation can produce agreement on a single dimension on which preferences are arrayed, thus ruling out the introduction of other dimensions to confound collective choice on the part of clever strategists (Miller 1992). It can also produce agreement on the range of alternatives considered acceptable. These are the two key aspects of preference meta-consensus described in chapter 5. As Arrow's theorem (1963) implies, if democratic processes cannot find a way to induce such agreements, the main available alternative is dictatorship. To the extent new democracies develop deliberative capacity, they can generate preference meta-consensus and so cope with the dangers identified by social choice theory: arbitrariness, instability, civil conflict, and a lapse into dictatorship (see chapter 5). Voting in both elections and in the legislature can then proceed without fear.

## Effectiveness in solving social problems

Deliberation is also a means for joint resolution of social problems. Of course, problems can be resolved in top-down, hierarchical, and technocratic fashion, or allocated to quasi-market mechanisms. But a large public policy literature now points to the effectiveness of deliberation on the part of those concerned with a common problem in generating solutions that are both effective and mutually acceptable (see, for example, Innes and Booher 2003) – and which can work when top-down solutions are resisted by those whose interests and arguments are overridden. This is not the place to assess the effectiveness of deliberation in comparison with its alternatives in social problem solving. But as long as some degree of pluralism of perspectives is seen as instrumental to effective decision (a staple of liberal democracy), deliberation can help generate mutual acceptance of the credibility of disputed beliefs: epistemic meta-consensus as discussed in chapter 5. Such mutual acceptance ought to be promoted to the degree actors try to state their positions, and their supporting beliefs, in terms acceptable to actors on the other side of an issue. Again, reciprocity comes into play. The absence of such acceptance means the other side is seen as trafficking in falsehoods – rather than a different perspective on common problems. Such alleged falsehoods might concern economic doctrines (Marxist or market liberal), interpretations of history (identifying oppressors, liberators, friends, and enemies), or theories about the impact of policy.

## Reflexivity and meta-deliberation

Elster, Offe, and Preuss (1998) liken the democratization and marketization of postcommunist systems to "rebuilding the ship at sea" – as opposed to the construction of a new ship from a set of plans. One aspect of deliberative capacity is a distributed ability to reflect critically on preferences, including preferences about the structure of the political system itself. Thus, the "meta" component of deliberative capacity ought to promote the ability of a system to identify its own shortcomings and further reform itself. Without this ability, reformers may be tempted by more authoritarian pathways. The anti-deliberationist Adam Przeworski (1991: 183) inadvertently puts the issue into stark perspective when he states that post-transition economic reforms "are based on a model of economic efficiency that is highly technical. They involve choices that are not easy to explain to the general public and decisions that do not always make sense to popular opinion." Similarly, Brucan (1992: 24) argues that "A reform policy is not one that emerges from broad participation, from a consensus among all the affected interests, from compromises." Przeworski and Brucan may be right, but only to the extent the society in question lacks capacity for deliberation in general and meta-deliberation in particular.

This reflexive quality may be enhanced inasmuch as the experience of deliberation itself increases the competence of political actors. There is some evidence that participating in a deliberative forum has an enduring effect on the political efficacy of citizen participants (Delli Carpini, Cook and Jacobs 2004: 334). However, this evidence to date comes mainly from deliberative polls in developed democracies, so it is not clear how generaliz-able the effect is – nor whether the effect extends to partisan political actors, as opposed to ordinary citizens.

Together, the ability to promote legitimacy, heal division, secure tractable collective choice, solve social problems effectively, and promote reflexivity mean that deliberative capacity contributes to state building as well as demo-cratic consolidation. Carothers (2002: 8–9) points out that many democracy promoters assume democratization is done to a well-functioning state, rather than having to proceed in tandem with state building. A deliberative capacity approach can appreciate this dual task, in part because it can be applied to situations with any degree of "stateness" – including zero.


## DELIBERATION WITHOUT TRANSITION

A deliberative capacity approach can also be applied to states where transition to something with the familiar characteristics of a liberal democratic state is not on the agenda – let alone consolidation of any such liberal democratic state. Western democracy promoters (as exemplified, for example, by most of the contributors to the *Journal of Democracy*) tend to assume that democracy comes in a well-defined package. Thus, democratization ought only ever to be assessed and pursued in relation to the adoption of this package, and asso-ciated rupture with the old authoritarian regime. But in many societies – including many Confucian and Islamic ones – this package is either widely seen as undesirable or is not feasible in any near future. In Confucian societies (exemplified by Singapore but perhaps also including China) that place high value on consensus and the common good, and on state-guided economic development, it is liberal individualism and the excessively adversarial char-acteristics of electoral democracy that may seem objectionable. (Though, of course, consensual versions of liberal democracy are available, and practiced in countries such as Switzerland and Denmark.) In Islamic societies, it is the secular and morally neutral aspects of liberalism that may be unwanted. Of course, it is possible to point to both Confucian and Islamic countries, whose states have adopted competitive elections and constitutions with liberal aspects. But countries featuring substantial resistance to these institutions are also not hard to find.

Countries that for whatever reason seem unlikely to adopt liberal electoral democracy may nevertheless develop deliberative capacity. Fung (2008: 9) argues that such capacity may be found wherever there are opportunities for public judgment (which can be categorized in terms of public space), transmission of public judgment to government, and some opportunity for "the public to sanction public officials and call them to account." Any development of these features – aspects of a deliberative system – can be interpreted as democratization. In an Islamic society, this might involve public debate over how the will of God is to be interpreted, and better consultation between leaders and people. In China, it already has involved substantial innovations at the local level that involve public meetings where criticisms of the decisions of party officials can be aired, public consultation, and experiments with deliberative forums. Any such developments will not necessarily be welcomed by promoters of the standard liberal democratic package, because development of such a capacity might actually forestall breakdown of the old regime of the sort democracy promoters generally believe to be necessary.

When it comes to China in particular, He and Warren (2008) are more careful than Fung to distinguish between deliberative and democratic aspects of political change. They interpret what they call "authoritarian deliberation" in China as an adaptation by the state to the plurality of political forces unleashed by rapid economic development. Party and state can benefit because they will be able to receive information about the effects of policies that would otherwise be suppressed, and their decisions may achieve a degree of legitimacy that would otherwise be missing. Public participation may also be a way to keep corruption under control, if instances of it can be exposed. But He and Warren believe deliberation of this sort has to be described as "authoritarian" because it remains within parameters set by the party – even when it involves public participation. Missing in China is any more free-wheeling public space. He and Warren are, however, more sanguine than Fung about the possibilities of these deliberative innovations being linked to more conventional notions of state democratization. What they call "deliberation-led democratization" may result if these innovations cannot be contained by the party, as they lead to demands for ever more effective inclusion – and eventually truly competitive elections. One could even imagine China developing some meta-deliberative capacity in which the place of deliberative innovation in China's political trajectory could itself be a matter for public deliberation. There are hints of such a meta-deliberative capacity in the 2005 White Paper issued by the Chinese government "Building of Political Democracy in China,"[2] which offers public interest justifications for a very non-liberal and noncompetitive approach to democracy. Again, though, any such path to state democratization is very different from that envisaged

---

[2] Online at http://english.people.com.cn/whitepaper/democracy/democracy.html, accessed on August 20, 2009.

by conventional liberal democracy promoters – who would seek breakdown of the authoritarian state, not its gradual transformation.


## THE DETERMINANTS OF DELIBERATIVE CAPACITY

Let me turn now from the impacts to the determinants of deliberative capacity. Deliberative capacity may be facilitated by

- *Literacy and education*, inasmuch as they influence the "communicative competence" of political actors and ordinary citizens. Sanders (1997) worries that at least in the United States, deliberative forums will be dominated by white, male, high-income, and well-educated participants. Cook, Delli Carpini, and Jacobs (2007) demonstrate that while inequalities in deliberative participation do exist, they are smaller in relation to income than in other forms of participation. But even if Sanders is right, deliberative capacity will benefit from more equal access to education.
- *Shared language.* Kymlicka (2001) suggests that democratic politics has to be "politics in the vernacular," implying democracy across language groups can be problematic – though the case of societies such as Switzerland or India with multiple languages suggests that this is not an insuperable barrier. A much bigger obstacle to deliberative capacity may be when elites cultivate a form of spoken or written language unavailable to the masses as a way of bolstering their standing and power (Anderson 2007). Historical examples here might include the use of High German by Prussian elites, of French by the Russian aristocracy (famously recounted by Tolstoy in the opening pages of *War and Peace*), the use of *futsubun* by politicians in pre-1945 Japan (Anderson 2007: 32), or even the distinctive accent of the British upper classes.
- *Voting system design.* Horowitz (1985) and Reilly (2001) recommend preferential voting for divided societies on the grounds it advances the prospects of moderate politicians and parties, for they can appeal for second or third preferences across the divide. Though not explicitly conceptualized by Horowitz and Reilly, deliberative capacity may also benefit because such appeal requires politicians to cultivate reciprocity: to communicate in terms voters from the "other" side can accept.
- *State structures and institutions.* Different sorts of state structures and institutions may be more or less conducive to deliberation. Obviously, parliaments and constitutional courts ought to be better than executives ruling by decree. Beyond such obvious comparisons, it is not always clear

which sorts of institutional combinations best promote deliberative capacity in particular settings, especially when these institutions are combined in a deliberative system. State structures may have unintended and surprising consequences that can be revealed only by empirical analysis. For example, the exclusive character of West German corporatism up until the mid-1980s provided few opportunities for political access to social interests other than business and labor, making any deliberation that did occur far from inclusive. However, political activity was therefore channeled into a deliberative public space at a distance from the state, where profound critiques of public policy were constructed by (among others) green, feminist, and peace movements. Even when those developing the critiques lacked formal access, their influence was felt on empowered space and so public policy: at first through protest action, later through the development of expertise through research centers associated with movement groups. Only when the walls of corporatism crumbled did erstwhile movement activists take their deliberative competence into government (Dryzek et al. 2003).

- *Political culture.* Deliberation may play out very differently in different kinds of political cultures. The comparative analysis of cultural determinants of deliberative capacity got off to a questionable start in Gambetta's evaluation (1998) of the deliberative possibilities in "analytical" cultures (the paradigm for which is the Oxford University committee) compared to "indexical" cultures. In indexical cultures such as Italy, "discursive machismo" means one cannot admit uncertainty, or any lack of competence or knowledge. A competent political actor in an indexical culture system has to be an expert on everything. Gambetta's provocative essay is high on entertainment value and anecdote but low on empirical evidence. "Discursive machismo" and its opposite, deliberation, are likely to appear in different ways in different locations in different political cultures (Sass 2006). Comparative empirical analysis might reveal the subtlety of their forms and locations. There are plenty of other hypotheses concerning the effects of political culture that merit empirical study. For example, it is plausible (but by no means certain) that deliberation travels more easily to Confucian, Islamic, and some indigenous cultures far more easily than do the adversarial politics associated with competitive elections or an individualistic conception of human rights. Aspects of deliberative democracy may resonate with the Confucian emphasis on reasoned consensus, Islamic emphasis on consultation, and the sorts of communicative approaches to conflict resolution found in many indigenous societies. Deliberation may play out in very different ways in different kinds of societies – just like democracy in general (Dryzek and Holmes 2002).

Deliberative capacity may be obstructed by

- *Religious fundamentalism.* Fundamentalist adherents of religious doctrines by definition struggle with deliberative reciprocity, because they see no reason to communicate in terms that respect the frameworks held by nonbelievers. Nor are they interested in the kind of reflection upon values and beliefs that is central to deliberation. Deliberative capacity is in trouble when fundamentalists control the state. Even here, though, it is not necessarily totally absent. Even in a country such as Saudi Arabia, Islamic traditions related to consultation can involve some modicum of deliberative capacity. And to the extent fundamentalists disagree among themselves about what the word of God really means, space for deliberation might eventually open.
- *Ideological conformity.* If the state has an official ideological doctrine that is not readily challenged then deliberative capacity is impaired. Moments of ideological conformity can impede the deliberative capacity of any polity – as illustrated by the case of the United States in the wake of the terrorist attacks of 9/11, when critics of dubious presidential initiatives could be stigmatized as unpatriotic.
- *Segmental autonomy.* Segmental autonomy is specified by Lijphart (1977) as one of the defining features of consociational democracy, conducive to stability in divided societies. But segmental autonomy means no opportunity for members of different blocks to communicate with one another. Consociationalists might argue that there is in fact a high degree of good deliberation in consociational systems, but this would apply only at the elite level, purchased at the expense of more socially pervasive capacity. Some divided societies feature ubiquitous and intense political talk; but this should not be confused with deliberative capacity, if people interact only with like-minded others. Enclave deliberation of this sort has a polarizing effect. Sunstein (2000) criticizes deliberation on the grounds that it induces groups to go to extremes, but his argument holds only to the extent a group contains no countervailing views at the outset. Religious fundamentalism, ideological conformity, and segmental autonomy all repress the variety in points of view necessary for deliberation to work.

## THE HISTORICAL DYNAMICS OF DELIBERATIVE CAPACITY

While the reflexive aspect of deliberative capacity intimates the possibility of a virtuous circle in which deliberative capacity begets more deliberative capacity, regress as well as progress is possible. Consider the following cases.

The history of the early bourgeois public sphere recounted by Habermas (1989) portrays a deliberative public space that arises with the development of capitalism in Europe. The emerging bourgeoisie was excluded from power by the landed aristocracy and the church. Thus, bourgeois political interaction was forced into an oppositional public sphere featuring debate in newspapers and coffee houses. With time, the bourgeoisie is accepted into the state – through liberal revolutions or more gradual processes. Newspapers become commercialized, compromising their ability to host robust political debate. Thus, the public sphere went into decline; its deliberative capacity was lost. The liberalization of politics that attends bourgeois entry into the state may mean an increase in contribution of empowered space to deliberative capacity (especially in parliaments), perhaps compensating for the loss in the contribution of public space. Only detailed comparative study across time could determine whether the gain in empowered space fully compensated for the loss in public space.

Old as well as new democracies can experience losses in deliberative capacity, for example, when national crisis enables critics of governmental policy to be labeled unpatriotic and so illegitimate participants in public debate. Some government policies can also involve a direct attack on deliberative capacity. For example, one approach to increasing efficiency in local government seeks to construct people as "customers" or "consumers" of government services, as opposed to citizens potentially engaged in the coproduction of governmental decisions (Alford and O'Neill 1994). To the extent that approach succeeds, *homo civicus* is displaced by *homo economicus*, who can make choices but not give voice.

The trade-off between deliberative capacity in public space and empowered space can be observed in connection with social movements. As noted earlier, West Germany until the mid 1980s featured a corporatist state that denied access to social movements. The Scandinavian countries, in contrast, actively incorporated social movements such as feminism and environmentalism into state structures, beginning in the late 1960s. Yet, this did not necessarily mean greater deliberative capacity in Scandinavia. For the inclusion of social movements was bought at the expense of their radicalism. So while Scandinavia featured moderate movements with small membership whose leaders (but only their leaders) could deliberate on policy-making committees, Germany featured a critical public sphere engaged by movement activists, and (in the case of environmentalism) an associated network of research institutes. In public space, Germany had a higher deliberative capacity than the Scandinavian countries (Dryzek et al. 2003). What this contrast suggests is that when it comes to the dynamics of democratization, authentic, inclusive, and effective public space ought to precede in time authentic, inclusive, and effective empowered space. If it is the other way around, the desirable kind of public space may be hard to generate.

The trade-off between deliberation in public and empowered space is illustrated by Poland. While the public space established by Solidarity did carry over to a degree after 1989, empowered space has since been problematic. Neoliberal economic reforms were accepted rather than deliberated, and subsequently parties led by populists and ethnic nationalists have prospered. While prerevolutionary deliberative capacity is important in determining the outcome of a crisis in the old regime (see the section on "Deliberation in transition"), its legacy in the long run is more uncertain.

Deliberation is a demanding activity, almost certainly not for all of the people all of the time. But it might be for most of the people some of the time. Ackerman (1991) interprets U.S. political history in terms of three decisive deliberative moments – the founding, the Civil War amendments to the constitution, and the Great Depression – which instigated society-wide deliberation about constitutional fundamentals. Politics had an unusual intensity and breadth in both public space and empowered space. Moments of similar intensity and impact can be found elsewhere in, for example, instances of "people power" directed against authoritarian leaders, or in the "color revolutions" in Georgia (2003) and Ukraine (2004/5).

The inclusiveness and intensity of deliberation that can surround transitional moments – what O'Donnell and Schmitter (1986: 48) call the "layers of an exploding society" – is hard to sustain. For Linz and Stepan (1996), the subsequent replacement of a "politics of truth" by a "politics of interests" is actually good for democratic stability. However, this does not mean that in the long democratic run we should forget about deliberation in favor of interest and strategy. As argued earlier, there are many reasons why democratic consolidation can benefit from authentic, inclusive, and consequential deliberation. These reasons shade into the numerous arguments that theorists and practitioners alike have advanced for the necessity of deliberation in democratic politics. Thus, the full intellectual, financial, and organizational resources of the global movement for the institutionalization of deliberative democracy can be brought to bear in building deliberative capacity that will look very different from that which explodes in transitional moments.

## CONCLUSION

Deliberation that is authentic, inclusive, and consequential is central to democracy, and so ought to be incorporated in any definition of democratization.

Deliberative capacity is instrumental in democratic transition, and crucial to democratic consolidation and deepening. It can also contribute to democratization when transition to the standard model of liberal democracy is not on the agenda. Examination of the development of this capacity does not require specifying any well-defined beginning or end, and so it can be applied in all kinds of political settings: under authoritarian regimes, in new and old democratic states, and in governance that eludes states.

# 8

## Mini-Publics and Their Macro Consequences

In chapter 1, the institutional, practical, and empirical turns that deliberative democracy has taken were noted. The institutional turn involves a focus on particular forums, the practical turn upon real-world political innovation and reform, and the empirical turn on more or less systematic study of deliberation in action. These three turns have converged on a particular kind of innovative forum, the mini-public, composed of ordinary citizens recruited to deliberate political issues that are often complex and contentious. Examples include citizens' juries, consensus conferences, deliberative opinion polls, planning cells, citizens' assemblies, the 21st Century Town Meetings first organized by the America*Speaks* Foundation, National Issues Conventions, and one-off exercises, such as the 2009 Australian Citizens' Parliament, and the "Narrow but Deep" element of the larger GM Nation consultation exercise organized by the UK government on genetically modified foods in 2003. This chapter investigates what mini-publics can actually tell us about the prospects for deliberative democracy, in light of the fact that a stress on particular forums may seem to sit uneasily with the emphasis on deliberative systems at the heart of the systemic turn endorsed in chapter 1. This chapter is completely grounded in empirical studies of mini-publics, and therefore also contributes to both illustration and celebration of the way that work inspired by the empirical turn can inform both the practice and the normative theory of deliberative democracy. These studies turn out to hold many lessons for deliberative democrats, in terms of what is possible and difficult for deliberating citizens to do, the nature of the tasks facing larger deliberative systems, the challenges that any deliberative democracy has to overcome, and how the content of deliberative innovation must be sensitive to the character of the states and political systems in which it is attempted.

Mini-publics are, as already stated, composed of ordinary citizens. At their smallest, citizens' juries and consensus conferences are composed of fifteen to twenty people. At their largest, 21st Century Town Meetings can have thousands of participants. In between, designs such as the deliberative poll seek a representative sample of the population, for which a minimum of about 150 people is necessary. Random sampling is the preferred method of recruitment, though for the forums with smaller numbers that will not necessarily produce the requisite variety, and so stratification on the basis of age, sex, education, ethnicity, and income may also be necessary. 21st Century Town Meetings for their part often feature a substantial measure of self-selection by participants, though most designers of mini-publics try to avoid self-selection (because it disproportionately attracts politically active, highly educated, high income, and older participants). For numbers above twenty, participants are divided into smaller deliberating groups. Deliberation normally takes place under the auspices of a facilitator, to ensure dialogue is civil and inclusive (though the precise rules for discussion can be specified by the participants themselves). Normally, participants will be provided with information about the issue at hand, and have access to experts and advocates on the issue. At the end of the process, they will usually produce a report and recommendations (though in the deliberative poll they simply complete a questionnaire). (For more details on mini-publics, see Smith (2009: 72–110); for a treatment that places them in the contexts of other sorts of forums, see Fung (2003)).

Now, these citizen-based mini-publics are not the only kind of designed deliberative forum. The "discursive designs" identified long ago by Dryzek (1987) as promising sites for deliberative experimentation mostly featured partisans with a history of political activity and activism on an issue. Discursive designs of this sort then sought to bring partisans, who might come from community groups, government, businesses, interest groups, or social movements, into productive engagement. The intent was to produce a kind of communicative action very different from the familiar strategic interaction that is the norm in liberal democratic politics. Discursive designs with partisan participants owed a lot to the field of conflict resolution, a connection eventually reestablished by Susskind (2006). Parties to a dispute are brought into a forum under the auspices of a neutral third-party mediator or facilitator. Such designs have found new life in what Innes and Booher (2003) and others call "collaborative governance."

This chapter shall set aside partisan forums in favor or those that emphasize the participation of ordinary citizens with no necessary history of involvement or activism on an issue: the mini-public. There are three reasons for this emphasis. The first is that mini-publics on the face of it offer fewer obstacles to authentic deliberation than do forums composed of partisans with a history of strategizing against each other. The second is that mini-publics are grounded in a broader public, and as such may be able to help deliver deliberative democracy's core promise of legitimation of collective decisions in the eyes of this broader public. And the third is simply that mini-publics have received much more in the way of attention from deliberative democrats in the recent past, as opposed to a more long-standing concern with partisan forums. Thus, they make a more appropriate focus for a book concerned with the frontiers of deliberative governance. The first two reasons should not necessarily be taken at face value, though Hendriks, Dryzek, and Hunold (2007) find empirical support for them in their comparative study of partisan forums and nonpartisan forums composed of lay citizens.

Deliberative democrats have, then, devoted substantial time and energy over the years to the design, evaluation, and occasional advocacy of innovative kinds of deliberative forums, and mini-publics in particular. At one level this is an obvious thing to do, because deliberation involves a particular kind of communication that is not always found in the give-and-take of ordinary politics. On the other hand, it is not obvious that the time and energy involved are well spent, given that any particular forum does not amount to a deliberative democracy. Chambers (2009) suggests all this attention to particular forums means the field is in danger of abandoning mass democracy, and so would be the antithesis of the systemic turn identified in chapter 1. While Chambers's fears are exaggerated, her underlying challenge is well-taken: what exactly is the point of devoting so much attention to these forums? It is also worth noting at the outset that many of these forums were originally designed and implemented by people who had little if any knowledge of the theory of deliberative democracy, prior to the rise of deliberative democracy (at least by that name) since 1990. So in their early years, at least, they did not need any input from deliberative democrats to make them happen. There has, however, been a convergence of interest between theorists and practitioners; and theorists have worked with practitioners on the design of deliberative forums (indeed, become practitioners themselves), for example, on the pioneering Australian Citizens' Parliament in 2008–2009 (Dryzek et al. 2009*b*).

This chapter is intended to convince the reader that all this attention devoted to mini-publics is time well spent – and in particular, that it does not mean turning our backs on mass publics and deliberative systems. Each of the next three sections examines a particular kind of macro use for a mini-public. There follows a demonstration of how the actual and potential uses of mini-publics vary quite dramatically across different kinds of political system.


## LESSONS FROM MINI-PUBLICS FOR POLITICAL SYSTEMS

The study of mini-publics can demonstrate exactly what we would like deliberation to accomplish in larger political systems – and, for that matter, what we would like to avoid in those systems. The next section addresses challenges to be avoided or overcome, but for the moment the concentration is on the generation of positive lessons for larger systems. It is possible to talk about what deliberation can do and must overcome from the armchair; but study of the dynamics of actual deliberations reveals so much more. These dynamics prove to be much easier to study in the relatively self-contained and controlled environment of a mini-public, compared to the larger and more disorganized public sphere, and that is a major justification for attention to what transpires in mini-publics. It turns out that Habermas (2006*b*: 414) is wrong when he says that "All these studies offer empirical evidence for the cognitive potential of deliberation. However, small-scale samples can only lend limited support to the empirical content of a deliberative paradigm designed for legitimation processes in large scale or national societies."

### First lesson: citizen competence

The most obvious finding from mini-publics relevant to the larger public sphere is that, given the opportunity, ordinary citizens can make good deliberators. Moreover, issue complexity is no barrier to the development and exercise of that competence. These findings contradict skeptics who highlight citizen incompetence, and proceed to argue for either nondemocratic or (more frequently) minimally democratic political arrangements (for recent examples of this long and dismal tradition, see Bartels (2003) and Caplan (2007)). Unsystematically, we can simply observe citizens within mini-publics – and see that in many cases individuals come in with little or no interest or capability in politics, yet leave as energized and competent actors. More quantitative evidence is available. This evidence shows that ordinary citizens may make better deliberators than partisan political actors on at least one dimension: the capacity to reflect and change their minds as a result of their participation in deliberation (Hendriks, Dryzek, and Hunold 2007: 369–71). As Mackie (2006) argues, it is hard for partisans to admit to having been persuaded in the context of a political forum (though, as Mackie rightfully points out, individuals who do not at once admit to being persuaded may reveal that they have been persuaded later, in a different setting, with different participants, where face will not be lost). Does this mean that deliberation in a lay citizen forum is normally of higher quality than in a partisan setting (deliberative or otherwise)? Comparing case studies of forums in Germany about genetic diagnostics and genetically modified food involving (respectively) ordinary citizens and partisans, Hendriks, Dryzek, and Hunold (2007: 371) conclude that this is indeed the case. It would be possible to do a more quantitative study of transcripts from different kinds of forums using the discourse quality index developed by Steiner et al. (2004); at the time of writing several such studies are under way, but there are no results to report yet.

Given empirical corroboration of the quality of lay citizen deliberation and the high potential for political competence it reveals, the democratic challenge then becomes how to achieve something similar on a broader scale. Of course, what we observe in mini-publics does not of itself tell us how to do that. But it does undermine the arguments of all those antidemocrats and dubious democrats who tell us that citizen incompetence means the task itself is pointless.

## Second lesson: displacing symbolic politics

To demonstrate another way macro lessons can be generated from mini-publics, it is possible to begin with the long-standing observation that symbolic politics in the public sphere can cause all kinds of distortions with adverse political consequences (Edelman 1964). The invocation of appealing symbols often drives out good arguments. Many kinds of actors are guilty of this. So environmentalists might find that fund-raising and public support benefit from claiming imminent environmental catastrophe rather than insidious long-term change; and threats to aesthetically appealing mammals rather than to whole ecosystems. When governments want to go to war, they may invoke nationalistic symbols such that opposition to the war looks like betrayal of the nation. In the United States, right-wing opponents of moderate reform to health care stigmatize it as socialist or communist, thus trying to end discussion. There is a close connection here to what Chambers (2009) denounces as the "plebiscitary" form of rhetoric. The idea of such rhetoric is to make sure that such preferences as citizens do express are manipulated by elites. Symbolic politics involves suppression of the autonomy of citizens, because their opportunity to reflect upon their preferences is restricted, and their capacity to endorse policy positions that would actually further their own values is overwhelmed.

Deliberative democracy as a normative theory is committed to the reflective autonomy of citizens. But can it be shown that deliberation in practice – as opposed to in the hopes of deliberative theorists – can actually dispel symbolic politics? There is considerable evidence that suggests such processes in operation. In the case of a citizens' jury reported by Niemeyer (2004), what happens is that symbolic claims that dominated media debate from partisans on both sides of an issue were largely dissolved in the process of the jury's deliberations. The issue concerned what to do with a track that had been illegally bulldozed through a coastal rainforest in Queensland. The claims that were dissipated concerned, respectively, the idea that the track was needed to provide access to remote properties, and that runoff from the track damaged inshore coral reefs. The jurors' deliberations enabled them to see through such claims. A symbolic discourse that highlighted anxiety about such claims on both sides of the issue was likewise dissolved in the process of deliberation. At the end of the process, the deliberators still disagreed about what should be done, but they had better reasons for the positions they held.

In another case concerning what to do about a bridge over Fremantle harbor in Western Australia, Niemeyer, Ayirtman, and Hartz-Karp (2008) observe a similar kind of reduction in symbolic politics. Prior to deliberation, symbolic anxieties relating to the heritage value of the existing bridge dominated debate, crowding out concerns relating to safety and access. After deliberation, heritage concerns remained, but were integrated into broader positions concerning what should be done with the bridge.

In both of these cases, what happened as a result of deliberation was not so much that individuals changed their minds about what should be done. Rather, the dominant mechanism is that their preferences were brought into alignment with their own subjective dispositions (as measured by Niemeyer's index of intersubjective consistency). Prior to deliberation, that connection was obscured by symbolic messages dominating media debate. These dynamics could be scrutinized in the mini-publics in question by administering preference surveys and Q sorts (to measure underlying subjective disposition) before, during, and after deliberation. The results show that prior to deliberation, there was only a weak relationship between subjective disposition and policy preference; after deliberation, the relationship was much stronger. In addition, the deliberation of the mini-public could itself be observed and both its substantive content and procedural qualities ascertained.

Observing these processes at the level of mass publics would be much harder: indeed, it would be hard to know what, when, and how to observe, using what instruments. Study of the two mini-publics just discussed revealed the precise mechanism through which symbolic politics is dissipated. The challenge when it comes to the broader public sphere is then to figure out how this mechanism could be replicated on a large scale. Just what procedures to adopt in the larger public sphere is a question without easy answers. If part of the blame lies with the way the media covers and presents issues, then perhaps media reform would be appropriate. But the structural problems of the media from a deliberative perspective run very deep. There is probably very little money to be made or audience share to be gained through journalism that tries to see through the symbolic claims made by the dominant political actors. Moreover, it is not just the media that is to blame, as often the media is just amplifying the sorts of symbolic claims made by partisan political actors. The obvious implication is that we need to find ways to engage partisans in more deliberative forms of political action. The one mechanism that we now know *does* enable ordinary citizens to see through symbolic politics as presented by partisan elites and amplified by the media is the mini-public itself. This recognition might suggest an expanded political role for such forums, which leads directly to some major questions about what roles mini-publics can and should play in larger deliberative systems. Those questions will be revisited later in the section on "Mini-publics in the deliberative system".

## HIGHLIGHTING THE CHALLENGES
## FACING LARGER SYSTEMS

### Polarization

Aside from suggesting what deliberation in the larger public sphere should be trying to achieve, studies of small-scale forums can also highlight challenges that are likely to pervade politics in general, and that need to be addressed by deliberative democrats. Here, the studies adduced by Sunstein (2002) in support of his alleged "law of group polarization" are relevant. Now, these are not studies of mini-publics (if they were, the "law" would be found not to apply). Mostly, they involve studies of mock juries and other small group experiments. Yet, the effect he identifies is real enough: if all members of a small group are disposed at the outset to varying degrees in a particular direction, their communication will lead their average position to a more extreme location than at the outset. However, as Fishkin (2009: 131–2) points out, the effects described by Sunstein do not occur in deliberative polls, because random selection means it is unlikely that at the outset all the participants will be disposed in the same direction, and because subsequently they receive information from varied points of view. The lesson from Sunstein and Fishkin for the larger public sphere is actually a very old pluralist one: it is important that all sides be heard in public deliberation. Polarization within deliberative enclaves may not be a bad thing if it enables the individuals or group involved subsequently to enter with confidence debates in the larger public sphere (see the discussion in chapter 4). Further, as Goodin (2009) argues, if in their pre-discussion positions individuals are hesitant and tentative, the observed average movement to an extreme may just reflect increased confidence in their positions on the part of participants. In that case, polarization may simply lead to collective moral clarity. The work that Sunstein summarizes alerts us to what may be a danger in macro-deliberative settings. The work of his critics shows that polarization is not always undesirable. But clearly Sunstein has pointed to some issues that need to be kept in mind at the systemic level.

## Systematic differences between elites and publics

The alleged law of group polarization is not derived from the actual study of mini-publics. But such study is quite capable of revealing some major challenges that need to be addressed in the larger system. One such challenge goes to the core claim of deliberative democracy, which is that legitimacy depends on the right, opportunity, and capacity of those subject to a decision (or their representatives) to participate in consequential deliberation about the content of the decision. But what if there is a systematic difference between the content of public decision and what deliberating publics would conclude? In one important set of cases, there does indeed prove to be a pervasive difference between what reflective publics conclude, on the one hand, and the policies that government elites choose, on the other. These kinds of cases concern risks associated with new technologies. The evidence comes from a comparative study of forums convened on the issue of GM foods, the most popular topic assigned to mini-publics for deliberation in many countries in recent years. There prove to be reasons to suspect the effect observed can be generalized to other risk-heavy technology-related public policy issues.

Ulrich Beck (1992) claims that risk-related issues have the potential to generate new kinds of politics, perhaps more participatory and deliberative than the norm in liberal democracies. The proliferation of mini-publics in connection with such issues corroborates his claim. The most popular such topic area to date concerns GM foods (though human biotechnology and nanotechnology may be catching up), which has featured citizens' juries, one-off exercises such as the UK government's "Narrow but Deep" forums held in conjunction with its larger "GM Nation" public consultation in 2003, and, above all, consensus conferences. The consensus conference model was developed by the Danish Board of Technology. The model begins with the selection of fifteen ordinary citizens from a larger random sample. The fifteen should reflect the variety of social characteristics (age, education, etc.) in the larger society. The main public session of four days is preceded by two preparatory weekends, which set the agenda (and may reframe the question as initially specified by an advisory committee). The citizens themselves select who they want to hear from and question out of a long list of experts and advocates generated by the advisory committee. At the main session, the fifteen citizens deliberate among themselves (under the auspices of a facilitator), and the process culminates with a press conference at which the findings and recommendations are presented. Despite their name, consensus conferences do not have to produce complete agreement on the values underpinning recommendations, so normative consensus is not required. These forums do strive for something like preference consensus, without necessarily achieving it. If preference consensus proves elusive, the consensus conference's recommendation can still constitute a working agreement (Eriksen 2006), or what Sunstein (1995) would call an "incompletely theorized agreement" responsive to the different priorities of the participants.

Consensus conferences on GM foods have been held in Denmark, the United States, Australia, Canada, France, Germany, Switzerland, and the United Kingdom, among other countries. What is found is that the reflective public of the consensus conference almost always reaches a conclusion that is more "precautionary" than that of policy-making elites (for greater detail on this study, see Dryzek et al. 2009a).

A precautionary discourse puts the burden of proof for safety on the proponents of new technologies (O'Riordan and Cameron 1994). Technologies are assessed not in isolation, but rather in terms of how they may interact with social and ecological systems in all their complexity. Concerns about risk are not subordinated to the drive for economic growth and (when it comes to food) efficiency and quantity of production. Promethean discourse, in contrast, has faith in the ability of economy and society to control social and ecological systems in the interests of human good (exposition of Promethean doctrine can be found in Simon (1996) and Lomborg (2001)). Technological progress is seen as required for economic growth, and any side effects amenable to management by further human ingenuity. Some Private Prometheans believe the market is best equipped to perform all these functions, others that governmental planning has some role to play. All believe there are no limits to the ability of humans to organize and manage the world and its resources.

Why are policy-making elites normally relatively Promethean? Sometimes it is a matter of ideological conviction, for example, in the presidencies of Ronald Reagan and George W. Bush in the United States. But such transient ideological enthusiasm matters less than the constraints upon national policy makers. The Promethean outlook pervades the most important institutions of the international political economy, such as the World Trade Organization (WTO), International Monetary Fund, and World Bank – and, equally important, the understanding of most actors operating in transnational markets and financial networks. Market liberalism is therefore embedded in the international political economy to a greater extent than in the economies of most and perhaps all states, and market liberalism bolsters Promethean discourse. Only occasionally does a heavy hand need to be wielded, for example, when in 2006 the WTO ruled that the European Union's existing limits on GM agricultural products constituted an illegal restraint on trade, and so would have to be removed. But even when they are not subject to formal rulings of this sort, most governments are very conscious of the fact that they are operating in a world economy run on market liberal lines. They know that they will be punished (by disinvestment, capital flight, and attacks on their currency) if they do not abide by both the formal rules and informal understandings that dominate this system, which therefore pushes them in a Promethean direction. Commitment to technology-led economic growth is part of the recipe the system imposes, and governments are expected to smooth the development and adoption of technologies.

Reflective citizens organized into consensus conferences and similar deliberative forums are of course not governments, and so are not subject to such constraints. They do not have to reach Promethean conclusions. Thus, it is no surprise that on average they reach fewer Promethean positions than do governments. But why should these reflective citizens actually reach precautionary conclusions? The answer may lie in the fact that often they are established by elites who think that risks as perceived by the general public are severe enough to warrant at least a gesture toward participation in policy making of informed public opinion. If there were no perceived risks, the mini-public would not be established to begin with. Thus, the lay citizens recruited to a mini-public actually have a mandate to worry. And they generally do so – even when the organizers of the mini-public or elites more generally try to persuade them to do otherwise.

These expectations are borne out in comparative empirical studies of lay citizen deliberations on GM foods. In *France* in 1998, a *Conférence de Citoyens* (which followed the consensus conference model) was held under the auspices of the *Office Parlementaire d'Evaluation des Choix Scientifiques et Technologiques* (OPECST), a technology assessment agency whose main task historically was to reassure the general public about the positives of technological progress (Vig and Paschen 2000: 14). The government that instructed OPECST (reluctantly) to organize the *Conférence* was mainly in favor of GM technology, so was the steering committee for the *Conférence*, and most of the presentations to it. Nevertheless, the citizen participants ended up highlighting risks, recommending substantial regulation, exhibiting some skepticism about economic benefits, and generally challenging the French tradition of top-down expert administration. The citizens' final report was not categorically against GM agriculture, but took a generally precautionary worldview (which is also revealed in an examination of the content of their prior deliberations).

In the *United States*, GM agriculture has been introduced on a large scale without anything much in the way of public consultation of any sort, and (in stark contrast to Europe) without a great deal of political controversy. The only lay citizen deliberations that have been held were organized by university academics as demonstration and academic exercises: in North Carolina in 2001 and New Hampshire in 2002. The New Hampshire consensus conference was unremittingly hostile to GM foods, perhaps not surprising given the leanings of its planning committee, and the inability of the organizers to find any representatives from the GM industry or pro-GM advocates willing to testify before the citizens. The North Carolina consensus conference had similar problems in getting representatives from industry to appear – but also faced skepticism from anti-GM groups, who thought the process would be biased against their position. Thus, the participants heard mainly from experts rather than advocates. The final report pointed to considerable uncertainty about the risks of GM agriculture, highlighted environmental problems, and criticized the lack of prior public debate on the issue. While allowing that GM foods might have economic benefits, the citizens called for substantial regulation of the industry. Thus, the two U.S. forums both produced reports much more precautionary in their content than the very Promethean position of the U.S. government.

In *Canada*, a 1999 consensus conference held in Calgary reached the most pro-GM conclusions that could be found, befitting a society that matches the United States in public acceptance of GM agriculture and its importance to the economy. However, the citizens' report also had plenty of precautionary caveats. Canada differed from the other reports studied in that the citizen participants took it as given that Canada had already taken the GM road – in the European countries in particular that was still an open question.

In 2003, the pro-GM *UK* government of Prime Minister Tony Blair launched a widespread (and, given its own commitments, ill-advised) public consultation exercise, GM Nation. The open meetings attracted mostly critics of GM foods. More instructively, questionnaires administered to participants in the "Narrow but Deep" lay citizen forums conducted at the same time revealed a solidification of opinion in the direction of skepticism and precaution about GM foods. Two subsequent citizens' juries conducted by the Politics, Ethics, and Life Sciences project at the University of Newcastle explicitly endorsed the precautionary principle.

In *Australia*, a 1999 consensus conference endorsed by the federal government likewise explicitly favored a precautionary approach – despite an opening speech by the Agriculture Minister that touted the benefits of GM food, and a steering committee that clearly leant in the pro-GM direction. In *Switzerland*, a 1999 *publiforum* was sponsored by a government less wholeheartedly committed to GM agriculture than in the other countries covered so far, though the Swiss government recognized the economic potential (and that the prominent GM company Novartis is based in Switzerland). The Swiss citizens recommended a moratorium on GM development – which was rejected in 2001 by parliament, but then supported by 55.7 percent of Swiss voters in a 2005 referendum.

The only case identified where there was in the end little difference between the position of government and that of the lay citizen forum was *Denmark*. In Denmark, the report of a 1999 consensus conference was hostile to GM agriculture – and in favor of alternatives such as organic farming. Agriculture was important to the Danish economy, but as of 1999 GM technology had not been adopted. Conventional and organic agriculture were highly profitable, and government and farmers saw little need to adopt the new technology. The discourse of ecological modernization that rejects market liberalism and Promethean discourse alike dominates environmental policy in Denmark, which is categorized by Mol and Sonnefeld (2000) as a "front-runner nation" when it comes to ecological modernization. Ecological modernization is committed to economic growth – but sees growth and environmental conservation as mutually reinforcing, so the environment does not have to be sacrificed for the economy. The precautionary principle is an integral part of ecological modernization.

While the details differ, the common story that emerges from all these cases except Denmark is of reflective publics that are much more precautionary than policy-making elites. Governments generally set up forums such as consensus conferences with the intention of increasing public legitimacy for their policies. Faced with broad public disquiet about potential risks, they adopt this apparent "technology of legitimation" (Harrison and Mort 1998). But the results almost always backfire, and as already indicated, call into question the very possibility of deliberative legitimation when it comes to issues of technological risk. It is ironic that these are exactly the issues that have been chosen most often by governments for deliberative treatment. At some point governments may realize that they are unlikely to win, and stop sponsoring citizen forums on risk issues. Deliberative democracy (at least by the mini-public route) will be the loser. More insidiously, governments may try to manage forums to produce the desired results, but our cases (France in particular) indicate this is very difficult. Denmark points to a happier outcome from the point of view of both environmental values and democratic legitimation of the positions taken by government. But the Danish result is contingent on government adopting a discourse of ecological modernization, which is not available everywhere.

In the GM case, systematic comparative analysis of the experience of mini-publics highlights a macro-problem for deliberative democracy: that policy legitimation by deliberative means may be in trouble, at least when it comes to issues of technological risk. Here at least, deliberative democracy and the economic imperatives of governments seem to be on a collision course. The empirically identified solution to this problem is for government to adopt a discourse of ecological modernization. If that is not available, then the very practical normative lesson for deliberative democrats applicable at the macro-systemic level is that, at least when it comes to risk-related issues, they should concentrate their efforts on deliberation in the public sphere at a distance from the state and its economic imperatives (Dryzek 1996*a*: 46–64). Other policy areas could benefit from the same empirical treatment. Another uncomfortable lesson is this: in the very area in which governments have sponsored the largest number of deliberative exercises, that sponsorship rests on mistaken assumptions about what deliberative exercises are likely to produce. At some point, governments may realize this and stop sponsoring mini-publics in these areas.

## MINI-PUBLICS IN THE DELIBERATIVE SYSTEM

We turn now from the lessons that mini-publics can generate for larger systems to the parts they can play in those systems. In chapter 3, it was shown how a mini-public could be conceptualized and convened as a formal "Chamber of Discourses," with participants selected as discursive representatives. Such a Chamber could conceivably take its place in the institutional architecture of government in a variety of ways: as a house of review in a bicameral legislature, as an additional branch of government deliberating proposals generated by other branches, or as a way to discharge legislative mandates for public consultation. Existing uses of mini-publics are much more limited (and none so far has selected its participants via discursive representation). This section looks at the parts that mini-publics currently can and do play in relation to the broader political system, paying special attention to the kinds of impacts that have been generated. The idea is to develop some conclusions about what deliberative innovation can accomplish. But before any such lessons can be applied with confidence, it is necessary to develop a more sophisticated understanding of the relevant ways larger political systems actually work in practice. In the following section, a comparative cross-national study shows that the constraints on and opportunities for mini-publics vary dramatically across different kinds of political system. Democratic innovators who do not attend to these facts of political life are likely to face nothing but frustration.

Ideally, we might want mini-publics to take their place in what Hendriks (2006) calls an "integrated deliberative system." In such a system, mini-publics would not be isolated exercises conducted by and for, and reporting only to, some well-defined governmental authority. Instead, they would have multifaceted and multidirectional relationships with other actors in the larger public sphere as well as government, with the intent of contributing to deliberation in that larger arena. Fishkin (2009) conceives of his deliberative polls in this light (which is why he always tries to get them televised). Such interchange would be facilitated by the involvement with mini-publics of interest organizations, social movement activists, politicians, and government bureaucrats. The mini-public would then constitute what Hendriks (2006) calls a "discursive sphere" – not just a place where citizens deliberate, but a place where these deliberations spark interaction between actors who would not normally engage each other, especially in deliberative fashion.

## The forms of impact of mini-publics

If mini-publics are to attract attention in a larger deliberative system, they do of course need to have some kind of impact within and upon that system. The impacts in question can be of varied types. They involve, notably, the following paths (most but not all of which are elaborated in Goodin and Dryzek (2006: 225–37)).

- Actually making policy in empowered space. This almost never happens. The closest case is where the mini-public has a guaranteed part in the policy process. The best example of this is the 2004 British Columbia Citizens' Assembly, which had a guarantee in advance from the provincial government that its recommendation for a new voting system for the province would be put to a referendum and, if passed, adopted. The single transferable vote (STV) system recommended by the Assembly received 57 percent of the vote in a 2005 referendum; this fell short of the absurdly high 60 percent threshold that had also been specified (see Warren and Pearse 2008).
- Being taken up in the empowered space of the policy process. This is at once less demanding and harder to ascertain than actually making policy, given the complexity of policy processes and the consequent difficulty of establishing "smoking gun" causation. In Denmark, there are clear examples of consensus conference recommendations finding their way into

legislation, for example, on restricting genetic screening by insurance companies and employers. Fishkin (2009: 152–3) claims such influence for some of his deliberative polls, notably concerning the adoption of renewable energy in Texas.

- Informing public debates. This is still less demanding, and still harder to ascertain given the cacophony of the public sphere, and the associated number of competing voices. The Australian consensus conference on GM foods mentioned earlier had some clear influence on the positions taken by Monsanto, the leading GM company, and by the Commonwealth Scientific and Industrial Research Organization, a pro-GM government body that realized it had to do more than just sell the benefits of technology to the public.

- Guiding public opinion. Broader publics do not necessarily need to *understand* what a mini-public has concluded on a complex issue, but they do need to *trust* it. Again the British Columbia Citizens' Assembly provides a key illustration. The 57 percent of voters who in the 2005 referendum voted for the proposed new system did so not because they understood STV, but because they trusted that the members of the Assembly that recommended STV were people like themselves (Warren 2009). When the STV proposal was put to a second referendum in 2009 there was no mention of the citizens' assembly, and the campaign was conducted as STV versus the simple plurality system that was the status quo. With less reason to trust the STV campaigners, only 41 percent of the voters supported STV this time around.

- Market testing of policy. A mini-public can be used to test acceptance of a policy. The "Listening to the City" forum convened by America*Speaks* in New York effectively vetoed all six proposals on offer for redevelopment of the World Trade Center site after the 2001 attacks.

- Legitimating policy. Parkinson (2006*a*) describes the case of a citizens' jury on hospital reorganization in Leicester in England that acted as a creative circuit breaker that helped policy move beyond impasse.

- Confidence building, whereupon participants become empowered as a result of their participation in a mini-public. The 2009 Australians Citizens' Parliament produced some dramatic effects on participants. Individuals with no prior interest or involvement in politics became active in contacting local media and elected representatives, advocating similar events in their own suburbs or towns, even launching political careers of their own.

- Popular oversight of public officials who have to give an account of existing policies and practices before a mini-public.

Direct influence on and in policy making is a hard test for mini-publics to pass. While examples exist of influence and impact, they are outnumbered by cases where a mini-public is established but turns out to have little or no effect on public decision making, let alone take its place in any integrated deliberative system. Why is that? Here, we need a sophisticated understanding of the relevant ways that real political systems actually work, and the implications for how mini-publics are likely to be both sponsored and received. This sophisticated understanding is typically not possessed by normative theorists of deliberative democracy (even very clever ones), or by practitioners and designers of mini-publics. The British Columbia Citizens' Assembly was exemplary in many ways, but its sponsors and designers should have realized that given the 60 percent threshold required in the referendum, there was virtually no chance of its recommendations being adopted. It is impressive that 57 percent was achieved; this is an exceptionally high positive vote in a constitutional referendum. In the next section, a particular kind of explanatory scheme is deployed that tries to show why the actual impacts of mini-publics often prove so at variance with the hopes of their advocates and designers. There prove to be massive differences across different kinds of political system in these respects.

## DELIBERATIVE INNOVATIONS HAVE DIFFERENT EFFECTS IN DIFFERENT SYSTEMS

The roles open to mini-publics vary significantly across different kinds of political system. To the extent that comparative empirical analysis reveals such difference, then normative theory and the practice of institutional innovation must also be sensitive to the opportunities and constraints that different political systems present. In order to demonstrate these points, the comparative analysis of mini-publics designed to deliberate the issue of GM foods can be further scrutinized. This time the focus is on the cases of France, the United States, and Denmark. The reason for this selection is that these three countries exemplify three kinds of states, based on a classification first developed in Dryzek (1996*b*) and since applied in a number of places. This classification reveals major implications for how mini-publics actually get used.

On one dimension, states can be classified as inclusive to exclusive. Inclusive states welcome a broad variety of social interests. Exclusive states are much more limited in the kinds of interests they accept as legitimate political players. On a second dimension, states can be either active or passive in their orientation to social interests.

*Actively inclusive* states intervene in civil society to manage the pattern of interest organization, and also construct formal channels of participation that organize these interests into the state. The best examples of active inclusion can be found in the Nordic countries, where concerns that in other countries would constitute social movements (such as feminism and environmentalism) are integrated from the outset into the state. Denmark provides a good example. In contrast, *passively inclusive* states provide a number of channels by which the influence of interests grounded in civil society and the market can exercise influence (lobbying, legal action, consultation, political party activism), but otherwise do not intervene to affect the pattern of interest organization in civil society, or organize groups into the state. The best example of passive inclusion is the relatively pluralist polity of the United States – "relatively" because it falls short of any pluralist ideal, but empirically is more pluralist than any other state (Lehmbruch 1984).

*Passively exclusive* states provide few channels for the influence of social interests beyond a favored few, but beyond that leave civil society alone. Examples can be found in the corporatist states of Europe, where traditionally labor federations and peak business organizations made policy in conjunction with top executive branch officials, with all other social interests left out. (Active inclusion in the Nordic states is therefore in a sense just an expansive form of corporatism.) Though not exactly corporatist (with labor in particular having no privileged access to policy making), France provides a good example of an exclusive state. Policy has traditionally been made in a top-down and highly centralized fashion. *Actively exclusive* states for their part intervene in civil society to try to undermine the basis for the organization of social interests. While such states abound in the world's autocracies, they are rare to the point of vanishing among contemporary liberal democracies, especially since the demise of Thatcherism in the United Kingdom (and its imitators elsewhere) since 1990. Thus, there is no case of a mini-public being organized in an actively exclusive state.

Let us now take a close look at what happens when a mini-public is organized in actively inclusive Denmark, the passively inclusive United States, and exclusive France (this study is reported in detail in Dryzek and Tucker (2008)). Fortunately, there is a strong basis for comparison because there is the same design, the consensus conference, being deployed on the same issue, GM foods, at around the same time.

In *Denmark*, the 1999 consensus conference was organized by the Danish Board of Technology (which had earlier invented the format), operating under a mandate from parliament. Consistent with Danish participatory and egalitarian traditions, the consensus conference had a high degree of legitimacy in the eyes of other actors in the political system, and among broader publics. As noted earlier, the recommendations on GM foods were not especially controversial in the Danish context. Under a 1995 law, the results of the consensus conference are conveyed to the appropriate parliamentary committee. But given the recommendations did not diverge much from existing government policy, it is hard to discern any obvious policy impact (such impact is easier to see in other consensus conferences in Denmark, concerning, for example, genetic screening and food irradiation). Key actors such as Greenpeace and biotechnology companies reported increased appreciation of informed citizen views, and politicians realized they could not dismiss public fears as irrational. Denmark exhibits an *integrative* use of the consensus conference model, which is tightly integrated into the political structure.

Matters worked out very differently in *France*, where a weak legislature has little power in relation to the executive (Kitschelt 1986: 64–5) and policy making is monopolized by an elite political class (Safran 2002). The main task of French government is to identify and implement the national interest defined in singular terms. The technology assessment agency, OPECST, exists not to engage the public but to inform and reassure the public (and parliament), so as to smooth the path of progress. The 1998 consensus conference on GM foods was imposed on a reluctant OPECST by the Prime Minister's office. The legitimacy of the consensus conferences was not accepted by members of parliament, because it looked like a challenge to their (tenuous) authority. The Green Party, even though part of the governing coalition at the time, opposed the consensus conference because they considered themselves the relevant authority when it came to environmental issues. The steering committee for the conference was composed of four OPECST members and several other scientists and social scientists, and played a very interventionist role in trying to reassure the citizen participants that they could trust the government on this issue. The steering committee was on balance pro-GM foods. As already noted, the citizens' report and (especially) the content of their deliberation was more precautionary than the government's position, though no radical policy departures were recommended. The consensus conference had little independent policy impact, and its standing remained controversial. It received some media coverage, but parliamentarians were for the most part barely aware of what it had recommended. As befits a centralized and exclusive state, the French consensus conference was deployed in *managerial* fashion by a government that wanted it to perform some helpful functions – but not to present any challenge to government policy. The main such function the government hoped for was to provide a relatively pro-GM representation of public opinion that could be contrasted with mass public skepticism about GM technology. The citizen participants did, however, prove more critical than expected. Thus, the French *Conférence de Citoyens* proved a disappointment to its sponsors, an irritant to parliament, a forum compromised by a pro-GM bias to the Greens and other environmentalists, and an unnecessary exercise in participation by many bureaucrats – including the agency charged with running it. Given its context, the French conference can hardly be said to have advanced the cause of deliberative democracy.

Unlike Denmark and France, the *U.S.* federal government has never shown any interest in organizing lay citizen forums. When federal agencies do run consultation exercises, they generally just advertise opportunities for whoever wants to show up or contribute to do so. The idea that agencies might actually organize the input of ordinary citizens does not register. No lay citizen mini-public has to date been run by the U.S. federal government. It does not even have an obvious agency to do so on issues of technological risk, the Office of Technology Assessment having been abolished in 1996 by Congress. Thus, it has been left to outsiders to organize such forums, and for such recommendations as they do produce having to compete with the cacophony of organized interests in the system. When it comes to GM foods, consensus conferences have been run by university researchers (with some support from private foundations and the public National Science Foundation – interested in consensus conferences only as social research exercises). The New Hampshire consensus conference described earlier was run with advice from the Loka Institute, whose mission is to promote public participation to help control risks associated with new technologies. This exercise attracted a bit more controversy than the North Carolina conference, though neither received too much attention from either government or the media. In a passively inclusive political system, inputs to public policy processes generally consist of advocacy. Expecting this, partisans on both sides of the GM foods issue thought these mini-publics could be biased against their own interests, and so were reluctant to play any role in either giving advice or testifying. In the case of New Hampshire (where only the pro-GM side withdrew), bias was something of a self-fulfilling prophecy. Overall, the consensus conferences in the United States were deployed in *advocacy* fashion. In New Hampshire, advocacy was for both process and for recognition of the risks of GM technology; in North Carolina, where the organizers took no position on the severity of risks, for process alone. This advocacy mode is the norm in the United States, especially at the federal level. Foundations such as Kettering and America-*Speaks* advocate and run deliberative processes featuring ordinary citizens, but they are just small voices in the pluralist multitude vying for political access and influence.

The common design of the consensus conference does, then, get deployed very differently in the three states. The kind of integrative use seen in Denmark, which enthusiasts elsewhere would like to copy, is actually contingent on the actively inclusive features of the Danish political system. In France, the political structure induces top-down managerial use of the consensus conference; in the United States, passive inclusion means that consensus conferences can only knock on the door from the outside, deployed in advocacy fashion.

What lessons can be drawn for deliberative democrats interested in introducing mini-publics? There is no realistic hope of rendering most other liberal democratic states into the actively inclusive Nordic form that makes full integrative use of the consensus conference possible in Denmark. At most, islands and moments of active inclusion are possible. For example, in 2003, testimony from the Loka Institute convinced Congress to include in an appropriations bill for nanotechnology some language that referred to "the convening of regular and ongoing public discussions through mechanisms such as citizens' panels, consensus conferences, and educational events" (though to date nothing has happened as a result). In the United States, more generally, sponsors of deliberative forums should be careful to avoid the embrace of advocacy groups with a well-defined policy agenda, for that can only delegitimate the forum in the eyes of other groups. In the United States in particular, media attention is going to be important in a mini-public having any influence, given there is no direct connection to the legislature as found in Denmark and France. But the media is generally not interested in reasoned discussion – only conflict and controversy. There might be some hope in the movement for "public journalism" that has taken hold in some U.S. regional newspapers (Dzur 2002), committed to more serious and sustained deliberation involving broader publics. In the absence of public journalism, the media is an especially problematic means for mini-publics to influence broader publics. The media deals in sound bites, not sustained dialogue; in moments of conflict, not in the search for reciprocal understandings; in personality and celebrity, not serious reflection; in the simplification of issues, rather than complex understandings of difficult choices. Sponsors of mini-publics, especially in passively inclusive political systems, realize they need the media. Indeed, media demands can (especially in deliberative polls) drive the way the event is organized, sometimes to the detriment of citizen deliberation itself (Gibson and Miskin 2002). The media is, as Parkinson (2006*b*) puts it, a "rickety bridge" for linking mini-public to larger publics.

In France, the seemingly unpromising potential for mini-publics may improve to the degree the centralized state yields to networked governance, as described in chapter 6. It is possible to imagine a consensus conference being networked into a variety of other actors. Such a process happened in Australia in 1999, where the consensus conference on GM foods was original-ly sponsored by the Consumers' Association, endorsed by government de-partments, after some hesitation recognized by anti-GM activists, and influenced the positions taken by the biotechnology industry (Hendriks 2004: ch. 5). Networked governance in France may, however, have a long way to go before these kinds of linkages become possible. In France and the United States alike, subnational levels of government may be more promising locations for mini-publics than national government. The exclusive features of the French state are less rigid at local and regional levels. Mini-publics have actually been sponsored by state and local governments in the United States.

We are now in a position to revisit the kinds of impacts that mini-publics can achieve in the deliberative system in light of an analysis of their experience in practice in three different sorts of states. Table 8.1 summarizes the possi-bilities. As this table illustrates, most of the possibilities that appear to be available in actively inclusive Denmark are not available in the other kinds of state. The bad news is softened to the extent that France and the United States represent relatively pure forms of, respectively, exclusive and passively inclu-sive states. So most states will not exhibit the problems they present to the uptake of deliberative mini-publics in quite such stark fashion. For example, Canada is a passively inclusive state – but less starkly than the United States, which enabled trust-based guidance of public opinion in the case of the referendum following the British Columbia Citizens' Assembly. The United Kingdom is a mixed case with large elements of passive inclusion, but it seems to allow mini-publics being used to legitimate policy. And as already noted, the United States can be different at state and local levels of government, with consequently greater scope for the influence of mini-publics.

Table 8.1  Potential impacts of mini-publics in different kinds of states

|  | Denmark (*actively inclusive*) | France (*exclusive*) | United States (*passively inclusive*) |
|---|---|---|---|
| Actually making policy | No | No | No |
| Taken up in empowered space | Yes | No | No |
| Informing public debate | Yes | No? | Yes |
| Guiding public opinion (trust) | Yes | No | No |
| Market testing policy | Yes | Yes | Yes |
| Legitimating policy | Yes | No | No |
| Confidence building | Yes | Yes | Yes |
| Popular oversight | Yes | No | No |

## CONCLUSION

While some of their enthusiasts would place their preferred design at the center of their hopes for democratic reform, a mini-public in and of itself never can and never should be mistaken for a deliberative democracy. Mini-publics in practice get deployed in very different ways in different political settings, and in all settings they ought to be assessed in terms of how the larger political system affects them – and how they can take effect in the larger system. Not all of their deployments in practice are very salutary from a democratic perspective. It is often very hard for mini-publics to have much impact at all. But any negatives just remind us of the need for vigilance and awareness of larger contexts.

Mini-publics have many attractive features. They provide space and support for deliberating citizens that can otherwise be very hard to find. They have little difficulty in achieving a measure of deliberative authenticity that normally eludes partisan political actors, professional participants in adversarial politics, and relatively neutral administration alike. They show what public opinion might look like if ordinary people had the chance for extensive and informed deliberation. They can have an impact on broader political debates. They provide all kinds of opportunities for social scientists to study the causes, consequences, and processes of deliberation. They highlight challenges that larger deliberative systems must somehow resolve. For all these reasons, deliberative democrats ought to applaud and encourage their spread.

# 9

## Global Politics

Democracy is starting to go global. Formal authority is exercised at the global level through (for example) the rulings of the World Trade Organization (WTO), the decisions of the International Monetary Fund (IMF) imposed on countries experiencing financial crisis, or the content of global agreements covering anything from human rights to climate change. Sometimes, the authority may not be very public but at the same time quite consequential, as in the production of collective decisions by transnational financial networks spanning private and governmental actors. Sometimes, relatively impersonal market forces will constrain the policies that any state can follow. Sometimes, dominant discourses such as market liberalism will reinforce those constraints. Whatever the precise mix of forces, the production of collective outcomes is increasingly a global affair. And if collective choice is global, then democracy must go global too. The only question is how. This chapter argues that the globalization of democracy can most fruitfully be conceptualized in deliberative terms. The focus is on the global and not just the transnational level. Of course, there is plenty of transnational governance that is not global, and some transnational contexts (notably the European Union (EU)) are relatively tractable – and relatively well studied in deliberative terms (e.g., Eriksen and Fossum 2007).

Deliberative democracy is particularly well placed to take on the global challenge, in part because elections do not constitute its sine qua non. It is so much more straightforward to think of global democracy in this way than in the terms of the standard lineup of competitive elections, constitutional specification and separation of powers, sovereign authority, a common legal framework, and binding moments of collective decision. The liberal democratic state does not provide any applicable model for global democracy (and if it did, it would be resisted by much of the world). Global politics may not currently be very deliberative or very democratic, but then the task is to make it more so. This chapter does not, however, attempt to go over all the proposals that have been made on behalf of the basic idea of deliberative democracy in international politics, because there are now several thorough treatments (including Thompson 1999; Dryzek 2000: 115–39; Brunkhorst 2002; Payne and Samhat 2004; Dryzek 2006; Bohman 2007; Young 2007: 145–55; Smith and Brassett 2008). Instead, the present concern with the *frontiers* of deliberative governance means looking less at the basic arguments for global deliberative democracy, more at some of the thornier issues, unresolved challenges, and new ideas.

Now, not all deliberative democrats are convinced that deliberative democracy belongs at the global level. So, for example, Habermas (2006*a*: 143) doubts that the dense solidarity and common civic identity that facilitate national democracy are achievable at the global level. However, experience of deliberation in the context of deep difference (see chapter 7; also Dryzek 2005; O'Flynn 2006) suggests that such shared identity is not necessary for deliberation to occur. And if deliberation is possible in settings where deep difference is present (e.g., international conflicts with a history of violence), it ought to be more straightforward in the many global settings where deep difference (in the form of incompatible assertions of identity) is not so salient. The key here is the generation of a public around a shared issue. Global publics can be found, for example, around the issue of climate change (where the scientists of the Intergovernmental Panel on Climate Change have played a key role), banning or controlling land mines and other weapons, biopiracy, and genetically modified (GM) agriculture. Crawford (2009: 107) points out that international politics may feature substantial communicative action because of the lack of any authoritative center of decision empowered to put an end to talk; joint action therefore necessitates persuasion. In short, communicative action is possible at many levels in global politics, therefore so is deliberation; but can that deliberation be democratic?

The scene for this chapter is set by a brief look at criticisms of global deliberative democracy alleging its failure to provide a strategy that is at once feasible and significant enough to make a difference. In constructing a response to the skeptics, the consequential roles that governance networks and the engagement of discourses can play in producing global outcomes are then stressed. If discursive hegemony is increasingly yielding to global contestation of discourses, the prospects for a global discursive democracy grounded in the engagement of discourses in public spheres begin to look better, though much turns on the conditions of this engagement. This discussion can be connected to the idea of global deliberative systems, building on the framework for the mapping and evaluation of such systems sketched in chapter 1. The global governance of climate change provides an illustration of how even when deliberative capacity is currently deficient, it is still both possible to analyze global politics in these terms, and seek deliberative improvement. The ideas about discursive legitimacy, meta-consensus, and discursive representation developed in earlier chapters all prove to be especially applicable to thinking about the deliberative capacity of global politics. Indeed, they prove in some ways more at home here than in the politics of states. There even turns out to be a place for mini-publics in global politics – as focal points for the construction of broader deliberative interactions, and as alternatives to problematic proposals for global parliaments.

## SKEPTICS

Scheuerman (2006, 2007) charges transnational deliberative democracy (especially to the degree it is inspired by Habermas's ideas) with oscillating between two indefensible extremes. One is radical and utopian, conjuring up all kinds of global institutions that would exercise benign authority (Scheuerman refers especially to Held (1995), who is not a deliberative democrat but has been influenced by Habermas's thinking about deliberation). The other extreme is, in Scheuerman's view, excessively defensive, pinning its entire hopes on global civil society in the face of recalcitrant global and national institutions that cannot be reformed (he refers to Bohman and Dryzek). Scheuerman (2006: 94) believes that abandoning the "commanding heights of decision making" means abandoning democracy. He himself offers no middle way between the two extremes (indeed, he offers no advice at all). However, his critique is a useful starting point.[1]

How then ought we to think about the commanding heights? The first problem we face is that there are in fact few tangible commanding heights in the existing global system whose democratization could be targeted. There are heights in the form of global organizations like the United Nations (UN), WTO, and World Bank, but they are not especially commanding. Rather, they are embedded within broader regimes and processes. Authoritative government resembling that of the sovereign state hardly exists at the level of the global system. While the IMF and World Bank exercise influence that is confined mostly to states that are in economic trouble, poor, or both, the WTO has a broader remit. But even the WTO is in large measure a creature of the states that built it and belong to it. It has a small staff, and can only take on a small proportion of trade disputes. Moreover, it relies on states to enforce its

---

[1] Unlike Kuper's critique of transnational deliberative democracy (2004: 47–74), which actually says little about anything transnational, and turns out to be just another philosophical critique of the possibility of deliberation involving large numbers of people; see chapter 2 for a solution to this problem.

decisions through trade sanctions against those that violate WTO rulings. In the end it is states that remain the dominant repositories of formal authority in global affairs. A prescription to democratize the commanding heights might therefore reduce to a prescription to democratize states. Yet, states that are democratic internally are quite capable of acting in coercive and authoritarian fashion in their international dealings. About all that can be said for them is that they do not go to war with each other (the "democratic peace" thesis – though really all this says is that Western liberal democratic states do not go to war with one another). Beyond that, democratic states do little for democratization of the global system, and we could not be sure that more deliberatively democratic states would do much better for the global system.

"Commanding heights" is a misleading metaphor. The global system may not actually have much in the way of commanding heights. Rather, its "fundamental institutions" (Reus-Smit 1999) are actually shared understandings about proper practice (such as diplomacy or multilateral negotiation). These fundamental institutions in turn condition decentralized forms of governance very different from the hierarchical image of government within the state. These forms of governance constitute very consequential sources of order that can be deliberatively evaluated – and democratized. Here, it is possible to begin with two related sources: *governance networks* and *discourses*. They are related because, especially in international affairs, governance networks can be coordinated and stabilized by discourses (though as will be seen, if done by a single discourse this is generally to their democratic detriment). How then might transnational governance networks be democratized?

## GLOBAL GOVERNANCE NETWORKS AND THEIR DISCOURSES

In chapter 6, it was pointed out that networks challenge democracy because they seem to dissolve public authority and render the exercise of power less visible. Transnational networks are actually less problematic in these terms than those within states because in the international system there is so little concentrated authority to disperse to begin with, and such concentrated authority as does currently exist is not at all democratic. Transnational networks can, however, feature substantial inequality in the distribution of power, so in this sense they are democratically problematic. Chapter 6 showed that the informal qualities of governance networks means they elude liberal constitutionalist conceptions of democracy. There it was suggested that thinking about the democratization of networks has to be post-Westphalian, post-liberal, and post-electoral. Yet because they are polycentric and coord-inated by the medium of language, networks ought to be amenable to deliberative democratization. Networks can be more or less inclusive, and more or less deliberative.

In chapter 6, it was suggested that the first normative principle for the deliberative democratization of networks is contestatory. A network should contain internal differentiation, especially when it comes to something in the way of public space at a critical distance from empowered space. The second normative principle is discursive representation, to ensure that a network is not dominated by a single discourse. A third is meta-consensus: if a network is not dominated by a single discourse, then productive interchange requires some degree of discursive meta-consensus. These conclusions apply quite straightforwardly to transnational and global networks.

Just about everything that is democratically deficient in existing transna-tional networked governance is illustrated by financial networks prior to the global financial crisis of 2007–2008. The global financial system can, as Castells (1996) points out, be interpreted as an interlocking set of networks. Those networks were dominated by a single discourse, that of market liberal-ism, organized around a core postulate of efficient markets. Competitive markets, especially capital and financial markets, were not supposed to have endogenous sources of systemic failure. As financial instruments and their associated networks became ever more complex and ever more beyond the reach of regulatory authority – partly because they were beyond the reach of anyone's understanding, and if something cannot be understood it cannot easily be regulated – this faith continued to underpin a collective judgment that nothing systemic could go wrong. There was no contestation from within the network. The usual sources of contestation in transnational politics – media and social movements – were conspicuously absent. The financial media acted as little more than cheerleaders for the dominant discourse. Social movements might have been interested in challenging the justice of global finance, and environmentalists still criticized the unregulated econom-ic growth that it spawned. But no movement contested the basic claims to efficiency and stability of the financial system itself, and so none of the critical discourses that did exist at a distance made the slightest difference to the way global financial networks worked.

The dominant discourse of market liberalism was eventually challenged not by any counter-discourse, but by the force of events as bad loans and the financial instruments built upon them precipitated a cascade of bankruptcy. In the wake of the crisis, the response involved the emergence of a regulatory counter-discourse, and the resurrection of old state-centric Keynesian ideas.

But the 2008 crisis did not lead to the establishment of any "commanding heights" global institution, such as a regulatory authority. Indeed, it led to no formal global institution building at all (beyond a slightly enhanced role for the IMF), let alone the democratization of any such formal institutions. Instead, regulation and Keynesian deficit spending were left to states to organize and implement (though key states did consult with one another on what to do). The network form survived the crisis, for better or for worse. However, the global governance network did gain a degree of differentiation and contestation that was missing before. In place of echoes and cheerleading, there emerged a critical public sphere that for a while caught the attention of global publics, now disgusted with the mendacity and greed of bankers. However limited, the birth of contestation in global financial networks was at least a baby step on the road to global democratization. Other areas of global politics have featured contestation for some time. Indeed, there may be a secular trend toward greater contestation, for reasons that can now be examined.

## HEGEMONY YIELDS TO CONTESTATION IN GLOBAL POLITICS

Global finance, though of course massively consequential in itself, may actually be an outlier when it comes to the degree of discursive hegemony in global affairs. Even within the global political economy, market liberalism did not go unchallenged prior to the 2007–2008 crisis. In the wake of the Asian financial crisis of 1997 that seemed to mark the demise of a cooperative Confucian capitalism and its associated discourse (Hall 2003), market liberalism in the form of the "Washington Consensus" for a while seemed hegemonic and triumphant in the international political economy. But beginning with the protests in Seattle in 1999, a counter-discourse of antiglobalization or global justice emerged from a variety of local struggles against the effects of market recipes. Ridiculed at first, this discourse eventually made itself felt within international economic institutions (Stiglitz 2002). What the events of 2007–2008 clarified was that this counter-discourse and the kinds of claims it made did not reach the core of global financial networks. And the power of those networks is ultimately much greater than that exercised by global organizations like the World Bank that were eventually reached by the antiglobalization discourse. The antiglobalization counter-discourse did, however, emphasize only non-efficiency values, such as social justice and environmental conservation, leaving the core economic efficiency claims of market liberalism unchallenged.

Looking beyond the international political economy, there appears to be a more general shift from hegemony to contestation in the configuration of discourses (Dryzek 2006: 8–19). International security was once dominated by a realist discourse that treated international politics as a Hobbesian anarchy at the edge of violence where the first concern of states had to be self-help and maximization of their relative power in relation to other states. As Wendt (1992) points out, "anarchy is what states make of it" – and so long as policy makers shared a realist understanding, it became the dominant reality of the system they both confronted and constituted. Eventually, challengers to this understanding came thick and fast: from liberal builders of cooperative international institutions, from Mikhail Gorbachev's "new thinking" in the 1980s, from proponents of a "democratic peace" that (contra realism) stressed the importance of internal factors in determining how a state behaved toward other states (Russett and Oneal 2001), and from idealistic neoconservatives in the United States who started a war in Iraq in 2003 that horrified realists. The demise of neoconservatism led to further discursive proliferation. So, for example, a "security first" U.S. foreign policy (Etzioni 2007) is based on the idea of making alliances with "illiberal moderates" throughout the world; not exactly a return of realism, because it too believes in the internal characteristics of state matters.

An era of unchallenged dominance of a rights discourse in international humanitarian affairs began in 1948 with the adoption by the United Nations of the Universal Declaration of Human Rights. Even when countries violated the rights of their own peoples, they paid lip service to the basic idea of human rights. Eventually, human rights came under challenge from a communitarian "Asian values" discourse, which characterized individual rights as a Western construct. After 2001, the West's commitment to rights discourse was weakened by the rise of a discourse of counterterror that prioritized the prevention of terrorism over the protection of rights. Counterterror was enthusiastically adopted by governments around the world who could brand their own insurgents as terrorists. It also further undermined the discourse of sovereignty, for it legitimated military intervention in states claimed to be harboring or supporting terrorists.

Until the late 1960s, the global environment barely registered as a matter of concern. A discourse of limits and survival that pervaded global environmental affairs in the 1970s (epitomized in the best-selling *Limits to Growth*; Meadows et al. 1974) gave way in the 1980s to sustainable development. However, the limits discourse never went away, and made a comeback in connection with climate change. It has been joined by a resurgent industrialism that denies ecological limits altogether, radical green discourses, and those that stress environmental justice.

The 1990s saw a resurgence of the politics of identity on the international stage, and identities are a product of discourses. The identities could be national, religious, or even in Huntington's terms (1996) "civilizational."

All these movements from hegemony to contestation of discourses in global politics are not a matter of coincidence. They stem from what Beck, Giddens, and Lash (1994) call "de-traditionalization." Traditions lose their authority as people become increasingly aware of alternative ways of experiencing the world. Reflexive modernization involves the rise of discourses (such as antiglobalization or sustainability) that challenge previously ingrained discourses. Reflexive traditionalization entails a retreat into religious fundamentalism, ethnic or national identity, or the comfort of counterterror (Dryzek 2006: 19–21). International relations scholars who have recognized the importance of discourses have mostly not caught up with these sorts of possibilities. These scholars tend to adopt a hard-line interpretation of Michel Foucault's orientation to discourses, treating them mostly as hegemonic sources of oppression (e.g., Walker 1993). Though styling themselves dissidents within international relations theory, such scholars actually perpetuate the long-standing lack of concern with democracy that pervades the field of international relations.[2] It is contending discourses that provide the grist for global discursive democracy.

## GLOBAL DISCURSIVE DEMOCRACY

In earlier chapters much was said about the importance for deliberative democracy of the contestation and engagement of discourses in public space (though of course a lot depends on the conditions of that engagement). This idea applies quite straightforwardly to global politics, which as we have seen can feature multiple discourses when it comes to any particular issue.

The main challenge when it comes to global politics is what to make of the general absence of decisive governmental authority at the system level. In part, this shifts the attention to transnational governance networks of the sort described in the previous section. Sometimes, such networks are present and consequential; sometimes, they are absent or weak.

---

[2] That lack of concern is now being corrected, with special issues of mainstream journals *Millennium* (2009) and *Review of International Studies* (2010) devoted to transnational democracy.

In the absence of central government authority and networks, a large part of the work of coordination of collective choices is done by discourses themselves – and by their relative weight as revealed in their contestation and engagement. The work that discourses do is not "defensive" in relation to formal authority (because often there is little in the way of formal authority to defend against, except that exercised by and within states). Rather, it is highly consequential. Much turns, for example, on the outcomes of engagement between market liberalism and sustainable development in international environmental affairs; and much depends too on how the discourse of sustainable development itself unfolds over time. Over time, sustainable development has been moved in a direction more friendly to business and relatively conventional notions of economic growth. Environmental movement activists have sometimes had to fight against this kind of transformation of the discourse, though some moderate environmentalists have embraced it.

Discursive contests are played out in global public space. It matters enormously whether or not such contests are influenced by corporate public relations machines, the short attention spans of tabloid journalism, more responsible journalism, the weighty pronouncements of intergovernmental bodies, the interventions of celebrity advocates of various kinds, civil society activism, the heavy hand of authoritarian governments, the lighter touch of states that try to be good global citizens, spin doctors, or the veiled threats of superpowers. Often, what goes on falls far short of any deliberative ideal.

These kinds of processes involving the engagement of discourses and their impact upon the exercise of political authority can be evaluated in terms of advance or retreat on three basic democratic criteria: scope, franchise, and authenticity (Dryzek 1996a: 4–9). An advance in scope means an issue previously off-limits to any semblance of popular control becomes recognized as a matter for collective political judgment; this will probably not happen without the emergence of counter-discourses to challenge previously hegemonic discourses. So, global financial crisis in 2007–2008 enabled the scope of democracy to be extended to areas of finance previously off-limits because they were dominated by hegemonic market liberal discourse. Franchise refers to the effective number of participants joining in control over collective decisions, in this case via their participation in the engagement of discourses. Historically, franchise meant the right to vote, but the basic idea can travel to contexts where voting is not available. So, for example, if the World Bank starts consulting nongovernmental organizations (NGOs) on its decisions, that is an increase in franchise (however small), especially if the NGOs are themselves in touch with larger constituencies. Authenticity is the degree to which control is substantive rather than symbolic, exercised by competent and reflective actors. Clearly, authenticity is closely connected to core deliberative concerns, though deliberative democrats also want deliberation to be inclusive (franchise) and consequential (scope).

The life and times of economic globalization in the decade after the beginnings of antiglobalization protests at Seattle in 1999 reveals advance on all three of these criteria. The protests brought a set of economic issues (notably international trade) out of technical authority and onto a public agenda, so scope increased (Stiglitz 2002). Social movements mobilized categories of people who previously did not have a voice, so effective franchise expanded. Deliberative authenticity for its part was advanced initially by the need for activists to negotiate their contradictory concerns (such as protecting workers in wealthy countries versus promoting the interests of developing countries and their workers). The discursive hegemony of market liberalism was then challenged by a counter-discourse of global justice, which led to deliberative engagements where none had previously existed.

## GLOBAL DELIBERATIVE SYSTEM: AN ILLUSTRATION FROM CLIMATE CHANGE

The engagement of discourses in global public spheres can be connected to the defining elements of a deliberative system introduced in chapter 1: public space, empowered space, transmission from public to empowered space, accountability of empowered to public space, meta-deliberation, and decisiveness. Empowered space need not feature state-like public authority – and that absence of course is the condition of global politics. Currently, the global polity features putatively deliberative systems that are mostly issue specific, concerning (for example) refugees, trade, finance, climate change, control of nuclear weapons proliferation, and biodiversity protection. Of course, these systems are not necessarily very deliberative in practice, but any more precise judgment here is a matter for empirical investigation. All are potentially deliberative to the degree they feature public space, empowered space, transmission from public space to empowered space, and some degree of accountability of empowered space to public space (however small).

Consider, for example, the global governance of climate change. This case is an extremely complex one, and the following account is not meant to be definitive – especially in the absence of requisite empirical studies (which are, however, under way at the time of writing). Public space on this issue is populated by a number of discourses. They include, most prominently, the following. A discourse of *ecological limits* is held by many of the natural scientists active on climate issues, who point to the degree to which the planet's ecosystems are stressed by climate change. A discourse of *skepticism* advanced mostly by right-wing journalists, some large energy corporations, and a few dissident scientists in their pay refuses to recognize the existence of anthropogenic climate change. *Promethean* discourse accepts that there can be problems and ecological scarcities, but believes that overall ecological limits vanish in the face of human ingenuity (especially when markets harness that ingenuity to overcome scarcities). *Climate justice* stresses the distributive aspects of climate change, highlighting the claims of developing countries against the wealthy countries that built their own economies on fossil fuel exploitation, but now seek to deny poorer countries that option. Climate justice in addition highlights the claims of those who suffer most from climate change (e.g., inhabitants of low-lying island states, or marginal agricultural regions) against those who caused it. This discourse can also encompass the claims of those likely to be hurt by mitigation practices (e.g., forest dwellers displaced by Reducing Emissions from Deforestation and Degradation schemes). *Energy security* involves linking climate issues to the need to reduce dependence on imported oil from unstable parts of the world. This discourse is prominent in the United States. *Ecological modernization* is a relatively optimistic discourse that sees economic growth and environmental protection as mutually reinforcing, provided the growth is of the right kind: "pollution prevention pays," as a popular slogan puts it. *Radical transformation* seeks structural change of the market liberal international political economy, with very different patters of production and consumption resulting.

These discourses among others populate public space, though not always in salutary fashion. Media treatment is often sensationalist, featuring dying polar bears rather than chronic ecosystem change. Skeptics can be subject to personal attack (though the source of their funding is a legitimate target, for it affects judgments about their *ethos* – see chapter 4). Climate activists can also suffer attack. Arguments for and against particular policy instruments can be suppressed (so, for example, in Australia, the Commonwealth Scientific and Industrial Research Organisation suppresses publication of papers that criticize Australian government policy). Corporate interests can bend ecological modernization to the point where policies such as emissions trading seem mostly designed to protect the profits of existing polluters and the existing energy mix they represent. However, there are some positives. Unlike the case of global finance before the crash of 2007–2008, there is no domination by a single discourse. Particular discourses rise and fall. The rise of climate justice discourse has been accompanied by the more effective inclusion of a variety of previously marginalized voices. The skeptical discourse still exists, but the days when some large energy corporations could pretend environmental concern through fronts such as the Global Climate Coalition (disbanded in 2002) while promulgating and financing skepticism are now probably gone. The contestation of discourses in public space is engaged by many competent and critical actors. The deliberative system on climate change has failures – but public space is not where they are concentrated.

It is less easy to discern much in the way of deliberative authenticity in empowered space. The obvious place to start would be with international negotiations, beginning at Kyoto in 1997 and continuing with various meetings under the heading of the United Nations Framework Convention on Climate Change (UNFCCC), culminating in the Conference of the Parties in Copenhagen in 2009. Such negotiations feature plenty of bargaining, as positions are stated, restated, and sometimes marginally refined. They probably do not feature much in the way of making of threats (which are more the currency of issues relating to security, or to enforce compliance with international economic agreements).

Now, communicative action and so deliberation are possible in international negotiations, even when tough issues of sovereignty and security loom large. That is, participants in negotiations do not just have to state positions, offer inducements, or make threats to get others to change their positions. Instead, they can issue warnings about what will happen if a particular path is not followed, and argue in terms of values that the other side may recognize. Risse (2000) points to many examples of communicative action, including negotiations between the United States, Germany, NATO, and the Soviet Union over German reunification in 1989. On Risse's account, Gorbachev and the Soviet negotiators were eventually persuaded that a unified Germany within NATO was no real threat, and a better idea than maintaining Soviet troops in a hostile Germany.

The degree to which communicative action exists in global negotiations on the climate change issue, and the relative weight of bargaining and arguing in those negotiations, are matters for further empirical investigation. Arguments themselves may proceed in terms that serve a state's interests. So it would be no surprise to hear a negotiator from a developing country deploy the language of climate justice, or from a country such as New Zealand or Norway rich in hydropower to emphasize the need for the world to switch to renewable energy. But even if that is how arguments start, what Elster (1998a: 12) calls the "civilizing force of hypocrisy" can make itself felt, as negotiators come to believe in the principles they advance, and induce other negotiators to state *their* positions in terms of more general principles.

The UNFCCC negotiations do not exhaust empowered space in the global governance of climate change. However, unlike (for example) international trade, there is no global organization with any remit for handling the climate change issue. There is a WTO with teeth; there is no World Environment Organization (still less environmental parallels to the World Bank and IMF). In the absence of any such authorities, empowered space is constituted mainly and predominantly by states. It is states that choose whether or not to adopt policies to reach targets agreed under international negotiations. In the case of the Kyoto protocol (covering only developed states), most of them chose not to adopt such policies, even if they ratified the protocol. Many of these states came nowhere near meeting the targets they agreed to in Kyoto, and most do not feature enough in the way of internal deliberation to make this shortfall seem to be much of a problem. There is no mechanism at all to punish them for their lack of compliance. Conceivably, however, a global deliberative system could exist in which the only actors in empowered space were states. This would mean that all deliberative and democratic transnational and global interaction would be confined to the public space of global civil society.

Transmission ought to have its source in global civil society, and its targets in international negotiations and states. Certainly, NGOs, scientists, and other activists try to secure transmission (and are much in evidence at UNFCCC negotiations). Whether they succeed or not is another question entirely. Transmission has succeeded at least to the extent of getting the climate change issue to the top of global and national policy agendas. This happened through largely deliberative means: key political actors in empowered space were persuaded. Getting the issue onto the agenda may be about the limit of deliberative transmission, but again more detailed empirical investigation is necessary.

Accountability is in questionable shape too. But the first thing to notice is that there is some degree of deliberative accountability, as governments try to give an account of the positions they adopt and the reasons for them. This can apply even to inaction: so when President George W. Bush announced the United States' withdrawal from the Kyoto protocol, he did so through explicit reference to the priority of economic over environmental values. What was missing in this case was transnational accountability, because Bush couched the issue solely in terms of the health of the U.S. economy. This illustrates a more general point: governments may be held to account by their own publics, but accountability that crosses national boundaries is very weak, and so in terms of the global deliberative system accountability is highly problematic.

Contemplation of the global governance of climate change may reveal a deliberative system in disrepair, especially when it comes to empowered space and accountability. That negative judgment can be tempered by recognition of the fact that it was once in much worse repair. There was once a time when energy companies and others financing specious science and sham concern could exert considerable weight in public space; that problem seems to be over with the demise of the Global Climate Coalition. And Kyoto, for all its problems, was at least an advance on what preceded it; because before Kyoto, there were no serious negotiations to act as a focal point for a global deliberative system. Revisiting the three democratization criteria of scope, franchise, and authenticity discussed earlier: Kyoto signaled that the climate change issue was a matter for common global concern, and so scope expanded. Franchise is a bit more problematic, but there has been some enfranchisement of states under particular threat (such as Tuvalu), climate scientists, and perhaps NGOs, now welcomed into the deliberative system. Authenticity has advanced in public space – but remains highly problematic in empowered space, with little discernible advance.

Any discernible advances are, however, limited in their significance and durability by the lack of any capacity for *meta-deliberation* in the global politics of climate change. Of the enormous quantities of effort that go into the global politics of climate change, hardly any addresses the global governance structure itself – let alone the deliberative qualities of that structure. All actors complain of the painful and prolonged character of international negotiations (which, remarkably, proceed in the absence of a formal decision rule), and the many difficulties that seem to inhibit progress. But few contemplate how the system itself might be different. Indeed, the UNFCCC series of negotiations create a kind of bubble: those inside the bubble, be they negotiators, NGOs trying to influence the content of proposals, scientists, journalists, or corporate lobbyists, come to believe that what goes on inside the bubble is all that matters. There are some extremely obvious improvements that deliberative democrats could suggest. First of all, why not conduct international negotiations along lines that have been very well established in the practice of conflict resolution (Susskind 2006) and designed deliberative forums? Such introduction could be done on a piecemeal basis, for example, in preparatory meetings leading up to the main negotiations.

Failure in meta-deliberation is compounded by failure in *decisiveness* of the deliberative system. Agreements that are negotiated rely on the voluntary actions of states for their implementation, which (as the Kyoto experience illustrates) is frequently not forthcoming. And the policy actions taken by states often respond in large measure to the weight of lobbying by powerful economic interests. Thus, emissions trading schemes are generally well stocked with exemptions or free permits for the biggest and most powerful emitters of greenhouse gases. Deliberative advances in public space may actually displace failure into empowered space. So energy corporations that have failed when it comes to sponsorship of a discourse of skepticism may simply turn to twisting the arms of governments, meaning the deliberative system as a whole loses decisiveness.

## THE FOUNDATIONS OF DELIBERATIVE GLOBAL GOVERNANCE

The main theoretical point of this discussion of climate change is to show that the basic idea of deliberative capacity and its operationalization in terms of the requirements of a deliberative system can be applied fruitfully to global politics – even in the absence of any binding public authority at the system level. What this means is that all the foundational concepts of deliberative democracy developed in earlier chapters can also be applied at this level.

To begin with *legitimacy*, the account of discursive legitimacy outlined in chapter 2 emphasized the resonance of collective outcomes with the provisional outcome of the engagement of discourses in the public sphere, to the degree such engagement is composed of reflective and competent actors. This conceptualization actually fits very well in the global system, far better than most alternative conceptions of democratic legitimacy, which are tied to a constitutional structure and set of accepted rules that do not exist at the global level.

The degree of diversity that global politics features, combined with the lack of formal institutionalization at the system level, means that *meta-consensus* of the kinds developed in chapter 5 is especially urgent (as noted earlier in the discussion of global networks). Meta-consensus is necessary to make collective choice more tractable. Constitutional rules can perform a similar function (by ruling in and out some kinds of evidence, some kinds of values, some kinds of options, some dimensions of collective choice), but such rules are generally not available in global politics. In their absence, meta-consensus generated by deliberative means is especially necessary. When it comes to conflicts between states and especially "the clash of civilizations," discursive meta-consensus is vital. What Huntington (1996) calls "civilizational" identities are, like any identity, the product of discourses. And if these particular discourses are not to embark on some kind of struggle to the death, discursive meta-consensus is necessary.

It was also argued in chapter 5 that the conditions under which meta-consensus is generated matter enormously, which means being especially wary of the generation of meta-consensus through symbolic distortion of various kinds. Such distortions are no less prevalent in global politics than elsewhere. The efforts of energy corporations and their allies to keep a discourse of denial in a global discursive meta-consensus were noted earlier. These efforts proceeded largely through deployment of public relations and the financing of studies whose skeptical conclusions were predetermined.

*Rhetoric* is likely to play a large part in any global deliberative system to the degree these systems are made up of large numbers of actors coming from very different kinds of backgrounds. In chapter 4, the role of rhetoric in bridging the perspectives of differently situated actors was highlighted. In global affairs, rhetoric is likely to be especially important in enabling transmission from public space to empowered space. And judgments about the *ethos* of speakers are likely to be especially important if their word is to be taken on technically complex global issues such as climate change. Several of the examples of the way rhetoric can be deployed in order to advance deliberative systems in chapter 4 were international in character. Gorbachev's rhetoric concerning a "common European home" helped create an international deliberative system in Europe in the late 1980s. One example in chapter 4 was global: the case of "ozone hole" rhetoric leading to the creation of an effective deliberative system in governance for the control of ozone-depleting chemicals. On the negative side, George W. Bush's rhetoric in the "war on terror" diminished the prospects for a global deliberative system to deal with terrorism and associated security issues.

*Discursive representation* too works particularly well at the global level. Representing discourses in transnational political action is actually more straightforward than representing persons (especially in the absence of elections). Indeed, it is already happening. In recent years, even economistic global institutions such as the World Bank and (begrudgingly) the IMF have begun programs of outreach to global civil society, meaning accountability no longer runs strictly to states. Who elects the NGOs? Nobody. Is there an identifiable constituency or category of people with which each NGO is associated, and to which it is accountable? Not usually. International relations scholars have started to think about accountability (Grant and Keohane 2005), albeit mainly in terms of how sanctions can be levied on advocates, rather than discursive accountability as characterized in chapter 3 (defined as continuing to communicate in terms that make sense in the discourse that is being represented). NGOs pushing for human rights, fair trade, sustainable development, demilitarization, transparency, and so forth, may, however, best be thought of as representatives of particular discourses in international politics. Is the world any more democratic for their activities? Clearly yes: the international governmental institutions they target now have to justify their activities in light of a variety of discourses, whereas previously they either felt no need to justify at all, or did so in narrowly economistic and administrative terms. Thus, the idea of discursive representation provides democratic validation for the activities of NGOs and other transnational activists.

This kind of transnational discursive representation is currently informal in character, but more formal representation can be imagined. Thompson (1999) suggests that cross-border policy impacts can be brought into democratic accountability by the device of a "tribune for noncitizens." Such a tribune could not easily be elected – the appropriate electorate would be dispersed and extraordinarily hard to organize. But for particular policy issues, it would be possible to identify relevant extra-national or transnational discourses, and identify a good representative for them. For example, there exists a very well-defined global discourse of sustainable development. Perhaps global sustainability tribunes could be identified to represent this discourse in particular national governments (states remain the most important actors in empowered space when it comes to global environmental affairs). The problem of course is that those representatives would be least welcome where they were needed most. One can imagine them being welcomed by countries that are exemplary international citizens (Sweden), but resisted by countries that are poor international citizens, those that subscribe to hardline notions of sovereignty, superpowers, and rogue states.

For most states, transnational discursive representation will probably have to be informal in any foreseeable future, constituted mostly by NGOs and networks of political activists in transnational public spheres exerting pressure. It is easier to envisage more formal Chambers of Discourses established in association with international organizations. Organizations such as the WTO, IMF, and World Bank have (as already noted) accepted the need to legitimate their activities beyond the states that are their members, funders, or clients. Constituting formal Chambers of Discourses would be one very public way of discharging this obligation. Chapter 3 canvassed the possibility of a formal "Chamber of Discourses" that started with more or less randomly selected citizens (selecting further on the basis of identification with particular discourses), and I did of course address possible roles for mini-publics in larger systems in chapter 8. Could such mini-publics play any part in global politics?

## MINI-PUBLICS IN THE GLOBAL SYSTEM

Among the many roles that mini-publics can play is that of a focal point for deliberative interaction that extends to actors beyond the citizen participants in the forum itself. This kind of effect could also exist for transnational mini-publics. To date, a few such forums have been held. Deliberative polls have been carried out involving all the nations of the EU, entailing translation between many different languages (notably the EUROPOLIS deliberative poll in 2009). No global mini-public has yet been held.

When global democrats turn to thinking about formal institutions at the system level, what they normally have in mind is an aspiration for some kind of elected assembly, called by Falk and Strauss (2001) a "popularly elected global assembly." The Campaign for a United Nations Parliamentary Assembly (UNPA) now has the support of thousands of political leaders from around the world (including former UN Secretary-General Boutros Boutros-Ghali) and has been endorsed by the European Parliament and the parliaments of several countries (http://en.unpacampaign.org). The proponents of UNPA accept that global elections are unlikely in any near future, and advocate a number of interim measures. These measures can involve a strengthened UN General Assembly with more formal powers. The problem with any interim measure is that it would have somehow to involve authoritarian states that resist national elections. These states might well agree to be involved – but the major democratic cost is that the Parliamentary Assembly would then include a large number of appointees of authoritarian governments. Proponents of UNPA get themselves into all kinds of tangles as they try to navigate this problem.

Global mini-publics are both more feasible and less problematic in democratic terms than the quasi-elected quasi-legislatures that are proposed by the Campaign for UNPA and others. Being global, the term "mini-public" does not sound quite right, so better to use the term "Deliberative Global Citizens' Assembly" (DGCA). Such a deliberative forum would in all likelihood do better than any body mixing directly elected representatives and state appointees because it would not be bedeviled by the short time horizons of elected politicians, the preoccupation of the political parties who would field candidates or select representatives with national concerns and, when it comes to international forums, advancing only the national interest. Randomly selected citizens would be in the DGCA as citizens of the world, and so be in a position to attend seriously to global public goods – not just to advance their own national interest. Experience of existing mini-publics shows that long-term considerations and public goods are exactly the sorts of values that tend to come to the fore through the process of citizen deliberation.

Proponents of a UN Parliament believe that it would become a focal point for political interaction – indeed, if it did not, it would be a failure. For Falk and Strauss (2001: 217–18), this interaction would be constituted by lobbying by NGOs, corporations, national governments, and others. But being composed of a mix of elected politicians and appointees of authoritarian governments, such an assembly would not be well placed to act as a focal point for more deliberative interaction. Its participants would all have a long history of associating politics with bargaining, strategizing, and command. In contrast, a DGCA would be deliberative in its internal workings, because, like any mini-public, it would be designed from the outset with that in mind. Thus, all actors coming to it from the outside would have to engage it in deliberative fashion. Lobbying in particular would have no place.

In addition, any DGCA need not look anything like a general purpose legislature, and could instead be issue specific (focusing perhaps on climate change or international finance). Thus, it would be much easier to introduce in experimental and piecemeal fashion than something like UNPA. It would be less likely to arouse the ire of the governments of authoritarian states because it would involve random selection of citizen participants and not nationally organized elections. While it has absolutely no interest at all in competitive national elections, the Chinese Communist Party hierarchy has been willing to experiment with deliberative forums involving citizen participation (see chapter 7). Equally important, a DGCA could involve less opposition from the United States. The UNPA web site lists endorsements from thousands of prominent leaders around the globe – but not a single member of the U.S. Congress appears on the list, indeed not a single mainstream U.S. politician. That is because it is the accepted view in the United States that there can be no authority higher than that established in the U.S. Constitution. The UNPA, with its aspiration to be directly elected, looks like a direct challenge to the elected institutions of U.S. national government. A DGCA would look like a completely different entity altogether, making no obvious challenge. As pointed out in chapter 8, mini-publics are unfamiliar in U.S. federal government, but that lack of familiarity does not betoken any hostility.

Of course, a DGCA would present some logistical challenges, concerning for example, how to organize deliberation in a multilingual and multicultural setting. But these are all problems that have been confronted in existing mini-publics, so there is a wealth of experience to draw upon. Mini-publics that have involved a majority of participants living in poverty in developing countries have yielded successful deliberation (e.g., citizens' juries on the issue of GM foods held in Mali in Africa and Andhra Pradesh in India in

2001), so they are not just institutions that suit wealthy liberal democracies. (More details on exactly how a DGCA would improve upon models for a global parliament that have electoral democracy in mind can be found in Dryzek, Bächtiger, and Milewicz (2009).)

## CONCLUSION

Deliberative democracy is well placed to go global, though the terms in which it does so mean leaving behind many of the taken-for-granted features of democracy within states. In particular, the electoral aspects of democracy have to take a backseat. It is possible nevertheless to think in terms of global deliberative systems. This is, indeed, where deliberative democracy must prove itself, for many of the toughest political challenges facing the world are going to require coordinated global action. To be legitimate – and to be effective – that action needs to be democratized. The only question is how. The deliberative path is both more feasible and more attractive than currently competing proposals.

# Part IV

# Conclusion

# 10

## Integrated Foundations and Long Frontiers

This book has, among other things, celebrated the ever-expanding reach of deliberative democracy. That does not mean applauding absolutely everything that has been done under the deliberative heading. An enterprise that spans political theory, empirical social science, practical applications, a reform movement, and political advocacy on its behalf that has become so big, so quickly is inevitably going to experience growing pains. Some critics have also made some telling points that require response (though other critics have missed the point by working with false and/or outdated stereotypes of deliberative democracy).

Now, one kind of growth, and one associated set of internal disputes, would begin from a common and shared core or foundation, such that disputes come only in the way the foundation is built upon. The field of deliberative democracy is not quite like this, and that is simply because it deals with political questions, around which contestation should properly occur. The foundations cannot then be taken for granted, but instead need to be worked upon. That was the task of Part II of this book. The chapters in Part II cannot claim to have settled the shape of the foundations of deliberative governance once and for all. Again the political aspects of the enterprise mean that agreement on those foundations would not be desirable. If it did happen, it would be a sign either of stagnation, or suppression of alternative understandings (of the sort we see, for example, in the discipline of economics). But it is still possible for foundations to be more or less secure, and the intention in Part II was to help put the field on a more secure footing.

### INTEGRATED FOUNDATIONS

Part II addressed core questions concerning legitimacy, representation, communication, pluralism, and consensus. While these topics do not necessarily sum to a comprehensive set of requirements for any arena of political theory and practice, the accounts of them in chapters 2–5 were intended to do more than simply generate and survey a disparate set of considerations. Instead, they fit together in a coherent whole, as follows.

Chapter 2 began by addressing the thorny question of how deliberative legitimacy can be achieved as the scale of politics increases, such that not all those affected by a collective decision can participate in direct simultaneous interpersonal deliberation about the content of the collective decision in question – still less in deliberation that is consequential in affecting the content of the decision. It was concluded that legitimacy in such conditions can be sought in the resonance of collective choices with public opinion, characterized as the provisional outcome of the engagement of discourses in public space as transmitted to public authority in empowered space. The vocabulary here locates this notion of legitimacy in the logical requirements of a deliberative system as sketched in chapter 1 (public space, empowered space, transmission from public to empowered space, accountability of empowered to public space, meta-deliberation, and decisiveness). Discursive legitimacy is achieved to the degree engagement and contestation are joined by a broad variety of competent actors.

This formulation of legitimacy remains imprecise without some way to identify relevant discourses in particular situations, and to figure out how these discourses can and should be represented. The account of discursive representation developed in chapter 3 meets this need. But discursive representation is not just a necessary complement to the theory of legitimacy in deliberative democracy. It is also a powerful and morally defensible account of representation in its own right, grounded in a subtle conceptualization of the way individuals are in part constituted by the discourses they engage. Aside from being well suited to a world experiencing a proliferation of representation claims, discursive representation also offers a very practical program of political innovation. This innovation could come in the form of a "Chamber of Discourses" that could conceivably take its place in the formal architecture of political systems – alongside more informal processes of discursive representation. Chapter 3 also showed how these informal sorts of discursive representation already exist in the generation and transmission of public opinion to public authority, and provided some guidelines for evaluating the activities of discursive representatives (be they social movement activists, celebrities, politicians, or even corporate public relations experts).

Good informal discursive representatives are likely to be good rhetoricians; and rhetoric in representation can be linked to the same kind of discursive psychology that underpins the account of discursive representation. Deliberative systems feature differently situated actors in multiple sites, and chapter 4 showed how rhetoric can establish links across these sites.

Rhetoric, the art of reaching and persuading others, is especially important when it comes to representing discourses in the public sphere to those in positions of public authority. Thus, the basic account of discursive legitimacy developed in chapter 2 will often demand effective rhetoric on the part of discursive representatives. Chapter 4 did of course also recognize the well-known hazards accompanying rhetoric, and so developed a systemic test for its admissibility. The key question here is whether or not the rhetoric in question contributes to the construction of an effective deliberative system linking competent and reflective actors. Thus, a strong connection is made back to the basic ideas about the deliberative system set out in chapter 1.

These accounts of legitimacy, representation, and communication join in the creation of deliberative and democratic capacity in political settings featuring plural discourses. What, then, happened to the leaning toward consensus as an ideal that attracted some support in the early days of deliberative democracy? Chapter 5 reconciles competing ideals of pluralism and consensus in political deliberation through reference to the idea that simple pluralism ought to be combined with, and regulated by, meta-consensus. Meta-consensus can be normative (concerning the legitimacy of disputed values), epistemic (about the credibility of disputed beliefs), preference (about the nature of disputed choices), and discursive (about the acceptable range of contested discourses, and so the identities generated by these discourses). In this light, deliberative forums and deliberative systems can be judged in terms of their ability to generate meta-consensus. However, the conditions under which meta-consensus is generated matter enormously. The deliberative generation of meta-consensus should feature uncoerced dialogue, not strategic action and symbol manipulation. Meta-consensus makes collective choice more tractable, whatever the procedure subsequently used to decide upon the content of those choices (be it voting, negotiation, working agreement, or mutual adjustment). This analysis then makes possible a more refined statement of the account of discursive legitimacy developed earlier. Legitimacy can be sought in the resonance of collective choices with public opinion, characterized as the provisional outcome of the engagement of discourses in public space as transmitted to public authority in empowered space, to the degree that engagement is regulated by free and reasoned meta-consensus reached by competent and reflective actors. This redefinition of legitimacy puts the finishing touches to the integration of the foundations of deliberative democracy.

## LONG FRONTIERS

Part II's integrated account of the foundations of deliberative democracy in the capacity of deliberative systems to secure legitimacy, representation, communication, and meta-consensus can be applied to a wide range of challenges facing democracy in general. Crucially, this account of deliberative democracy is sufficiently general that it does not require the developed formal institutions of a liberal democratic state (including elections), and so can travel to many contexts where nothing like these institutions is available. Governance networks, into which the authority of once sovereign states is increasingly dispersed, can be interpreted as deliberative systems, and so evaluated in deliberative terms. A normative theory of democratic network governance as intimated in chapter 6 would highlight the importance of contestation within nodes of governance, regulated by meta-consensus of the kind developed in chapter 5.

The democratization of authoritarian states can be interpreted in terms of their development of effective deliberative capacity, which in turn requires all the elements of the deliberative system outlined in chapter 1. This deliberative approach has the advantage over conventional treatments of state democratization in that it can be applied to situations where there is not much in the way of a functioning state; and in settings such as China where the immediate adoption of competitive national elections is unlikely. The development of deliberative capacity turns out to be instrumental in many phases of democratic transition and consolidation; but can also be sought when transition to liberal electoral democracy is a remote prospect.

The ever-growing popularity of mini-publics discussed in chapter 8 can be linked to the more systemic concerns of deliberative democracy, because processes that are straightforward to study in mini-publics have their counterparts in macro systems where such processes are much harder to study. Thus, mini-publics provide lessons about what those larger systems need to accomplish, as well as helping to identify problems that larger systems must overcome, and dangers these larger systems need to avoid. But mini-publics are more than just sites of research and demonstration. They can also be deployed in consequential fashion in macro political systems, with potential impacts on collective decisions as well as upon broad public debate. However, their macro potential proves to vary substantially, depending on the kind of political context in which they are employed (e.g., inclusive versus exclusive states). At their best, they can act as a focal point for larger deliberative systems – and chapter 9 suggested this might even include the global system, so international mini-publics are worth exploring and developing.

The discussion of global politics in chapter 9 did, though, focus much more intensively upon the engagement of discourses in global public spheres and its contribution to remedying the currently massive democrat deficit in global politics. Governance networks and discourses prove to be especially consequential sources of order in the global system. The outcome of the contestation of discourses is often particularly important in global politics due to the lack of "commanding heights" institutions at the level of the system as a whole, which would function in a fashion analogous to the sovereign state. But it is possible to interpret and evaluate global politics in deliberative terms – again demonstrating the ability of deliberative democracy to travel to contexts without elections and without anything like the institutions of a state exercising sovereign authority. In light of problems such as climate change, the construction of effective global deliberative systems is an urgent task. Discursive legitimacy facilitated by transnational discursive representation and regulated by meta-consensus can be sought in such a system – and to the degree that is achieved, solving global problems becomes more tractable.

## LIBERAL CONSTITUTIONALISM FALTERING AT THE FRONTIERS

The foundations and frontiers of deliberative governance that have been set out in this book do not of course exhaust the range of available approaches to deliberative democracy. Some are very different: most notably, a liberal constitutionalist approach. There was once a time when the theory of deliberative democracy seemed to be on the verge of assimilation to liberal constitutionalism. This assimilation could be advanced for several reasons (Dryzek 2000: 10–17). First, deliberative principles could be deployed to justify some of the standard liberal rights (because they are needed to protect a sphere of free public reasoning). Second, liberal constitutions can be designed in large part to promote deliberation in both the formal institutions of government and the larger public sphere. Third, the development of constitutions can itself be a deliberative process. In light of these three sources of affinity, deliberation would be properly and primarily within, about, and regulated by the institutions of a liberal democratic state. Prominent works in the 1990s gave impetus to this combination of liberal constitutionalism and deliberative democracy (e.g., Gutmann and Thompson 1996; Rawls 1997; Sunstein 1997; Bohman 1998).

Liberal constitutionalist deliberative democracy was perhaps well suited to the years of liberal democratic triumphalism that followed the fall of the Berlin Wall in 1989. Francis Fukuyama (1989, 1994) celebrated the "end of history," in which liberal democracy plus capitalism set the parameters of all future political projects, including, presumably, deliberative democracy. But that triumphalism was eventually challenged from a number of directions. These included:

- The rise of a seemingly confident yet undemocratic polity overseeing a booming capitalist market in China, along with a less economically successful but ever more authoritarian Russia.
- The resurgence of religious fundamentalisms: Christian in the developed West (especially the United States), Jewish in Israel, Muslim in many countries, and Hindu in India.
- The retreat of developed Western states (especially the United States) from their liberal commitments in response to the terrorist attacks of 9/11.
- The rise of networked governance of a sort that eludes constitutional regulation and the formal sovereign authority of government.
- Globalization, which moved authority away from states (whether or not they are liberal democratic) and into seemingly undemocratic global structures.

In the wake of these developments, the future no longer seemed to belong quite so clearly to the liberal democratic state.

Now, it is possible to fight rearguard actions against all these developments on behalf of the sovereign liberal democratic state (and the kind of deliberative democracy that might accompany it). Liberal democrats can hope that economic growth in China might eventually require for its further development and management a more complex kind of society and associated pluralization of social forces that eventually challenge the Communist Party's monopoly on power. They can, if necessary, fight wars against fundamentalism abroad, and pass laws to regulate its excesses at home. They can insist on – and have done so with modest success – a return to liberal principles after the excesses of the "war on terror" led to suspension of these principles. They could try (but so far seem not to have tried) to remove authority from governance networks and return it to the formal institutions of the sovereign state, and so make it subject to more visible and accountable public authority (exercised, for example, by an elected legislature). They can (and do) assert the power of the sovereign state against the claims of globalization (Hirst and Thompson 1996) – provided only that it does not succumb to the *discourse* of globalization. Such globalization skeptics can point to the fact that it was sovereign states that rescued the global economy amid financial crisis in 2008. The rescue did not feature any transnational institutions, markets, or networks capable of responding in the quick and decisive fashion of state mobilization against crisis.

What all of these responses share is that they try to turn the clock back. Sometimes the response may work, for example, in the (modest) restoration of liberal rights after the "war on terror." Sometimes the response may work, but only for a while. After states stepped in to resolve the 2008 financial crisis, the transnational economic forces that had previously undermined their authority soon sprang back to life. Banks too big to fail also proved too big to regulate effectively.

Sometimes, the clock stubbornly refuses to be reset to a time when the sovereign and confident liberal democratic state seemed to have the world in its hands. Liberal democrats, and so liberal constitutionalist deliberative democrats, do not quite know what to do when confronted with authoritarian states where transition to liberal democracy does not seem part of any realistic agenda. If their populations seem uninterested in adopting the developed Western liberal democratic state model, prescribing it for them looks a bit like undemocratic imperialism. If authoritarian states develop consultative forms that do not seem to be leading to transition, liberal constitutionalists can (and do) only dismiss them as irrelevant to the main democratization game. Liberal constitutionalist deliberative democratic theory remains silent in the face of the continued rise of networked governance. Assertion of the rightful public authority of high-visibility sovereign institutions (such as the legislature) simply does not do justice to all the factors that led to the rise of networked governance in the first place.

If reasserting the power of the sovereign state fails to tame globalization, liberal democrats can always seek to replicate the institutions of liberal democracy at the global level. But any such global institutions – featuring electoral democracy, courts with universal and effective jurisdiction, and effective embodiment of liberal rights, all united under compelling constitutional structure – are remote prospects.

All of these attempts to reassert the sovereignty and primacy of the liberal democratic constitutional state (or its replication at the global level) fail to do justice to the challenges in question in their own terms. Because it is so attached to the model of a functioning liberal democratic state, liberal constitutionalist deliberative democracy does not travel well to the frontiers identified in the chapters of this book.

## FURTHER FRONTIERS

Chapter 1 began by listing the fields, disciplines, and areas of practice into which deliberative democracy is being taken, ranging from criminal justice to development studies, the writings of presidents to the establishment of deliberative citizen forums. Beyond the items on this list, other topics worth exploring range from the deliberative potential of the Internet to cultural variations in the way deliberation is and can be practiced (there are almost certainly no cultures without some deliberative capacity). Deliberation may be sought – and sometimes found – in seemingly unpromising locations (e.g., the military, bureaucracies, corporations, and markets). Its interrelationships with (as opposed to determination of) the "output" side of governance (concerning, for example, impartiality, effectiveness, and fairness) merit further exploration. When it comes to collective choice, nothing much is off limits: not the courts, not bureaucracy, not international negotiations, and certainly not the economy. Deliberation does belong in the economy, especially to the degree it is a *political* economy, and so departs (as it always must) from the textbook depictions of self-regulating and welfare-maximizing markets. Not everything in collective life has to be deliberative – that would be impossibly demanding – but all of the key features of that life must at some point have to be amenable to analysis and justification in deliberative terms. Of course, there are plenty of feasibility constraints, and some areas of collective life will prove much more welcoming toward deliberative innovation than others.

At this point, the more voracious deliberative democrat might justifiably look forward to an ever-expanding domain of theoretical and conceptual development, empirical study, and practical application. These three are increasingly linked. The political theory of deliberative democracy informs the design of practical applications, which in term can have empirical studies built into them. The findings of such empirical studies can both pose further problems for theory, and lead to refinement or rethinking of practical applications. Other kinds of empirical studies – especially macro studies of existing deliberative systems – make little or no use of designed applications (such as mini-publics), but they too can contribute to rethinking the theory, as well as developing prescriptions for macro-systems improvement. Deliberative democracy is a project to which many hands have contributed, and to which many hands will surely make further contributions.

With expansion comes the danger that deliberative democracy may come to encompass too much. Here, the history of liberalism is instructive. With time, liberalism has managed to assimilate many of the doctrines that once challenged it: socialism (after it moderated to become social democracy), feminism, communitarianism, and even critical theory (Dryzek, Honig, and Phillips 2006: 14–23). Critical theory began in the Frankfurt school as a thoroughgoing critique of just about the totality of modern society, but eventually started to look very liberal in the later work of Habermas. Is a similar fate in store for deliberative democracy? In part this is a matter of pull from the outside, as many of those working on communication in general now style what they cover as "deliberative." While such claims should not be taken at face value, they can and should be engaged. Much more of the expansive impetus comes from the inside, as deliberative thinkers have incorporated into their accounts elements of pluralism, disruption, agonism, rhetoric, enclave communication, and polyphonic interaction in broader public spaces. All this might look like there are few limits to the deliberative democratization of just about everything. But then the danger is if deliberative democracy is everything, maybe it is nothing. There have to be some things that deliberative democracy is not. Deliberative democracy is not command, deception, strategizing, coercive bargaining, play, poetry, violence, therapy, friendship, patronage, religion, private experience, or conformity with social norms and traditions. And even when it comes to new places where deliberative democracy might be taken, it is important to maintain a hard critical edge that looks for subtle forms of domination and exclusion.

The long history of deliberative democracy stretches from ancient Greece to the present day. The long frontier of deliberative governance has extended from a president of the United States to local politics in China, from minipublics to the global system. There is no shortage of work for those who want to extend the history and push back the frontiers, in political theory, social science, and political practice.

# Bibliography

Ackerman, Bruce A. 1991. *We the People I: Foundations.* Cambridge, MA: Harvard University Press.
—— and James S. Fishkin. 2004. *Deliberation Day.* New Haven, CT: Yale University Press.
Alford, John and Deidre O'Neill, eds. 1994. *The Contract State.* Melbourne: Deakin University Press.
Alker, Hayward and David Sylvan. 1994. Some Contributions of Discourse Analysis to Political Science. *Kosmopolis* 24 (3): 5–25.
Anderson, Richard D. 2007. Discourse and the Export of Democracy. *St. Antony's International Review* 2 (2): 19–35.
Ankersmit, Frank R. 2002. *Political Representation.* Stanford: Stanford University Press.
Armony, Ariel C. and Hector E. Schamis. 2005. Babel in Democratization Studies. *Journal of Democracy* 16: 113–28.
Arrow, Kenneth J. 1963. *Social Choice and Individual Values,* 2nd edn. New York: Wiley.
Austen-Smith, David and Timothy J. Feddersen. 2006. Deliberation, Preference Uncertainty and Voting Rules. *American Political Science Review* 100: 209–17.
Baber, Walter F. and Robert V. Bartlett. 2005. *Deliberative Environmental Politics: Democracy and Ecological Rationality.* Cambridge, MA: MIT Press.
Bächtiger, André, Simon Niemeyer, Michael Neblo, Marco Steenbergen, and Jürg Steiner. 2010. Disentangling Diversity in Deliberative Democracy: Competing Theories, Their Empirical Blind-Spots, and Complementarities. *Journal of Political Philosophy,* 18: 32–63.
——, Marco R. Steenbergen, and Simon Niemeyer. 2007. Deliberative Democracy: An Introduction. *Swiss Political Science Review* 13: 485–96.
Barry, John, and John Proops. 1999. Seeking Sustainability Discourses with Q Methodology. *Ecological Economics* 28: 337–45.
Bartels, Larry M. 2003. Is Popular Rule Possible? Polls, Political Psychology, and Democracy. *Brookings Review* 21 (3): 12–15.
Beck, Ulrich. 1992. *Risk Society: Towards a New Modernity.* London: Sage.
——, Anthony Giddens, and Scott Lash. 1994. *Reflexive Modernization: Politics, Tradition, and Aesthetics in the Modern Social Order.* Cambridge: Polity.
Beetham, David. 1991. *The Legitimation of Power.* Basingstoke: Macmillan.
——. 1999. *Democracy and Human Rights.* Cambridge: Polity.
Bell, Stephen and Andrew Hindmoor. 2009a. *Rethinking Governance: The Centrality of the State in Modern Societies.* Cambridge: Cambridge University Press.
—— ——. 2009b. New Frontier for Governance without Government: The Case of the Forest Stewardship Council. Unpublished paper, School of Political Science and International Studies, University of Queensland.
Benhabib, Seyla. 1990. Communicative Ethics and Contemporary Controversies in Practical Philosophy. In Seyla Benhabib and Fred Dallmayr, eds., *The Communicative Ethics Controversy* pp. 330–70. Cambridge, MA: MIT Press.

——. 1996. Toward a Deliberative Model of Democratic Legitimacy. In Seyla Benhabib, ed., *Democracy and Difference: Contesting the Boundaries of the Political*, pp. 67–94. Princeton, NJ: Princeton University Press.

Berlin, Isaiah. 1969. *Four Essays on Liberty*. Oxford: Oxford University Press.

Bessette, Joseph M. 1980. Deliberative Democracy: The Majoritarian Principle in Republican Government. In Robert A. Goldwin and William A. Shambra, eds., *How Democratic Is the Constitution?* pp. 102–16. Washington, DC: American Enterprise Institute.

——. 1994. *The Mild Voice of Reason: Deliberative Democracy and American National Government*. Chicago, IL: University of Chicago Press.

Bevir, Mark. 2006. Democratic Governance: Systems and Radical Perspectives. *Public Administration Review* 66: 426–36.

—— and R. A. W. Rhodes. 2003. *Interpreting British Governance*. London: Routledge.

Black, Duncan. 1948. On the Rationale of Group Decision-Making. *Journal of Political Economy* 56: 23–34.

Bohman, James. 1995. Public Reason and Cultural Pluralism: Political Liberalism and the Problem of Moral Conflict. *Political Theory* 23: 253–79.

——. 1996. *Public Deliberation: Pluralism, Complexity and Democracy*. Cambridge, MA: MIT Press.

——. 1998. The Coming of Age of Deliberative Democracy. *Journal of Political Philosophy* 6: 399–423.

——. 2007. *Democracy Across Borders: From Dêmos to Dêmoi*. Cambridge, MA: MIT Press.

Braithwaite, John. 2007. Contestatory Citizenship, Deliberative Denizenship. In Geoffrey Brennan, Frank Jackson, Robert Goodin, and Michael Smith, eds., *Common Minds*, pp. 161–81. Oxford: Oxford University Press.

——. 2008. *Regulatory Capitalism: How It Works, How to Make It Work Better*. Cheltenham: Edward Elgar.

Brennan, Geoffrey and Loren Lomasky. 1993. *Democracy and Decision*. Cambridge: Cambridge University Press.

Brown, Steven R. 1980. *Political Subjectivity: Applications of Q Methodology in Political Science*. New Haven, CT: Yale University Press.

Brucan, Silvio. 1992. Democracy at Odds with Market in Post-Communist Societies. In Michael Keren and Gur Ofer, eds., *Trials of Transition: Economic Reform in the Former Soviet Bloc*, pp. 19–25. Boulder, CO: Westview.

Brulle, Robert J. 2000. *Agency, Democracy, and Nature: The U.S. Environmental Movement from a Critical Theory Perspective*. Cambridge, MA: MIT Press.

Brunkhorst, Hauke. 2002. Globalizing Democracy without a State: Weak Public, Strong Public, Global Constitutionalism. *Millennium* 31: 675–90.

Caplan, Bryan. 2007. *The Myth of the Rational Voter: Why Democracies Choose Bad Policies*. Princeton, NJ: Princeton University Press.

Carothers, Thomas. 2002. The End of the Transition Paradigm. *Journal of Democracy* 13: 5–21.

Carson, Lyn and Brian Martin. 1999. *Random Selection in Politics*. Westport, CT: Praeger.

Castells, Manuel. 1996. *The Information Age*, Volume I: *The Rise of the Network Society*. Oxford: Basil Blackwell.

Castiglione, Dario and Mark E. Warren. 2006. Rethinking Representation: Eight Theoretical Issues. Paper presented to Conference on Rethinking Democratic Representation, University of British Columbia, Vancouver, BC.

Chambers, Simone. 1996. *Reasonable Democracy: Jürgen Habermas and the Politics of Discourse*. Ithaca, NY: Cornell University Press.

——. 2003. Deliberative Democratic Theory. *Annual Review of Political Science* 6: 307–26.

——. 2004. Behind Closed Doors: Publicity, Secrecy, and the Quality of Deliberation. *Journal of Political Philosophy* 12: 389–410.

——. 2009. Rhetoric and the Public Sphere: Has Deliberative Democracy Abandoned Mass Democracy? *Political Theory* 37: 323–50.

—— and Jeffrey Kopstein. 2001. Bad Civil Society. *Political Theory* 29: 837–65.

Cohen, Joshua. 1989. Deliberation and Democratic Legitimacy. In Alan Hamlin and Philip Pettit, eds., *The Good Polity*, pp. 17–34. Oxford: Basil Blackwell.

Collier, David and Steven Levitsky. 1997. Democracy with Adjectives: Conceptual Innovation in Comparative Research. *World Politics* 49: 430–51.

Connolly, William E. 1991. *Identity/Difference: Democratic Negotiations of Political Paradox*. Ithaca, NY: Cornell University Press.

Conover, Pamela Johnson, Donald D. Searing, and Ivor M. Crewe. 2002. The Deliberative Potential of Political Discussion. *British Journal of Political Science* 32: 21–62.

Cook, Fay Lomax, Michael X. Delli Carpini, and Lawrence Jacobs. 2007. Who Deliberates? Discursive Participation in America. In Shawn Rosenberg, ed., *Deliberation, Participation and Democracy: Can the People Govern?*, pp. 24–44. Basingstoke: Palgrave Macmillan.

Crawford, Neta C. 2009. Homo Politicus and Argument (Nearly) All the Way Down: Persuasion in Politics. *Perspectives on Politics* 7: 103–24.

Crocker, David A. 2008. *Ethics of Global Development: Agency, Capability, and Deliberative Democracy*. Cambridge: Cambridge University Press.

Dahl, Robert A. 1970. *After the Revolution?* New Haven, CT: Yale University Press.

Davies, B. B., K. Sherlock, and F. Rauschmayer. 2005. "Recruitment," "Composition," and "Mandate" Issues in Deliberative Processes: Should we Focus on Arguments Rather than Individuals? *Environment and Planning C-Government and Policy* 23: 599–615.

De Grieff, Pablo. 2002. Deliberative Democracy and Punishment. *Buffalo Criminal Law Review* 5: 373–403.

Delli Carpini, Michael X., Fay Lomax Cook, and Lawrence R. Jacobs. 2004. Public Deliberation, Discursive Participation, and Citizen Engagement: A Review of the Empirical Literature. *Annual Review of Political Science* 7: 315–44.

Dewey, John. 1927. *The Public and Its Problems*. New York: Henry Holt and Co.

Dovi, Suzanne. 2002. Preferable Descriptive Representatives: Will Just Any Woman, Black, or Latino Do? *American Political Science Review* 96: 729–43.

Dryzek, John S. 1987. Discursive Designs: Critical Theory and Political Institutions. *American Journal of Political Science* 31: 656–79.

——. 1990. *Discursive Democracy: Politics, Policy and Political Science.* New York: Cambridge University Press.

——. 1995. Political and Ecological Communication. *Environmental Politics* 4: 13–30.

——. 1996*a*. *Democracy in Capitalist Times: Ideals, Limits and Struggles.* New York: Oxford University Press.

——. 1996*b*. Political Inclusion and the Dynamics of Democratization. *American Political Science Review* 90: 475–87.

——. 2000. *Deliberative Democracy and Beyond: Liberals, Critics, Contestations.* Oxford: Oxford University Press.

——. 2001. Legitimacy and Economy in Deliberative Democracy. *Political Theory* 29: 651–69.

——. 2005. Deliberative Democracy in Divided Societies: Alternatives to Agonism and Analgesia. *Political Theory* 33: 218–42.

——. 2006. *Deliberative Global Politics: Discourse and Democracy in a Divided World.* Cambridge: Polity Press.

——. 2007*a*. Networks and Democratic Ideals: Equality, Freedom, and Communication. In Eva Sørensen and Jacob Torfing, eds., *Theories of Democratic Network Governance*, pp. 262–73. Basingstoke: Palgrave Macmillan.

——. 2007*b*. The Empirical Turn in Deliberative Democracy. Presented to the Conference on Deliberation and Democratic Governance, SCORE, Stockholm, May 3–4.

——, André Bächtiger, and Karolina Milewicz. 2009. Toward a Deliberative Global Citizens' Assembly. Centre for Deliberative Democracy and Global Governance, Australian National University.

——, with Luca Belgiorno-Nettis, Lyn Carson, Janette Hartz-Karp, Ron Lubensky, Ian Marsh, and Simon Niemeyer. 2009*b*. The Australian Citizens' Parliament: A World First. *Journal of Public Deliberation* 5 (1).

——and Jeffrey Berejikian. 1993. Reconstructive Democratic Theory. *American Political Science Review* 87: 48–60.

——David Downes, Christian Hunold, David Schlosberg, with Hans-Kristian Hernes. 2003. *Green States and Social Movements: Environmentalism in the United States, United Kingdom, Germany, and Norway.* Oxford: Oxford University Press.

——Robert E. Goodin, Aviezer Tucker, and Bernard Reber. 2009*a*. Promethean Elites Encounter Precautionary Publics: The Case of GM Foods. *Science, Technology, and Human Values* 34: 263–88.

——and Leslie T. Holmes. 2002. *Post-Communist Democratization: Political Discourses Across Thirteen Countries.* Cambridge: Cambridge University Press.

——Bonnie Honig, and Anne Phillips. 2006. Introduction. In John S. Dryzek, Bonnie Honig, and Anne Phillips, eds., *The Oxford Handbook of Political Theory*, pp. 3–41. Oxford: Oxford University Press.

——and Christian List. 2003. Social Choice Theory and Deliberative Democracy: A Reconciliation. *British Journal of Political Science* 33: 1–28.

——and Simon Niemeyer. 2006. Reconciling Pluralism and Consensus as Political Ideals. *American Journal of Political Science* 50: 634–49.

Dryzek, John S. and Simon Niemeyer. 2008. Discursive Representation. *American Political Science Review* 102: 481–93.

——and Aviezer Tucker. 2008. Deliberative Innovation to Different Effect: Consensus Conferences in Denmark, France, and the United States. *Public Administration Review* 68: 864–76.

Dworkin, Ronald. 1977. *Taking Rights Seriously.* Cambridge, MA: Harvard University Press.

Dzur, Albert W. 2002. Public Journalism and Deliberative Democracy. *Polity* 34: 313–36.

Eberly, Rosa. 2003. Plato's Shibboleth Delineations; Or, the Complete Idiot's Guide to Rhetoric. In Gerard A. Hauser and Amy Grim, eds., *Rhetorical Democracy: Discursive Practices of Civic Engagement*, pp. 45–52. Mahwah, NJ: Lawrence Erlbaum.

Eckersley, Robyn. 2000. Deliberative Democracy, Ecological Representation, and Risk: Towards a Democracy of the Affected. In Michael Saward, ed., *Democratic Innovation: Deliberation, Association, and Representation*, pp. 117–32. London: Routledge.

Edelman, Murray. 1964. *The Symbolic Uses of Politics.* Urbana, IL: University of Illinois Press.

Edwards, Derek and Jonathan Potter. 1992. *Discursive Psychology.* London: Sage.

Eggins, Rachael A., Katherine J. Reynolds, Penelope J. Oakes, and Kenneth I. Mavor. 2007. Citizen Participation in a Deliberative Poll: Factors Predicting Attitude Change and Political Engagement. *Australian Journal of Psychology* 59: 94–100.

Ekiert, Grzegorz and Jan Kubik. 1999. *Rebellious Civil Society: Popular Protest and Democratic Consolidation in Poland, 1989–1993.* Ann Arbor, MI: University of Michigan Press.

Elster, Jon. 1986*a*. The Market and the Forum. In Jon Elster and Aanund Hylland, eds., *Foundations of Social Choice Theory*, pp. 103–32. Cambridge: Cambridge University Press.

——, ed. 1986*b. The Multiple Self.* Cambridge: Cambridge University Press.

——. 1998*a*. Introduction. In Jon Elster, ed., *Deliberative Democracy*, pp. 1–18. New York: Cambridge University Press.

——. 1998*b*. Deliberation and Constitution Making. In Jon Elster, ed., *Deliberative Democracy*, pp. 97–122. Cambridge: Cambridge University Press.

——, Claus Offe, and Ulrich Preuss. 1998. *Institutional Design in Post-Communist Societies: Rebuilding the Ship at Sea.* Cambridge: Cambridge University Press.

Eriksen, Erik Oddvar. 2006. Deliberation and the Problem of Democratic Legitimacy in the EU: Are Working Agreements the Most that can be Expected? ARENA working paper 8, University of Oslo.

—— and John Erik Fossum. 2007. Reconstituting Democracy in Europe. Framing paper for the Reconstituting Democracy in Europe (RECON) project. Oslo: ARENA.

——, Christian Joerges, and Jürgen Neyer, eds. 2004. *European Governance, Deliberation and the Quest for Democratisation.* Oslo: ARENA.

Esmark, Anders. 2007. Democratic Accountability and Network Governance – Problems and Potentials. In Eva Sørensen and Jacob Torfing, eds., *Theories of Democratic Network Governance*, pp. 274–96. Basingstoke: Palgrave Macmillan.

Estlund, David. 2007. *Democratic Authority: A Philosophical Framework.* Princeton: Princeton University Press.

Etzioni, Amitai. 2007. *Security First: For a Muscular, Moral Foreign Policy.* New Haven, CT: Yale University Press.

Falk, Richard and Andrew Strauss. 2001. Toward Global Parliament. *Foreign Affairs* 80 (1): 212–20.

Femia, Joseph. 1996. Complexity and Deliberative Democracy. *Inquiry* 39: 359–97.

Ferguson, James. 2006. *Africa in the Neoliberal World.* Durham, NC: Duke University Press.

Fishkin, James. 1991. *Democracy and Deliberation: New Directions for Democratic Reforms.* New Haven, CT: Yale University Press.

——. 1995. *The Voice of the People: Public Opinion and Democracy.* New Haven, CT: Yale University Press.

——. 2009. *When the People Speak: Deliberative Democracy and Public Consultation.* Oxford: Oxford University Press.

Føllesdal, Andreas. 2006. The Legitimacy Deficits of the European Union. *Journal of Political Philosophy* 14: 441–68.

Fontana, Benedetto, Cary J. Nederman, and Gary Remer. 2004. Introduction: Deliberative Democracy and the Rhetorical Turn. In Benedetto Fontana, Cary J. Nederman, and Gary Remer, eds., *Talking Democracy: Historical Perspectives on Rhetoric and Democracy,* pp. 1–25. University Park, PA: Pennsylvania State University Press.

Forester, John. 1999*a*. Dealing with Deep Value Difference. In Lawrence Susskind, Sarah McKearnan, and Jennifer Thomas-Larmer, eds., *The Consensus-Building Handbook,* pp. 463–94. Thousand Oaks, CA: Sage.

——. 1999*b*. *The Deliberative Practitioner.* Cambridge, MA: MIT Press.

Frantzius, Ina von. 2004. World Summit on Sustainable Development Johannesburg 2002: A Critical Assessment of the Outcomes. *Environmental Politics* 13: 467–73.

Fraser, Nancy. 1992. Rethinking the Public Sphere: A Contribution to the Critique of Actually Existing Democracy. In Craig Calhoun, ed., *Habermas and the Public Sphere,* pp. 109–42. Cambridge, MA: MIT Press.

Fukuyama, Francis. 1989. The End of History? *National Interest* (summer): 3–18.

——. 1994. *The End of History and the Last Man.* New York: Free Press.

Fung, Archon. 2003. Recipes for Public Spheres: Eight Institutional Design Choices and their Consequences. *Journal of Political Philosophy* 11: 338–67.

——. 2008. Pragmatic Democratization: Preliminary Reflections on Conceptions of Reform for Non-Liberal Societies. Paper presented at the Annual Meeting of the American Political Science Association, Boston, MA, August 28–31.

Gallie, W. B. 1956. Essentially Contested Concepts. *Proceedings of the Aristotelian Society* 56: 121–46.

Galston, William A. 2002. *Liberal Pluralism: The Implications of Value Pluralism for Political Theory and Practice.* Cambridge: Cambridge University Press.

Gambetta, Diego. 1998. Claro! An Essay on Discursive Machismo. In Jon Elster, ed., *Deliberative Democracy,* pp. 19–43. Cambridge: Cambridge University Press.

Garsten, Bryan. 2006. *Saving Persuasion: A Defense of Rhetoric and Judgment.* Cambridge, MA: Harvard University Press.

Gastil, John. 2000. *By Popular Demand: Revitalizing Representative Democracy Through Deliberative Elections.* Berkeley, CA: University of California Press.

——. 2008. *Political Communication and Deliberation.* Thousand Oaks, CA: Sage.

Gastil, John and Peter Levine, eds. 2005. *The Deliberative Democracy Handbook*. San Francisco, CA: Jossey Bass.

Gibson, Rachel K. and Sarah Miskin. 2002. Australia Deliberates? The Role of the Media in Deliberative Polling. In John Warhurst and Malcolm Mackerras, eds., *Constitutional Politics*, pp. 163–76. St. Lucia: University of Queensland Press.

Goodin, Robert E. 1986. Laundering Preferences. In Jon Elster and Aanund Hylland, eds., *Foundations of Social Choice Theory*, pp. 75–102. Cambridge: Cambridge University Press.

——. 2000. Democratic Deliberation Within. *Philosophy and Public Affairs* 29: 79–107.

——. 2003. *Reflective Democracy*. Oxford: Oxford University Press.

——. 2005. Sequencing Deliberative Moments. *Acta Politica* 40: 182–96.

——. 2008. *Innovating Democracy: Democratic Theory and Practice After the Deliberative Turn*. Oxford: Oxford University Press.

——. 2009. Rationalising Discursive Anomalies. *Theoria* 119: 1–13.

—— and John S. Dryzek. 2006. Deliberative Impacts: The Macro-Political Uptake of Mini-Publics. *Politics and Society* 34: 219–44.

Gould, Carol C. 1988. *Rethinking Democracy*. Cambridge: Cambridge University Press.

Grant, Ruth W. and Robert O. Keohane. 2005. Accountability and the Abuse of Power in World Politics. *American Political Science Review* 99: 29–44.

Gray, John. 1996. *Isaiah Berlin*. Princeton, NJ: Princeton University Press.

Gunnell, John G. 1986. *Between Philosophy and Politics: The Alienation of Political Theory*. Amherst, MA: University of Massachusetts Press.

Gutmann, Amy and Dennis Thompson. 1996. *Democracy and Disagreement*. Cambridge, MA: Harvard University Press.

Habermas, Jürgen. 1988. On the Distinction Between Poetic and Communicative Uses of Language. In Maeve Cook, ed., *On the Pragmatics of Communication*, pp. 384–98. Cambridge, MA: MIT Press.

——. 1989. *Structural Transformation of the Public Sphere: An Inquiry into a Category of Bourgeois Society*. Cambridge, MA: MIT Press.

——. 1996. *Between Facts and Norms: Contributions to a Discourse Theory of Law and Democracy*. Cambridge, MA: MIT Press.

——. 2006a. *The Divided West*. Cambridge: Polity Press.

——. 2006b. Political Communication in Mass Society: Does Democracy Still Enjoy an Epistemic Dimension? The Impact of Normative Theory on Empirical Research. *Communication Theory* 16: 411–26.

Häikiö, Liisa. 2007. Expertise, Representation and the Common Good: Grounds for Legitimacy in the Urban Governance Network. *Urban Studies* 44: 2147–62.

Hajer, Maarten A. 2009. *Authoritative Governance: Policy-Making in the Age of Mediatization*. Oxford: Oxford University Press.

—— and Wytske Versteeg. 2008. The Limits to Deliberative Governance. Paper presented at the Annual Meeting of the American Political Science Association, Boston, MA, August 28–31.

—— and Hendrik Wagenaar, eds. 2003. *Deliberative Policy Analysis: Understanding Governance in the Network Society*. Cambridge: Cambridge University Press.

Hall, Rodney Bruce. 2003. The Discursive Demolition of the Asian Development Model. *International Studies Quarterly* 47: 71–99.

Hansen, Allan Dreyer. 2007. Governance Networks and Participation. In Eva Sørensen and Jacob Torfing, eds., *Theories of Democratic Network Governance*, pp. 247–61. Basingstoke: Palgrave Macmillan.

Harré, Rom and Grant Gillett. 1994. *The Discursive Mind.* Thousand Oaks, CA: Sage.

Harrison, Stephen and Maggie Mort. 1998. Which Champions, Which People? Public and User Involvement in Health Care as a Technology of Legitimation. *Social Policy and Administration* 32: 60–70.

Hauser, Gerard A. and Chantal Benoit-Barne. 2002. Reflections on Rhetoric, Deliberative Democracy, Civil Society, and Trust. *Rhetoric and Public Affairs* 5: 261–75.

He, Baogang and Ethan J. Leib. 2006. Editors' Introduction. In Ethan J. Leib and Baogang He, eds., *The Search for Deliberative Democracy in China*, pp. 1–19. Basingstoke: Palgrave Macmillan.

—— and Mark Warren. 2008. Authoritarian Deliberation. Paper presented at the Annual Meeting of the American Political Science Association, Boston, MA, August 29–September 1.

Held, David. 1995. *Democracy and the Global Order: From the Nation-State to Cosmopolitan Governance.* Cambridge: Polity Press.

Hendriks, Carolyn M. 2004. Public Deliberation and Interest Organisations: A Study of Responses to Lay Citizen Engagement in Public Policy. PhD thesis, Australian National University.

——. 2005. Consensus Conferences and Planning Cells: Lay Citizen Deliberations. In John Gastil and Peter Levine, eds., *The Deliberative Democracy Handbook*, pp. 80–110. San Francisco, CA: Josey Bass.

——. 2006. Integrated Deliberation: Reconciling Civil Society's Dual Role in Deliberative Democracy. *Political Studies* 54: 486–508.

——. 2008. On Inclusion and Network Governance: The Democratic Disconnect of Dutch Sustainable Energy Transitions. *Public Administration* 86: 1009–31.

——. 2009. The Democratic Soup: Mixed Meanings of Political Representation in Governance Networks. *Governance* 22: 689–715.

—— and Lyn Carson. 2008. Can the Market Help the Forum? Negotiating the Commercialization of Deliberative Democracy. *Policy Sciences* 41: 293–313.

——, John S. Dryzek, and Christian Hunold. 2007. Turning up the Heat: Partisanship in Deliberative Innovation. *Political Studies* 55: 362–83.

—— and John Grin. 2007. Enacting Reflexive Governance: The Politics of Dutch Transitions to Sustainability. *Journal of Environmental Policy and Planning* 9: 333–50.

Hibbing, John R. and Elizabeth Theiss-Morse. 2002. *Stealth Democracy: Americans' Beliefs About How Government Should Work.* Cambridge: Cambridge University Press.

Hirst, Paul and Grahame Thompson. 1996. *Globalization in Question: The International Economy and the Possibilities of Governance.* Cambridge: Polity.

Hochschild, Jennifer L. 1981. *What's Fair? American Beliefs About Distributive Justice.* Cambridge, MA: Harvard University Press.

Honig, Bonnie. 1993. *Political Theory and the Displacement of Politics.* Ithaca, NY: Cornell University Press.

Honig, Bonnie. 1996. Difference, Dilemmas, and the Politics of Home. In Seyla Benhabib, ed., *Democracy and Difference: Contesting the Boundaries of the Political*, pp. 257–77. Princeton, NJ: Princeton University Press.

Horowitz, Donald. 1985. *Ethnic Groups in Conflict*. Berkeley, CA: University of California Press.

Hughes, Michael A., John Forester, and Irene Weiser. 1999. Facilitating Statewide HIV/ AIDS Policies and Priorities in Colorado. In Lawrence Susskind, Sara McKearnan, and Jennifer Thomas-Larmer, eds., *The Consensus-Building Handbook*, pp. 1011–29. Thousand Oaks, CA: Sage.

Huntington, Samuel P. 1996. *The Clash of Civilizations and the Remaking of World Order*. New York: Simon and Schuster.

Innes, Judith E. and David E. Booher. 2003. Collaborative Policymaking: Governance Through Dialogue. In Maarten A. Hajer and Hendrik Wagenaar, eds., *Deliberative Policy Analysis: Understanding Governance in the Network Society*, pp. 33–59. Cambridge: Cambridge University Press.

Jacobs, Lawrence R., Fay Lomax Cook, and Michael X. Delli Carpini. 2009. *Talking Together: Public Deliberation and Political Participation in America*. Chicago, IL: University of Chicago Press.

Kanra, Bora. 2005. Islam, Democracy and Dialogue: The Case of Turkey. *Government and Opposition* 40: 515–40.

——. 2007. Binary Deliberation: The Role of Social Learning in the Theory and Practice of Deliberative Democracy. Paper presented at the Joint Sessions of the European Consortium for Political Research, Helsinki, May.

Keane, John. 2009. Democracy Failure: Politics and the Great Recession. Evatt Foundation paper, online at http://evatt.org.au/publications/papers/216.html.

Keck, Margaret. 2003. Governance Regimes and the Politics of Discursive Representation. In Nichola Piper and Anders Uhlin, eds., *Transnational Activism in Asia*, pp. 43–60. London: Routledge.

Kempton, Willett, James S. Boster, and Jennifer A. Hartley. 1995. *Environmental Values in American Culture*. Cambridge, MA: MIT Press.

Kitschelt, Herbert P. 1986. Political Opportunity Structures and Political Protest: Anti-Nuclear Movements in Four Democracies. *British Journal of Political Science* 16: 57–85.

Knight, Jack and James Johnson. 1994. Aggregation and Deliberation: On the Possibility of Democratic Legitimacy. *Political Theory* 22: 277–96.

Knops, Andrew. 2007. Agonism as Deliberation: On Mouffe's Theory of Democracy. *Journal of Political Philosophy* 15: 115–26.

Kock, Christian. 2007. Norms of Legitimate Dissensus. In H. V. Hansen, ed., *Dissensus and the Search for Common Ground*, CD-ROM. Windsor, Ontario: OSSA.

Kuhn, Thomas. 1970. *The Structure of Scientific Revolutions*. Chicago, IL: Chicago University Press.

Kuper, Andrew. 2004. *Democracy Beyond Borders: Justice and Representation in Global Institutions*. Oxford: Oxford University Press.

Kuran, Timur. 1998. Insincere Deliberation and Democratic Failure. *Critical Review* 12: 529–44.

Kymlicka, Will. 2001. *Politics in the Vernacular*. Oxford: Oxford University Press.

Landa, Dimitri and Adam Meirowitz. 2006. Game Theory, Information, and Deliberative Democracy. Working paper, Department of Politics, New York University.

Lehmbruch, Gerhard. 1984. Concertation and the Structure of Corporatist Networks. In John H. Goldthorpe, ed., *Order and Change in Contemporary Capitalism*, pp. 60–80. Oxford: Clarendon Press.

Leib, Ethan J. 2004. *Deliberative Democracy in America: A Proposal for a Popular Branch of Government*. University Park, PA: Pennsylvania State University Press.

Levitsky, Steven and Lucan Way. 2002. The Rise of Competitive Authoritarianism. *Journal of Democracy* 13: 51–65.

Lijphart, Arend. 1977. *Democracy in Plural Societies: A Comparative Exploration*. New Haven, CT: Yale University Press.

Lindblom, Charles E. 1965. *The Intelligence of Democracy: Decision Making Through Mutual Adjustment*. New York: Free Press.

Linz, Juan J. and Alfred E. Stepan. 1996. *Problems of Democratic Transition and Consolidation: Southern Europe, South America, and Post-Communist Europe*. Baltimore, MD: Johns Hopkins University Press.

List, Christian. 2002. Two Conceptions of Agreement. *The Good Society* 11(1): 72–9.

——. 2007. Deliberation and Agreement. In Shawn Rosenberg, ed., *Deliberation, Participation and Democracy: Can the People Govern?* pp. 64–81. Basingstoke: Palgrave Macmillan.

Litfin, Karen. 1994. *Ozone Discourses: Science and Politics in Global Cooperation*. New York: Columbia University Press.

Lomborg, Bjørn. 2001. *The Skeptical Environmentalist: Measuring the Real State of the World*. Cambridge: Cambridge University Press.

Lowi, Theodore J. 1969. *The End of Liberalism*. New York: W.W. Norton.

——. 1999. Frontyard Propaganda. *Boston Review*.

MacIntyre, Alasdair. 1984. Does Applied Ethics Rest on a Mistake? *The Monist* 67: 498–513.

——. 1988. *Whose Justice? Which Rationality?* Notre Dame: University of Notre Dame Press.

Mackie, Gerry. 1995. Models of Democratic Deliberation. Paper presented to the Annual Meeting of the American Political Science Association, Chicago, IL.

——. 2003. *Democracy Defended*. Cambridge: Cambridge University Press.

——. 2006. Does Democratic Deliberation Change Minds? *Philosophy, Politics, and Economics* 5: 279–303.

McLean, Iain, Christian List, James Fishkin, and Robert Luskin. 2000. Can Deliberation Induce Greater Preference Structuration? Evidence from Deliberative Polls. Paper presented at the Annual Meeting of the American Political Science Association, Washington, DC.

Manin, Bernard. 1987. On Legitimacy and Political Deliberation. *Political Theory* 15: 338–68.

Mansbridge, Jane. 1990. Feminism and Democracy. *American Prospect* 1: 126–39.

——. 1999a. Everyday Talk in the Deliberative System. In Stephen Macedo, ed., *Deliberative Politics: Essays on Democracy and Disagreement*, pp. 211–38. New York: Oxford University Press.

Mansbridge, Jane. 1999*b*. Should Blacks Represent Blacks and Women Represent Women? A Contingent "Yes." *Journal of Politics* 61: 628–57.

———. 2003. Rethinking Representation. *American Political Science Review* 97: 515–28.

Meadows, Donella H., Dennis L. Meadows, Jørgen Randers, and William Behrens III. 1974. *The Limits to Growth*. New York: Universe Books.

Meidinger, Errol E. 2003. Forest Certification as a Global Civil Society Regulatory Institution. In Errol E. Meidinger, Chris Elliot, and Gerhard Oesten, eds., *Social and Political Dimensions of Forest Certification*, pp. 265–89. Remagen-Oberwinter: Forstbuch Verlag.

Miller, David. 1992. Deliberative Democracy and Social Choice. *Political Studies* 40 (special issue): 54–67.

———. 2002. Is Deliberative Democracy Unfair to Disadvantaged Groups? In Maurizio Passerin d'Entreves, ed., *Democracy and Public Deliberation*, pp. 201–25. Manchester: Manchester University Press.

Mol, Arthur P. J. and David Sonnefeld. 2000. Ecological Modernization Around the World. *Environmental Politics* 9: 3–16.

Montanero, Laura. 2008. The Democratic Legitimacy of "Self-Authorized" Representatives. Paper presented at the Workshop on Rethinking Representation: A North-South Dialogue. Italy, September 30–October 3.

Morrison, Kevin M. and Matthew M. Singer. 2007. Inequality and Deliberative Development: Revisiting Bolivia's Experience with PRSP. *Development Policy Review* 25: 721–40.

Mouffe, Chantal. 1996. Democracy, Power and "The Political". In Seyla Benhabib, ed., *Democracy and Difference: Contesting the Boundaries of the Political*, pp. 245–56. Princeton, NJ: Princeton University Press.

———. 1999. Deliberative Democracy or Agonistic Pluralism? *Social Research* 66: 745–58.

———. 2000. *The Democratic Paradox*. London: Verso.

Mutz, Diana. 2006. *Hearing the Other Side: Deliberative versus Participatory Democracy*. Cambridge: Cambridge University Press.

———. 2008. Is Deliberative Democracy a Falsifiable Theory? *Annual Review of Political Science* 11: 521–38.

Neblo, Michael. 2005. Thinking Through Democracy: Between the Theory and Practice of Deliberative Politics. *Acta Politica* 40: 169–81.

Niemeyer, Simon J. 2002. *Deliberation in the Wilderness: Transforming Policy Preferences Through Discourse*. PhD thesis. Australian National University, Canberra.

———. 2004. Deliberation in the Wilderness: Displacing Symbolic Politics. *Environmental Politics* 13: 347–72.

———, Selen Ayirtman, and Janette Hartz-Karp. 2008. Achieving Success in Large Scale Deliberation: Analysis of the Fremantle Bridge Community Engagement Process. Deliberative Democracy Research Group, Australian National University.

Niño, Carlos. 1996. *The Constitution of Deliberative Democracy*. New Haven, CT: Yale University Press.

Norgaard, Richard B. 2007. Deliberative Economics. *Ecological Economics* 63: 375–82.

Norval, Aletta J. 2007. *Aversive Democracy: Inheritance and Originality in the Democratic Tradition*. Cambridge: Cambridge University Press.

O'Donnell, Guillermo. 1994. Delegative Democracy. *Journal of Democracy* 5: 55–69.
—— and Philippe Schmitter. 1986. *Transitions from Authoritarian Rule.* Baltimore, MD: Johns Hopkins University Press.

O'Flynn, Ian. 2006. *Deliberative Democracy and Divided Societies.* Edinburgh: Edinburgh University Press.

O'Neill, John. 2002. The Rhetoric of Deliberation: Some Problems in the Kantian Theory of Deliberative Democracy. *Res Publica* 8: 249–68.

O'Riordan, Timothy and James Cameron, eds. 1994. *Interpreting the Precautionary Principle.* London: Earthscan.

Obama, Barack. 2006. *The Audacity of Hope: Thoughts on Reclaiming the American Dream.* New York: Crown Publishers.

Parkinson, John. 2006a. *Deliberating in the Real World: Problems of Legitimacy in Deliberative Democracy.* Oxford: Oxford University Press.

——. 2006b. Rickety Bridges: Using the Media in Deliberative Democracy. *British Journal of Political Science* 36: 175–83.

——and Declan Roche. 2004. Restorative Justice: Deliberative Democracy in Action? *Australian Journal of Political Science* 39: 505–18.

Payne, Roger A. and Nayef H. Samhat. 2004. *Democratizing Global Politics: Discourse Norms, International Regimes, and Political Community.* Albany, NY: State University of New York Press.

Peter, Fabienne. 2007. Democratic Legitimacy and Proceduralist Social Epistemology. *Politics, Philosophy and Economics* 6: 329–53.

Pettit, Philip. 1997. *Republicanism: A Theory of Freedom and Government.* Oxford: Oxford University Press.

Phillips, Anne. 1995. *The Politics of Presence.* Oxford: Clarendon Press.

Pierre, Jon and B. Guy Peters. 2000. *Governance, Politics and the State.* Basingstoke: Palgrave Macmillan.

Pitkin, Hannah F. 1967. *The Concept of Representation.* Berkeley, CA: University of California Press.

Piven, Frances Fox and Richard Cloward. 1971. *Regulating the Poor: The Functions of Social Welfare.* New York: Vintage.

Popper, Karl R. 1966. *The Open Society and Its Enemies.* London: Routledge and Kegan Paul.

Przeworski, Adam. 1991. *Democracy and the Market: Political and Economic Reform in Eastern Europe and Latin America.* Cambridge: Cambridge University Press.

Putnam, Robert. 2000. *Bowling Alone: The Collapse and Revival of American Community.* New York: Simon and Schuster.

Rawls, John. 1971. *A Theory of Justice.* Cambridge, MA: Harvard University Press.

——. 1993. *Political Liberalism.* New York: Columbia University Press.

——. 1997. The Idea of Public Reason Revisited. *University of Chicago Law Review* 94: 765–807.

Reber, Bernard. 2007. Technology Assessment as Policy Analysis: From Expert Advice to Participatory Processes. In Frank Fischer, Gerald J. Miller, and Mara S. Sidney, eds., *Handbook of Public Policy Analysis*, pp. 493–512. Boca Raton, FL: CRC Press.

Rehg, William. 1997. Reason and Rhetoric in Habermas's Theory of Argumentation. In Walter Jost and Michael Hyde, eds., *Rhetoric and Hermeneutics in our Time*, pp. 358–77. New Haven, CT: Yale University Press.

Reilly, Benjamin. 2001. *Democracy in Divided Societies: Electoral Engineering for Conflict Management*. Cambridge: Cambridge University Press.

Rescher, Nicholas. 1993. *Pluralism: Against the Demand for Consensus*. Oxford: Clarendon Press.

Reus-Smit, Christian. 1999. *The Moral Purpose of the State: Culture, Social Identity, and Institutional Rationality in International Relations*. Princeton, NJ: Princeton University Press.

Rhodes, R. A. W. 1994. The Hollowing out of the State. *Political Quarterly* 65: 138–51.

——. 1997. *Understanding Governance: Policy Networks, Governance, Reflexivity, and Accountability*. Buckingham: Open University Press.

Riker, William H. 1982. Liberalism Against Populism: A Confrontation Between the Theory of Democracy and the Theory of Social Choice. San Francisco, CA: W.H. Freeman.

——. 1996. *The Strategy of Rhetoric: Campaigning for the American Constitution*. New Haven, CT: Yale University Press.

Risse, Thomas. 2000. "Let's Argue!" Communicative Action in World Politics. *International Organization* 54: 1–39.

Rokeach, Milton. 1979. *Understanding Human Values: Individual and Societal*. New York: Free Press.

Rosenau, Pauline V., ed. 2000. *Public–Private Policy Partnerships*. Cambridge, MA: MIT Press.

Rosenberg, Shawn, ed. 2007. *Deliberation, Participation, and Democracy: Can the People Govern?* Basingstoke: Palgrave Macmillan.

Rostbøll, Christian F. 2008. *Deliberative Freedom: Deliberative Democracy as Critical Theory*. Albany, NY: State University of New York Press.

Russett, Bruce and John Oneal. 2001. *Triangulating Peace: Democracy, Interdependence, and International Organizations*. New York: W.W. Norton.

Ryfe, David M. 2005. Does Deliberative Democracy Work? *Annual Review of Political Science* 8: 49–71.

Sabel, Charles, Archon Fung, and Bradley Karkainnen. 1999. Beyond Backyard Environmentalism: How Communities are Quietly Refashioning Environmental Regulation. *Boston Review*.

Safran, William. 2002. *The French Polity*, 6th edn. New York: Longman.

Sagoff, Mark. 1988. *The Economy of the Earth: Philosophy, Law and the Environment*. Cambridge: Cambridge University Press.

——. 1999. The View from Quincy Library: Civic Engagement and Environmental Problem Solving. In Robert Fullwinder, ed., *Democracy and Civic Renewal*, pp. 151–83. Lanham, MD: Rowman and Littlefield.

Salamon, Lester M., ed. 2002. *The Tools of Government: A Guide to the New Governance*. Oxford: Oxford University Press.

Sanders, Lynn. 1997. Against Deliberation. *Political Theory* 25: 347–76.

——. 1999. Poll Envy: An Assessment of Deliberative Polling. *The Good Society* 9 (1): 9–14.

Sass, Jensen. 2006. Does Culture Count in Political Deliberation? Claro! Paper presented to the Conference on Dialogue Across Difference, Australian National University.

Saward, Michael. 2000. Less Than Meets the Eye: Democratic Legitimacy and Deliberative Theory. In Michael Saward, ed., *Democratic Innovation: Deliberation, Representation, and Association*, pp. 66–77. London: Routledge.

——. 2009. Authorisation and Authenticity: Representation and the Unelected. *Journal of Political Philosophy* 17: 1–22.

Schaap, Andrew. 2006. Agonism in Divided Societies. *Philosophy and Social Criticism* 32: 255–77.

Schedler, Andreas. 1998. What is Democratic Consolidation? *Journal of Democracy* 9: 91–107.

Scheuerman, William E. 2006. Critical Theory Beyond Habermas. In John S. Dryzek, Bonnie Honig, and Anne Phillips, eds., *The Oxford Handbook of Political Theory*, pp. 85–105. Oxford: Oxford University Press.

——. 2007. *Frankfurt School Perspectives on Globalization, Democracy, and the Law.* New York: Routledge.

Schlosberg, David. 1999. *Environmental Justice and the New Pluralism: The Challenge of Difference for Environmentalism.* Oxford: Oxford University Press.

Schumpeter, Joseph A. 1942. *Capitalism, Socialism, and Democracy.* New York: Harper.

Shapiro, Ian. 1999. Enough of Deliberation: Politics is About Interest and Power. In Stephen Macedo, ed., *Deliberative Politics: Essays on Democracy and Disagreement*, pp. 28–38. New York: Oxford University Press.

Simmons, John A. 2001. *Justification and Legitimacy.* Cambridge: Cambridge University Press.

Simon, Julian. 1996. *The Ultimate Resource 2.* Princeton, NJ: Princeton University Press.

Smith, Graham. 2009. *Democratic Innovations: Designing Institutions for Citizen Participation.* Cambridge: Cambridge University Press.

—— and Corinne Wales. 2000. Citizens' Juries and Deliberative Democracy. *Political Studies* 48: 51–65.

Smith, William and James Brassett. 2008. Deliberation and Global Governance: Liberal, Cosmopolitan, and Critical Perspectives. *Ethics and International Affairs* 22: 69–92.

Sørensen, Eva and Jacob Torfing. 2007. Introduction: Governance Network Research: Towards a Second Generation. In Eva Sørensen and Jacob Torfing, eds., *Theories of Democratic Network Governance*, pp. 1–21. Basingstoke: Palgrave Macmillan.

Spragens, Thomas A., Jr. 1990. *Reason and Democracy.* Durham, NC: Duke University Press.

Steiner, Jürg. 2008. Concept Stretching: The Case of Deliberation. *European Political Science* 7: 186–90.

——, André Bächtiger, Markus Spörndli, and Marco R. Steenbergen. 2004. *Deliberative Politics in Action: Analysing Parliamentary Discourse.* Cambridge: Cambridge University Press.

Stiglitz, Joseph. 2002. *Globalization and its Discontents.* New York: W.W. Norton.

Sunstein, Cass R. 1993. *The Partial Constitution*. Cambridge, MA: Harvard University Press.
——. 1995. Incompletely Theorized Agreements. *Harvard Law Review* 108: 1733–72.
——. 1997. Deliberation, Democracy, Disagreement. In Ron Bontekoe and Marietta Stepaniants, eds., *Justice and Democracy: Cross-Cultural Perspectives*, pp. 93–117. Honolulu, HI: University of Hawai'i Press.
——. 2000. Deliberative Trouble? Why Groups go to Extremes. *Yale Law Journal* 110: 71–119.
——. 2002. The Law of Group Polarization. *Journal of Political Philosophy* 10: 175–95.
——. 2007. The Empirical Turn in Deliberative Democracy. Presented at the Annual Conference of the American Political Science Association, Chicago, IL.
Susskind, Lawrence. 2006. Can Public Policy Dispute Resolution Meet the Challenges Set by Deliberative Democracy? *Dispute Resolution Magazine* (winter): 5–6.
——, Sara McKearnan, and Jennifer Thomas-Larmer, eds. 1999. *The Consensus Building Handbook*. Thousand Oaks, CA: Sage.
Talisse, Robert B. 2005. *Democracy After Liberalism: Pragmatism and Deliberative Politics*. New York: Routledge.
Tesh, Sylvia Noble. 2000. *Uncertain Hazards: Environmental Activists and Scientific Proof*. Ithaca, NY: Cornell University Press.
Thompson, Dennis. 1999. Democratic Theory and Global Society. *Journal of Political Philosophy*, 7: 111–25.
——. 2008. Deliberative Democratic Theory and Empirical Political Science. *Annual Review of Political Science* 11: 497–520.
Torgerson, Douglas. 1999. *The Promise of Green Politics: Environmentalism and the Public Sphere*. Durham, NC: Duke University Press.
Uhr, John. 1998. *Deliberative Democracy in Australia: The Changing Place of Parliament*. Cambridge: Cambridge University Press.
Urbinati, Nadia and Mark E. Warren. 2008. The Concept of Representation in Political Theory. *Annual Review of Political Science* 11: 387–412.
Van Mill, David. 1996. The Possibility of Rational Outcomes from Democratic Discourse and Procedures. *Journal of Politics* 58: 734–52.
Vig, Norman J. and Herbert Paschen, eds. 2000. *Parliaments and Technology: The Development of Technology Assessment in Europe*. Albany, NY: State University of New York Press.
Waldron, Jeremy. 2004. Liberalism, Political and Comprehensive. In eds., *The Handbook of Political Theory*, Gerald Gaus and Chandran Kukathas, pp. 89–99. London: Sage.
Walker, R. B. J. 1993. *Inside/Outside: International Relations in Political Theory*. Cambridge: Cambridge University Press.
Walter, Ryan. 2008. Foucault and Radical Deliberative Democracy. *Australian Journal of Political Science* 43: 531–46.
Walzer, Michael. 1999. Deliberation, and What Else? In Stephen Macedo, ed., *Deliberative Politics: Essays on Democracy and Disagreement*, pp. 58–69. Oxford: Oxford University Press.
Warren, Mark E. 2009. Two Trust-Based Uses of Mini-Publics in Democracy. Paper presented at the Conference on Democracy and the Deliberative Society, University of York, June 24–26.

—— and Hilary Pearse, eds. 2008. *Designing Deliberative Democracy: The British Columbia Citizens' Assembly.* Cambridge: Cambridge University Press.

Watson, Gary. 1975. Free Agency. *Journal of Philosophy* 62 (8): 205–220.

Weaver, Kimberlee, Stephen M. Garcia, Norbert Schwarz, and Dale T. Miller. 2007. Inferring the Popularity of an Opinion from its Familiarity: A Repetitive Voice can Sound Like a Chorus. *Journal of Personality and Social Psychology* 92: 821–33.

Wendt, Alexander. 1992. Anarchy is What States Make of It: The Social Construction of Power Politics. *International Organization* 46: 391–425.

Yack, Bernard. 2006. Rhetoric and Public Reasoning: An Aristotelian Understanding of Political Deliberation. *Political Theory* 34: 417–38.

Young, Iris Marion. 1990. *Justice and the Politics of Difference.* Princeton, NJ: Princeton University Press.

——. 1996. Communication and the Other: Beyond Deliberative Democracy. In Seyla Benhabib, ed., *Democracy and Difference: Contesting the Boundaries of the Political,* pp. 120–35. Princeton, NJ: Princeton University Press.

——. 1998. Inclusive Political Communication: Greeting, Rhetoric and Storytelling in the Context of Political Argument. Paper presented at the Annual Meeting of the American Political Science Association, Boston, MA.

——. 2000. *Inclusion and Democracy.* Oxford: Oxford University Press.

——. 2007. *Global Challenges: War, Self-Determination and Responsibility for Justice.* Cambridge: Polity Press.

Zablocki, Benjamin. 1980. *Alienation and Charisma: A Study of Contemporary American Communes.* New York: Free Press.

Zagacki, Kenneth S. 2003. Rhetoric, Dialogue, and Performance in Nelson Mandela's "Televised Address on the Assassination of Chris Hani." *Rhetoric and Public Affairs* 6: 709–35.

Zakaria, Fareed. 2003. *The Future of Freedom: Illiberal Democracy at Home and Abroad.* New York: Norton.

# Index

Lightning Source UK Ltd.
Milton Keynes UK
UKHW040613210819
348299UK00006B/1461/P